Personality

AND

Religion

~~~~~~~~~~~~~~~~~~

Personality

AND

Religion

PAUL E. JOHNSON

~~~~~~

Abingdon Press

NEW YORK   NASHVILLE

PREFACE

The starting point of modern psychology is generally marked as the year 1879 when Wundt opened a psychological laboratory in Leipzig, and William James began similar work at Harvard. One of the first interests of this young science was to undertake psychological studies of religion. In 1881 G. Stanley Hall presented a study of religious conversion, to be followed by a continuing stream of publications from many investigators in the psychology of religion.

By now psychology has moved into every area of behavior and human relations, where an amazing volume of research is at work with different tools and concepts in specialized interest. At the same time religion has been enriched by historical and cultural research, as well as exciting developments in theology and philosophy. Is it possible to relate the whole of psychology to the whole of religion? When each is so complex it may be contradictory to bring the diversity of one up against the variety of the other.

One field of psychology is coming to central importance among all others, the study of personality. There is need to relate this core study of personality to what is central in religious experience. What does it mean psychologically and religiously to be a person? And how does a person become whole through the resources of psychoreligious growth?

This book is devoted to such a study. Four leading theories of personality come before us. What can we learn from these viewpoints about the complex nature and dynamic of personality? Biographical case studies give an inside view of what it means to be a growing person in the context of living. Eventually, we arrive at a dimensional view of personality seeking to integrate the partial theories into a unity of relationships. This may be called neo-personalism, or as we have designated it, dynamic interpersonalism.

The course which we follow here is indebted to many minds and lively communications. The references and bibliography can cite only

5

a few of them, but to these and others unnamed I desire to acknowledge my profound gratitude. My thanks are offered especially to Evelyn G. Johnson and Viola W. Staveley for secretarial work, to Orlo and Mary Strunk for compiling the index, and to Robert P. Price for assistance in proofreading. And to those who will journey along this trail with me as readers, I send a hearty greeting and welcome to further exploration.

PAUL E. JOHNSON

CONTENTS

~~~~~~

I. To Be a Person

II. To Be Religious

III. To Be Whole

CONTENTS

9

PART I

To Be a Person

~~~~~~

CHAPTER ONE

THE MYSTERY
OF PERSONALITY

1. What Is a Person?

It was one of those September mornings you wait for. The sun was pouring out of a blue sky upon the bronzed faces of students walking across the university campus. Reluctantly they broke away from conversation knots and moved toward their classrooms as the bell sounded. A professor bounded up the steps a minute behind schedule. Within his classroom was an air of subdued excitement, the mood of the first day, alert with anticipation yet charged with uncertainty and anxiety. Would it be worth the effort, or another notch on the handle of routine educational monotony?

The professor might well be wondering too, for he looked quizzically at the class, trying to sense and respond to their mood. A hush fell upon the room while students and professor eyed each other indecisively. Quietly the professor began to speak, pensively as if in soliloquy, yet uneasily as if he suspected he was being overheard.

There is a mystery about this thing called personality. Actually, it is no thing at all. My body does occupy space and register 148 pounds upon the bathroom scales. You can push me over and I fall like any other thing, but there is more to me than a pile of bricks. For I know I am falling and wonder why you pushed me. I feel the pain of striking the cement walk. The cut on my hand at length stops bleeding and starts healing by its own self-repairing devices. I recall similar experiences when as a boy a bully tried to subdue me, and I begin to resent you for the indignity of my downfall. What have I done to deserve this fate, I wonder? Have I offended you or society or God? Evidently, I am full of mysteries; and possibly you are too! Who are you anyway, and what do you have to say for yourself?

By this time the students were verging on consternation at this unorthodox beginning, which was bypassing the safe formality of academic procedure. It was startling to encounter a teacher who was

13

talking openly about himself, and asking them to expose themselves also. Before the hour was over each student had introduced himself with some account of his life as a person. Then the students were invited to form groups of six to eight by choosing the persons who interested them most for group-mates.

At the end of the hour came the assignment to write one page on "Who Am I?" and be prepared to discuss their views at the meeting of their small group the following Wednesday. Each group was leaderless, except for a secretary to record decisions and notify members, when there was occasion to do so. The teacher would visit from group to group in the order of invitations received.

When the professor met with Group 4 the following Wednesday, they had been through the cafeteria line and were gathering on the roof of the Student Union Building with midmorning coffee and doughnuts. Seating themselves around a table under an umbrella sunshade, they enjoyed small talk until the doughnuts were dunked and downed. Then they began to consider what it means to be a person, and how they would reply to the question "Who am I?"

"Who do you think you are, John?"

The group came to focus upon John and waited while he cleared his throat.

"I'm just a number to most people. To selective service I am one number, and to social security another. To the department of motor vehicles I'm a license number. To the telephone company I am the number listed in the directory."

"Sure, we got your number," Mae put in, "but you're more than the numbers they classify you by."

"What do you mean more?"

"Well, the number is your classification for filing and reference," Mae parried. "But you are a body of flesh and blood, a biological organism."

"But that's not the whole story either," Don broke in. "We mean different things to different people. To my neighbor I'm the guy next door. Ask my wife and I'm her sweetheart. Ask my children and I'm the greatest man on earth. Ask one I've harmed and I'm his enemy. Ask one I've helped and I'm his friend."

"Ask me," John retorted, "and I'm confused. God only knows who I am."

"If God knows," said Lee, taking up the thread, "that makes a

14

real difference. Then I count for something in the whole scheme of things, and what I do or what happens to me has significance."

"That's what you think," John countered. "But how do you *know?* You have to know it all to know that!"

"But do you?" the professor queried. "We get along by piecing together bits of knowledge and making sense out of them. We never know it all or have the whole story, yet we make a lot of sense with what we put together in the puzzle of life. The astronomer measures the unknown by what he knows. The historian works with the evidence he can find. The research scientist shapes a hypothesis and searches for more data to add up one way or the other."

"Yes, but how can I know that I am an eternal soul," John protested. "How can I be sure that God created me for a purpose and has a plan for my life?"

"That is the mystery of personality," Lee replied. "There is a lot more to me than I know about myself. How do I know what I mean to you, and here you are right across the table?"

"Do you want to know?" There was a twinkle in John's eye, and he added, "Do you think you could bear up under it?"

"Go ahead. Shoot if you must at this old gray head," Lee intoned. "If you take me for a damn fool, you might as well out with it. Then I could reply like the polite Frenchman when so accused: 'I think *you* are a perfect gentleman, but then we could *both* be wrong!' The fact is we *could* both be wrong."

"Exactly what I am saying," John came back. "How then can we know who we are in any ultimate sense?"

"But I do know that I am I," Mae proposed. "I do remember what I had for breakfast yesterday. In fact, I recall how I hated cooked cereal when I was five years old, and know that I am the same person who has not changed my mind about it since."

"Oh, that's a woman's privilege," Ted bantered. "We wouldn't hold that against you. You don't need to pose like Venus on a pedestal."

"It is not I who put me on a pedestal; that's just your childish attitude toward your mother-image. I can change my mind anytime I want to about you."

"Come now, let's not make an indecent exposure of our prejudices," said Ted. And then to defend himself, "We have all changed our ideas about our parents since we were children. And maybe they have changed as much as we have."

"There is a paradox here, isn't there?" Summing up, the professor continued: "Isn't it amazing how through all the changing experiences of life there is personal identity, so one person is able to remember the past and project himself purposely into the future? Do you agree that self-consciousness is the most personal of all our characteristics? To know oneself is the capacity to be a person. From this self-knowledge arises the unique quality of personal identity. And from this self-awareness, rises the dynamic striving for the goals I seek, and the struggle to become what I want to be."

Returning to his study that evening the professor pondered over the statements which the students had written about themselves. A student from Mexico had written of moving forth from one culture to another which he wanted to make his own.

Who am I? Exactly, I do not know, for the task of knowing myself is not yet complete. When I knew my parents gave a name to distinguish me from others as something unique, the quest for my own self started. Since then many times I have dived into the innermost of my self hoping to find me and to know me.

I was born in an insignificant town in Mexico, and the people there were farmers. Beyond the few cotton plantations were the desert and the mountains. My parents were of Spanish and Indian ancestry; they spoke Spanish, professed the Catholic religion, and reared eight children. When I was nineteen years old I was converted to Protestantism and for three years lived in conflict with my family and my society, until I came to this city. Right now I perform the work of janitor while attending school. I am single and struggling to adapt myself to my new culture.

In attempting to know myself there are three facts which doubtless tell me who I am. First, I am like all other men for I was born like them; we have the same basic needs, and someday our bodies will become dust. The second fact is that I am like some of the other men; I speak Spanish as some millions do; with them I share the same cuisine style, and we may have the same faith. Also, I know I am unique; I am not like all other men. My nose is different from all the other men's. Not only that, but my real self refuses to be part of the other selves. I do not know yet who I am, but through faith I believe I am one of the many persons God has created and that some day he will help me to discover myself.[1]

[1] Names and data given in personal documents throughout the book are often changed to respect the confidential nature of the information. For permission to use these documents I am deeply grateful to the authors.

The student tells us a good deal about himself in this brief statement. He confesses humility about what he can know, yet he is undergirded by a faith that God will help him understand the meaning of the life he earnestly strives to fulfill. He suffers from a sense of inferiority, noted in his "insignificant" birthplace, humble family, and culture which he rejects for a new life in another country. It was not easy to break with his family and church, yet he endured the conflict to become independent and follow his own convictions. He acknowledges his unity with all men, and the traits that bind him to the ones he has departed from; yet he is acutely aware of his unique self that "refuses to be part of the other selves," and hopefully forges ahead through anxieties and frustrations to discover a better life.

A student from Germany also views himself in the context of social contrasts, in which he determines to assert his inner religious faith against the despair of the outer world.

What should I tell you in a few words about myself?

The *outer aspect* would be: I was born in a country which lived under tyranny many years and now it is destroyed and divided into two parts. One part is under tyranny up to the present. What is a person in this machinery of the world? Who can stop the destroying movement of history? I thought: the human being is nothing.

I was born as a child of a physician and wanted to become a physician too, when I came back from the war. It is a good idea to work healing human beings from their illness. But I perceived that the root of the worst illness is in the soul of human beings. This brought me to study religion.

Now I come to the U.S.A., where the people didn't experience much of the war-destruction, where the people live in peace and health, but nevertheless: What is a person here in this country, which believes in the freedom and dignity of every person? I saw, there are many things to prohibit the people being free. I guess that most people are so busy in their work and like the amusements presented by the technic so much, that they haven't time to meditate and stay to themselves. They lay the whole soul in their daily activity. What is a person? Only a function of the society, a function of his work?

The *inner aspect* is my faith. I believe that God created the human being to belong to him and to serve him in a life valuable to be lived. God is interested in every human being; he gave his son in the death to liberate them from sin and death. He gave everybody an eternal destination.

It is hard to keep this hope in view of the present world, its despair

17

and disorder. But I have to relate my faith with the outer life. Where is the way to develop this life, demanded by God, in an inverted world?

In such circumstances many persons have given up to the dark mood of despair, cursing their fate or nursing their weakness in self-pity and futility. But it is otherwise with our German student, who blinks no evil facts, denies none of the losses of his people, the sorrows of tyranny, or the bondage of conformity to social patterns of democracy. Yet he finds in his Christian faith dynamic resources to confront the world and devote himself with courage to the wresting of good from evil. He would like to heal human beings from their illness, as his father has done in the work of a physician; but he perceives that the deeper illness is of the soul and decides to give his life to a religious vocation, wherein he may start from the center of life and work outward to a better world community.

2. Inner and Outer Worlds

The chasm between the inner self and the outer world is so basic that it affects all of one's experience. A person may spend his energies in seeking to win that outer world of things and people for himself. Or, failing that, he may in another mood retreat from the world in defiance to guard what he can of his inner treasure from the attacks of others and the threats of further loss and disappointment. The subject stands ever in contrast to the object in knowing as well as doing. Every person is a minority of one, who wonders how to assert his individuality and when to claim refuge in the common life.

But there are conflicts also within the complex forces of personality. These conflicts are recognized by the student who writes:

I am a person with deep undercurrents. Doubts beset me. Fears possess me and shackle me. A depleted reserve of confidence puts a blight on my effectiveness at times. Moods transport me up and down. Storms rage within me. Anxiety nearly overwhelms me ofttimes. Resentments bring on a paralysis. Hate blocks out love.

Who am I? I am this complex of a person. This total person. Effective only because God somehow has used me, overruling my weaknesses, to minister to those who have frustrations, anxieties, broken wills, and diseased spirits.

What of the persons who do not speak of inner conflicts? Are they the fortunate mortals who are somehow saved from the stresses of life, free from anxiety and indecision to lead a placid life at peace within and without? Or is it truer to human nature to infer that the silent ones have their conflicts also but are less vocal about them? In moments of confidential conversation we have heard persons who appear calm insist they are seething in torment underneath.

Is it from such turmoil and perplexity that one comes to avow himself agnostic? Since appearances are so often deceptive and finite viewpoints so fragmentary, who can presume to grasp the whole truth about personality? It is quite possible, therefore, that whatever we claim is too much. The more we say the larger the possibility of error. Perhaps, after all, the part of wisdom in the face of so great a mystery is to cover one's head in modesty and admit one does not know.

Who am I? Breath of the Eternal or apperceptive mass? Spirit of God manifest in this phenomenal world or an inconsequential drop of spray from the vast Niagara called *Life?* Whatever or whoever I am ultimately, I do not know. Han-shan wrote:

> "Am I really an idiot?" I reflect.
> But my reflections fail to solve the question;
> I do not know who the self is,
> And how can another know who I am?
> I just hang my head—what use of more asking?

From many cultures we hear sentiments like these, and they speak eloquently to the dismay we also feel that our grandest pretensions and protestations may be vain. For after all we are but dust, poised for our little day on the ash heap of precarious values. We clutch frantically, knowing that before long we, too, are doomed to die. Is there nothing beyond the inevitable descent into the grave of dissolution? Is the invisible hand of an unseeing fate to write *finis* at the end of every human hope?

This puzzling question of man's ultimate destiny may be postponed, yet never escaped. In the role of scientist the psychologist may have nothing to say about human destiny, but as a mortal man he will in turn face the finalities of death and decide how to cope with the "threat to nonbeing." [2] A student approaching this question in the perspective of theology talks back to the naturalist from the heart of a genuine conviction:

[2] Paul Tillich, *The Courage to Be* (New Haven, Conn.: Yale University Press, 1952).

19

Who am I? Of this one thing I am sure, I am somebody. I may not be able to conclude with any degree of exhaustiveness my entire existence, but the fact remains that I am somebody. Furthermore, I am confident of the fact that I will always exist no matter what forces or men may say and do because I am more than dust. I am dust with life, and life that's eternal because it springs from the Eternal. Thus my entire confidence of the fact hinges upon the Author of life, and it is through faith in him that I realize I am somebody. I am somebody with a purpose. All creation has a purpose, a very definite purpose. Of this I am a part, a speck of dust with a purpose, a purpose to glorify him in the channel of his will which I may either choose or reject.

Yes, I am somebody; and yet when I view the rest of creation about me, when I count the stars, understand the atom, fathom all mysteries, I am reduced to nothing. My insignificance speaks of annihilation and I fear. But in this fear I find strength, for I learn to lean upon the Eternal arms. I see how through the ages of time God has taken a "Mr. Somebody" and revealed to him he was a "Mr. Nobody," and used that "Mr. Nobody" to His glory. And then I rest.

Such a confession of faith may not speak the language or argue the logic of the natural sciences. But it does rise out of honest self-searching and the legitimate need to count for something in the vastness of a universe of light years and atomic explosions. There is in this search for value a recognition of one's littleness and transience contradicting the evidence of a higher purpose. Yet there is the larger sense of a purpose of eternal dimensions one may find and follow through every circumstance. And there is the intimation of an undying meaning that has survived across many generations, the religious affirmation that human weakness may be a creative opportunity to learn and try a better way of co-operation with a God who sees more clearly and knows more truly than we. To offer oneself to this Purpose, he believes, may be the open road to self-transcendence, a step forward to break the deadlock of skeptical despair, and to move out to larger possibilities than he had glimpsed before.

3. Viewpoints for Looking at Persons

In these searchings of students to understand themselves we have a series of viewpoints from which to look at persons. To follow these views progressively is to imply that no one answer is final; that in the quest for the meaning of personality one assertion may demand and lead to another in a dialectic advance like that pursued by Socrates and his students in *The Dialogues*.[3] It is evident that no one who opens his mouth can speak the whole truth in one sentence or many sentences. The focus upon one aspect is to select this, rather than that, item to consider. And when I have had my say it is only fair that I wait to hear how it looks to you. By inter-viewing the situation we may discover other aspects, at first neglected, to sharpen the focus and enlarge the perspective.

Each declaration is significant equally for what it reveals and for what it omits. We are grateful that so much has been noted, yet aware that the subject is by no means exhausted. To go on quoting other descriptions from an endless procession of viewers would be enlightening but not conclusive. There would always be more to discover, especially at the center of personality. No bill of particulars, no summation of external appearances, no listing of traits and characteristics will do. What is needed is to clarify our view of what is most essential and significant in the unique yet universal character of the person.

To define the essential person is a thankless and presumptuous task. We have already agreed that no view can be exhaustive, that every assertion is selective, incomplete, and probably biased by one's particular viewpoint. Is it better then to point and not to attempt a verbal definition, which will only be cut up or cut down as a hollow phrase, a misleading abstraction meaning something quite different to you than to me? It would be safer not to open one's mouth; but communications would then be even less intelligible, for gestures are a feeble language and silence is always open to misinterpretation. Perhaps we had better take the risk of putting our meanings into words, which can then at least be tossed around in the open playing field of conversation, until by the interacting process of speech behavior, persons can reveal more clearly who they are and what they mean to each other.

4. Behind the Mask

To have room enough for this interplay of tossing words around, let us turn to the spacious forum of history. In ancient Rome a cen-

---

[3] Plato, *The Dialogues*. There are many editions in Greek and other languages. Benjamin Jowett has translated the Dialogues into English with analyses and introductions.

tury before Christ, the term *persona* was already current. It was originally used to designate the theatrical mask introduced from Greek drama to convey to the audience in a large amphitheater the character of an actor. The term was probably derived from the Latin *per sonare,* meaning "to sound through," evidently referring to the large mouth of the mask through which the voice of the actor sounded. At first the term was applied to the mask, and then it came to mean the actor behind the mask. These two contradictory meanings have been extended into as many as fifty different uses which survive in the European languages today.[4]

Cicero (106-43 B.C.) employed the term *persona* in at least four ways: (1) external appearance, (2) the role one plays in life, (3) personal qualities that fit a man for his work, (4) the dignity one bears. From these uses emerged other meanings that extend through many realms of discourse among theologians, jurists, sociologists, and psychologists.

Allport defines personality as what a man really is, or in more specfic terms, "the dynamic organization within the individual of those psychophysical systems that determine his unique adjustments to his environment." [5]

Personality is indeed an inexhaustible source of meaning to those who are willing to explore. The mask is likely to attract attention first since it is so obvious, as plain as the nose on your face. It is not surprising that a great deal of interest and no little effort are directed to the external appearance of the person. But this is not the whole of the subject, as we find when we study it more thoroughly, and it may not be the most important part.

Behind the mask is something real which concerns both religion and psychology. The discovery of the soul in primitive animism may be taken as the beginning of religion. Primitive man was not so dull or slow-witted as moderns are likely to think. He, too, was apt to wonder at the mystery of life and ponder over the hidden links of cause and effect in the coming of life and death, the relatedness of visible to invisible powers, and the vivid contrasts of good and evil. In his dreams he followed adventures that led him far afield, and

---

[4] These meanings are well presented by Gordon W. Allport in his *Personality: A Psychological Interpretation* (New York: Henry Holt & Co., Inc., 1937), pp. 24-50. Used by permission.

[5] *Ibid.,* p. 46.

waking to find his body reposing at home, he was able to identify the soul as distinct from the body. So preoccupied was he with the inner side of causation that he projected a soul into every living thing and held the spiritual in priority over the physical.

As the Hebrew tribes advanced from primitive culture to more clearly formulated religious concepts they noted *breath* (*ruach*) as the essential condition of life, that invisible yet pervading stuff moving within every creature so long as he remains alive. This symbolized the spirit of man, the mysterious vitality that enables him to live and act with energy. The dramatic story of creation recorded in Genesis[6] portrays the coming of life to Adam by means of the Creator's breathing into his nostrils the breath of life. In this religious view, spirit is the essence of reality whether in God or man, creating and sustaining the universe of heaven and earth as well as the life within us. Man is a living soul who is distinct from animal life in his capacity to know himself and other creatures by name, and to be conscious of self in relation to other selves.

The seat of life was also located in the *heart* (*lebab*), and not without reason, for the beating of the heart is a well-known indicator of continued living. The heart refers to the center of one's being in more than a spatial sense; it is the moving source of life-giving energy in the pulsating circulation of the bloodstream to nourish growing cells and carry off waste products. The ancients may not have comprehended the details of the blood system, but they did recognize the heart as the dynamic center of healthy vitality empowering life to outgoing activity. In a larger symbolic sense, heart came to mean the inner life in contrast to the external appearance, the personal sense of how life feels to the one who is living it. "The heart is deep" (Ps. 64:6 K.J.V.) and not easy to understand, yet decisive in providing the motives for good or evil in life. "Keep thy heart with all diligence; for out of it are the issues of life." (Prov. 4:23 K.J.V.)

When Samuel was searching for a successor to the ailing Saul, he was attracted at first to a man of commanding physical stature, who might impress the people with his prowess; but Samuel was reminded:

Look not on his countenance, or on the height of his stature; . . . for the Lord seeth not as man seeth; for man looketh on the outward appearance, but the Lord looketh on the heart. (I Sam. 16:7 K.J.V.)

[6] Biblical scholars find two creation stories, the J document dated about 850 B.C. (Gen. 2:4b-25) and the P document dated about 500 B.C. (Gen. 1:1–2:4a).

The outer appearance is a deceptive mask, not to be taken at face value, for if one is to understand a person there are deeper characteristics to be known. Religion like love is an affair of the heart, prompted by one's deepest feelings and arising by inward response to another being.

Psychology is equally concerned with what goes on behind the mask of persona. However psychologists may differ (and their differences are no secret), they are all engaged with one accord in searching the deeper truth beneath the surface appearance of personality. In Allport's chart[7] summarizing the fifty definitions of personality, the concept of the mask is extended to definitions in terms of appearance. Juristic and sociological viewpoints also accent the external characteristics of personality. On the other hand, the concept of the player leads to definitions in terms of the inner and essential nature. Theological, philosophical, ethical, and romantic viewpoints accent the inner characteristics of personality. Psychological definitions descend from the player rather than the mask, and specifically from Cicero's third meaning "an assemblage of personal qualities" constituting the true self. His own definition Allport places centrally between the outer and the inner views of personality to draw together the wisdom of the past and the scientific research of recent times. Yet it is evident that the inner is more essential than the outer for Allport, as for other psychologists who hold the dynamic view of motivating causes arising within the person himself.

The dynamic view of personality is indebted to Freud, whose pioneer work in neurology and psychiatry led him to the hidden causes motivating human behavior. We have noted how primitive man was instructed by his dreams in discovering his soul. It was Freud's analysis of dreams that revealed the deeper causes at work in personality, the latent wishes repressed by ego censorship, operating behind symbols which screened them with a mask of respectability. All behavior emerges from within personality, first by a primary system of wishes to gain pleasure and avoid pain which he called *libido;* and then by a secondary system of devices to cope with the primary drives, through modification of persisting impulses. Much of this interplay of psychic forces is so deeply repressed as to be unconscious.

Other psychologists approach personality from different standpoints, which will be noted later. For the present we have two axioms to

[7] *Op. cit.,* p. 49.

recognize as self-evident propositions which may be obvious enough to serve as premises for the discussion to follow: (1) Personality is more than a mask of external appearances; there is deeper inner reality to understand if we are to know the essential nature and dynamics of personal life. (2) Personality moves outward into a broadening field of active relationships to fulfill inner needs and realize values with other persons. These two premises we may call the *dynamic* axiom and the *interpersonal* axiom. They are basic to adequate understanding of personal behavior, from my point of view, and perhaps from your point of view as well if you so decide.

In seeking to understand what it means to be a person we may either start from the inner subjective view and move outward, or we may start with the outer objective view and move inward. Each approach has its merit, and each its limitation. The inner view has the merit of vivid first-person experience, but it suffers from lack of a larger context to appraise the experience in true perspective. The outer view has the merit of a common frame of reference known as "scientific objectivity," in which observers may meet to verify their impressions by checking with the reports of others, but it suffers from externalism in relying upon appearances which may be either superficial or deceptive.

To rectify the bias of either approach it seems necessary to compensate for one-sidedness by alternating the viewpoint from which we perceive. This we do constantly in everyday observation, as when we look at a table, for example, by walking around it and trying it out for intentional uses. Or as we may do in simple experiments in visual imagery by seeing a diagram first in one perspective as a descending staircase, and then in another perspective as an ascending staircase. So in viewing a personality we understand him better if we follow his varying moods and see him in successive relationships in which other aspects of his character may be revealed. Porter and Rogers[8] invite the counselor to take "the internal frame of reference" as viewed by the client to perceive what life means to him. Observers of the group process, however, may be concealed behind a one-way screen to have a detached and objective view of the situation from external analysis. Or the group may ask one of their number to be a "participant ob-

---

[8] E. H. Porter, *An Introduction to Therapeutic Counseling* (Boston: Houghton Mifflin Co., 1950) ; and Carl R. Rogers, *Client-Centered Therapy* (Boston: Houghton Mifflin Co., 1951).

server," whose role is to synthesize the inner and outer points of view, to be presented at intervals to the group for consideration.[9]

5. Person and Personality

To distinguish these two ways of studying personal life, let us employ the term *person* to denote the self or soul as perceived from within. This internal view will arise either from introspection of one's own conscious experiences, or from empathy by which one puts himself in another's place to sense how it feels to be that person and see what life means as through his eyes. Admitting that consciousness is not the whole of personality, we may identify it as the awareness a person has of the meanings that provide the continuities of memory and intention, the relationships which he can recognize, and the efforts to make sense and value out of his experiences. From this approach let us define the term internally as follows: "A person is a unique center of experience seeking values through dynamic relationships."

On the other hand, let us employ the term *personality* to denote the total functioning human individual as perceived from without. This external view may begin with the physical appearances of stature, build, facial expression, gestures, speech, style of behavior, etc. All of these will be taken as symptomatic manifestations of his character, i.e., the essential inner man behind the mask of his persona. Other clues such as family history, previous events, reactions to a variety of situations, performance in school or vocation, and test scores will be sought in reference to goals and purposes. Personality is therefore seen to be more than the core of self-conscious experience; it will include unconscious processes, behavioral stimuli and responses, the imprint of environment and culture, and the inner meaning of face-to-face relations with persons and groups, as well as the genetic unfolding of all past experiences in the developing process of one's life. From this approach let us define the term externally as follows: "Personality is a developing integration of goal-seeking life processes, arising from multidimensional needs and persisting through interacting relationships to experience meaning and achieve a community of values with other persons."

It will not be easy to keep these inner and outer views distinct, for we alternate taking internal and external standpoints in perceiving

[9] Dorwin Cartwright and Alvin Zander, eds., *Group Dynamics: Research and Theory* (Evanston, Ill.: Row, Peterson & Co., 1953).

self and others, to find what life means by transposing melodies from the key of experience to the key of observation and vice versa. But insofar as possible we are agreeing to refer to a *person* as "a unique center of experience," and a *personality* as "a developing integration of goal-seeking life processes."

From these definitions it may appear that consciousness flows like a stream in one direction, as inevitably as water flows down to the sea. But no life is simple, and the more conscious the more complications. What values to seek by what steps at what times in view of what alternative possibilities, can become a very complex nest of dilemmas to choose among. And personality is even more complex due to the endless series of determinants that interplay within and upon the human individual unconsciously. Behind the scenes of conscious awareness a great deal transpires of undeniable significance to the person on the stage. What we see in the spotlight of focal awareness is the product of numerous backstage operations hidden from view at any moment of rapt or tragic eloquence, yet integral with the whole developing plot of goal-seeking life processes.

To illustrate the constant interplay of inner and outer choices and determinants, a case study will be introduced. Jeanne Andrews is a young woman, twenty-nine years of age, who grew up in an apparently nonreligious family to become a religious person. She is now the wife of a Christian minister and the mother of four children, seeking to fulfill her religious ideals in the family and community of which she is a vital member. Her life story is written by the minister who is her husband, to trace the psychological motives of her inner life and the social influences which play a part in her religious development.

This will further illustrate the basic approaches whereby one person may come to understand another. To the young man who wrote this story Jeanne first appeared as a personality with external characteristics which attracted his interest. As they came to know each other better, he was able to appreciate the inner desires and motives arising to conscious awareness, and so to perceive her as a person. At the same time Jeanne was undergoing a similar transition in her awareness of the personality who first interested her to the person she loved enough to marry. Jeanne has talked freely in order to give her husband an inside view of what her life has meant to her. In writing the story her husband has sought to integrate the objective with the subjective views until Jeanne could be portrayed as one living *personality*.

CHAPTER TWO

JEANNE ANDREWS

~~~~~~

Jeanne was born in a windswept Nebraska village. Her father, Jack Schmidt, was only twenty when he met and married Marie Baker. Marie's parents had come to Colorado in a covered wagon. Her father was a stern, authoritarian taskmaster. Her mother was a whining, irresponsible woman with little emotional stability. The contagion of such a home environment dominated Marie's adolescence. Jack apparently paid attention to her. She retreated to the refuge of his affection and they were married. In about a year a daughter, Lila, was born. Nineteen months later Delbert, their only son, was born. Then came Jeanne. She is seventeen months younger than Delbert. Eight months after the birth of Jeanne young Jack Schmidt piled the family into his "jalopy" and headed west. With his wife, three children, and carpenter's tools, he hoped to build a new life in the state of Arizona. Coleen, a fourth child, was born a few months after their arrival.

The Schmidts settled in a city of some forty thousand people. Jack, working diligently, became known as a trustworthy carpenter. He even dared to contract two houses and was standing on the threshold of a new "career." But his plans were interrupted. It was 1929—the year of the great depression. Jack couldn't get credit. He couldn't pay his old debts. Building was at a standstill. The Schmidts "crashed" with hundreds of thousands of other Americans. And though but pebbles caught up in the currents of a mighty stream, they would never again find life to be the same. The most decisive years in the lives of the children would be a time of wandering, of insecurity, of fear and moral confusion.

The years following 1929 saw Schmidt as an iceman, a maintainer for the state road department, a truck driver, a W.P.A. worker (he hated this; it humiliated him), and a carpenter, doing odd jobs whenever and wherever he could find them. He moved from town to town, down as far as the Mexican border and up into the northern part of the state, always taking his family with him. His health was good, except for a strained back and a mild kidney ailment that developed while he was operating heavy road equipment. That is, his physical health was good. But the mental health of the family was quite another matter. During this time of frightening insecurity the Schmidts were "very emotional." They have been ever since. Jack would come home and just growl around. He was tired and irritable. Mrs. Schmidt was very high-strung. Life with her own parents had not prepared her for this. She would yell at the children for no reason at all. If the children troubled her she would scream at them one moment and spank them the next. The children thought that she was very unreasonable. Both she and Jack were harsh disciplinarians.

When Lila was but nine she began assuming a major responsibility in the care of the family. She was the official baby sitter. She would comfort the others when they were hurt, or when they were recoiling from the harshness of parental tongue and hand. It is significant that when Jeanne started menstruating it was Lila who interpreted the experience for her. Jeanne had had no instruction. She knew nothing of the "facts of life." She didn't even know how babies came. Thus, the menstrual flow presented a terrifying mystery. Was she pregnant? She didn't know. She told no one about her predicament for days. Finally she came crying to her older sister. Lila took over. She said that it had happened to her in the same way. She had been expecting it in Jeanne's case but didn't know how to open the subject. She explained the few basic facts and then took Jeanne to a dresser drawer where she had thoughtfully placed all of the necessary aids for the physical care and cleanliness of a menstruating adolescent. Jeanne had been initiated into one of the mysteries of female life without one word from her mother. That embarrassed and tragic silence would continue through the years.

It goes without saying that a close bond has existed since early childhood between Lila and Jeanne. Yet Delbert was always Jeanne's special playmate. Their ages were closer together. He was the typical big brother, proud of his protective role. They would climb trees, play house, and play kick-the-can together. Many of these games, probably most of them, were boy's games, but Jeanne was always there and they were together. Coleen, on the other hand, was the "baby." The others had to give in to her. She threw tantrums with quite successful results. Apparently she had inherited (a dangerous word) her mother's temperament and was to reflect the same patterns of behavior through subsequent years. However, she was one of the children too. And at this time they seemed to stand as "four musketeers" against the world of their parents.

The Schmidt children, during early childhood, were threatened not only by temperamental and emotional storm clouds, but they were also threatened by their parents' moral confusion as well.

The moral carelessness of Jack and Marie Schmidt was most noticeable during their stay in San Pablo, a town of some four thousand inhabitants on the Mexican border. San Pablo's chief claim to fame rested in its moral laxity. The older Schmidts soon adjusted to their new surroundings with hilarious abandon, oblivious to the needs of a growing family. For two long years the parents played and the children suffered.

Every week end brought its drinking bout, with frequent trips across the border into Mexican dives. Lila was left in charge of the family during these excursions. Night after night, Jack would come home from his road work with a quart bottle of beer tucked under his arm. He and Marie would drink while the children played unnoticed by their parents. The drinking became compulsive.

Often several families would meet at the Schmidt home for a party. All of the children would be put to bed early. The parents would play cards and drink. There would be a good deal of sex play continuing far into the night. The image of giggling parents running from bedroom to bedroom in their night clothes is still vivid in the mind of Jeanne. Her reaction to these early impressions was negative. She hated everything she saw.

The church was not an important factor in the lives of the Schmidts. In his boyhood Jack had occasionally attended a Baptist Sunday school. Marie's grandfather had been a Methodist "local preacher," but his piety had not seeped down through succeeding generations. The Schmidts never attended church, though in San Pablo they did send the children to the Baptist Sunday school.

One summer, during the vacation Bible school held in the Baptist church, an evangelist had been engaged to preach to the children. He stressed God's judgment and wrath, and described heaven and hell luridly. He insisted on an immediate decision on the part of each child, lest Christ's imminent second coming deprive them of that opportunity and damn them forever. A scared little Lila tearfully went forward and applied for baptism. For several weeks she was in a nervous state.

Her father "blew up." The children were not regular in their Sunday school attendance after that. When Jeanne was ten years old she stopped going to Sunday school altogether. She recalls that "the teachers always made you read." She was self-conscious about her reading and refused to expose herself to threatened disgrace.

Jeanne is most sensitive about her parents' failure to give her any feeling of security in their affection. Her parents, though in some strange way devoted to each other, were constantly involved in verbal bouts. On at least one occasion the hostility led Jack to strike his wife with brutal force before the children. Even so, the children observed moments of tenderness and physical expressions of endearment between their parents. Jeanne feels that such affection was withheld from her.

She has always been loyal to her father, yet she feels that he did not give her the love that many fathers bestow upon their children. When correcting or scolding the children he would swear at them unmercifully. His crudeness built barriers that were hard to overcome. During her later adolescence, he seemed to favor Jeanne and they had moments of genuine communication and love. Yet, these were rare and the barriers still existed.

If Jeanne is sensitive concerning her father's failure, she deeply resents her mother's failure. She feels that her mother rejected her from the beginning. Mrs. Schmidt has been intensely jealous of Jack's favorite sister. The sister, a successful business woman, has delighted through the years in giving nice gifts to her brother's children. When Jeanne was a child her aunt seemed to single her out for special attention. One of Marie's own sisters likewise seemed to have special regard for Jeanne. Jeanne was considered a "sweet" child, though not unusually pretty. Her mother, instead of appreciating this attention, reacted in violent opposition to it. One day when a stranger complimented Mrs. Schmidt on her lovely children, and made special reference to Jeanne, Jeanne recalls that "Mother looked at me as if she hated me." Jeanne hasn't forgotten. She cannot recall a single instance in which her mother expressed genuine affection for her. This lack of emotional security seriously affected Jeanne's childhood and youth.

When Jeanne was five years old she had a very serious mastoid operation. For many days her life hung in the balance. When the critical stage of her illness had passed the Schmidts rejoiced, and there

31

followed some of the happiest months of Jeanne's life. The family had not yet moved to San Pablo, and life was fairly normal. For long weeks she was the center of attention. Anxious parents, sisters and brother, aunts and uncles—everyone seemed to care. It was a meaningful experience to be loved by her family.

When she was ten or eleven years old, the children were playing ball in the yard. The ball got lost. Everyone was looking for it. Joining in the search, Jeanne ducked into a shed to look. She had been there but a moment when a friend of her parents, quite drunk, stumbled in after her. He made some suggestive remarks and advanced toward her. He unfastened his trousers, exposing his genitals. Terrified, Jeanne screamed. The man's son, a seventeen-year-old boy, heard the scream and came and led his father away. Jeanne ran into the house and into her bedroom, almost hysterical. Her mother came into the room. She assured her daughter that the man had meant no harm. He had just been drinking. Looking back Jeanne says, "She seemed to feel that I was just a baby. I didn't trust her. She was covering up for him, and he had tried to attack me." It was years before she had overcome the shock of that experience, if she ever has. Her first reaction was one of extreme revulsion. She couldn't stand to have her own father touch her. She was afraid of her favorite uncle. Sex became a dirty and frightening "something" on the horizon. And her mother had failed her once again.

School opened up a new world for Jeanne. She was never an outstanding student but she always made good grades. She worked hard and sought the approval of her teachers. She cannot remember her parents ever helping her with her studies. They didn't have time for that.

Her third-grade teacher took special interest in her. She was affectionate and Jeanne responded. Her work improved in the third grade. Her sixth-grade teacher was also the school principal. Looking back Jeanne says, "She liked me, and accordingly I tried to please her."

In the seventh grade she had a teacher who stressed penmanship and who gave certificates and awards for excellence. Jeanne practiced and practiced until she had achieved what was desired. "She thought I was the best in the room." At this particular stage in her life, a tall and skinny girl who wore horn-rimmed glasses needed to be "the best in the room."

Jeanne had always excelled in active games and sports. In the ninth grade her physical education teacher saw promise in her and coached her. She became active in the Girls' Athletic Association and was elected its vice-president. She was selected to lead the girls from her junior high school as they participated in a city-wide field day. She was transported on a little stand so that everyone following her lead might see her. Hundreds of parents and youngsters looked on. She remembers that she was very nervous and very, very proud. Neither of her parents was present.

Lila made a fine record in school and Jeanne was expected to live up to it. Her scholastic record did not always compare favorably with Lila's, and she was reminded of this by her parents. She dreaded examinations and was frequently sick before a test. This was no feigned illness. She was not secure. She had very little self-confidence and she feared failure. Thus, when she was being tested at examination times the organism rebelled and she became ill.

Jeanne apparently had no boy-crazy stage. She never quite trusted the boys. Delbert continued to be her best friend. His pals were her pals. Jimmy Younger, slightly older than Delbert and his closest buddy, played an important role in Jeanne's life. Jimmy was her pal. He was older and she looked up to him, idealized him. His parents were settled people. They were active in church work and their home was always open. Jimmy was one of several brothers and sisters. All of them were encouraged to bring their gangs home with them. Mr. and Mrs. Younger represented a way of life that Jeanne had not known before. And Jimmy became her most trusted friend and advisor.

When she was fourteen, Jeanne began attending the youth group of a Congregational church. She went with school friends. There she came in contact with young people who represented a different social and cultural world than the one she had known. There was Randy, the banker's son, and Lucy, the merchant's daughter. There was Charles, whose father was a university professor, and Joe, whose father was a lawyer. Jeanne was maturing now. She was new to the group. The boys thought she was "cute" and the girls befriended her. She was accepted, and what a difference that made!

Jeanne's first dates were with boys in this church group. The banker's son and professor's son competed for her favors. The banker's son was the first boy to kiss her. He kissed her several times when taking her home from various church functions. But, when it appeared that he was getting "serious," or when others in the group started petting, she would manufacture an excuse and insist on being taken home. She was still haunted by the memory of a drunken man in an old shed. One night one of the older boys tried to park with her. She refused. He argued with her, defending the propriety of what he had in mind as he drove her home. When he parked in front of her house he attempted to caress her. Panicky, she hit him and ran from the car. She was still "scared to death" of sex. It is interesting to note that it was Mrs. Younger, not Mrs. Schmidt, who was to share these experiences with Jeanne and help her adjust to them.

Jimmy Younger had been urging Jeanne to visit the youth group in his church for a long time. He was no more religious than most seventeen-year-old boys, but he was an active leader in his youth fellowship. Jeanne trusted Jimmy implicitly. In fact, at this particular time, as she recalls it, she "worshiped the ground he walked on." She explains it by saying, "He never touched me. Some of the older boys in the neighborhood would be suggestive—not Jimmy. He didn't try to get romantic." She accepted his invitation and visited his church.

Jimmy's closest friend in the church group was Jerry Andrews, a chaplain's son. Jerry, a tall slender boy, was just a few months older than Jeanne. He was a competent athlete, something of a show-off, and quite popular within the group. Jimmy, boylike, had thought that it would be nice if Jeanne and Jerry could "get together." Little did he realize the dynamics of the relationship that he helped to create. Within two years, Jeanne and Jerry would be married.

Thus two young people, approaching sixteen, were thrown together. They liked each other immediately and began to date. They went to shows and went swimming. They bowled. They walked to and from school together and held hands in the school halls. Later, Jerry was to get his first car, an old Model "A" Ford. Then they would drive to the mountains, to the desert, or to the lake. It was a wonderfully fascinating new world for Jeanne. She says that for the first time a boy liked her for what she was. "It was the first time in my whole life that I felt loved and needed." She had discovered a relationship that gave her both significant status and affection.

Unfortunately for both Jeanne and Jerry, they became so absorbed in each other that their other interests dwindled. They were "steadies," always together at school, at home, and at church. Jeanne continued to grow, physically, socially, and spiritually, but it was a growth marked more by intensity than breadth.

Her first important brush with religion since the vacation Bible school episode came when Jeanne was sixteen. A conservative Methodist evangelist was conducting a revival in the church which the young people attended. Jeanne went with Jerry and his parents. Jerry went forward one night in response to the invitation. Jeanne wanted to but was afraid that people would think she was doing it simply because Jerry had. She waited until the following night to make her commitment. Looking back, Jeanne says that she was seeking something; she didn't quite know what. The experience "seemed like a conversion" and made a deep impression, but the emotional glow didn't last very long.

A few weeks later Jeanne was baptized and united with the church. She sat with the Andrews family; the Schmidts were not present.

The Schmidts were coming back into their own now. At long last, Jack Schmidt was a building contractor. He could not operate on a large scale. He maintained small crews and built only two or three houses at a time. Sometimes he skirted dangerously close to the brink of bankruptcy. But, when a house was sold, he made money. As he made it he spent it. The Schmidts lived in a nice home (later they were to lose it, then come back again). They had a nice car. Jack bought Marie beautiful clothes and showered gifts upon the children. He was compensating for long years of hardship and want.

The Schmidts were not drinking so much, and their lives were somewhat more steady. The emotional outbursts were still a part of their daily routine. There was constant quarreling and much hostility. Even so, things had been worse. Within a few weeks after her high-school graduation Lila was married. Delbert was a senior in high school and worked for his father in his free time. He would marry at eighteen. Coleen was the problem child. She was a defiant rebel with a frightful temper and a biting tongue. She was considered "fast" with the boys. She, too, would marry at eighteen, but her married life would be riddled with domestic strife. As Lila, Delbert, and Coleen married, they all settled in the city where their parents lived. Both Lila's and Coleen's husbands, as well as Delbert, would work for Schmidt. The Schmidts attempted to dominate the lives of their children and much tension resulted. In spite of the apparent closeness of the families, the fact that all of the younger Schmidts married before they were nineteen indicates their desire to escape parental domination and their rejection of parental standards.

What did the Schmidts think of Jeanne's relationship to Jerry? They seemed to like Jerry all right, though they didn't understand his parents' world. Mr. Schmidt seemed to sense the dangers involved in the constant association of the youngsters, but he didn't know how to approach the subject. He did try to caution Jeanne once, but as she recalls it, "He couldn't convey what he was thinking."

Jeanne and Jerry were secretly married four months before they were to graduate from high school. They thought that they were very much in love. Some of their older friends were marrying. They continued on, finishing school, and then announced their action. The Schmidts accepted it as a matter of fact. Chaplain Andrews accepted it philosophically, though he seemed hurt. Mrs. Andrews was embittered by it for a time. She had had such dreams for her Jerry. Chaplain Andrews solemnized the vows in a church ceremony, and a new way of life was launched for two very young people.

The first home of the young Andrews couple was a tiny two-room apartment over a frame garage. Jerry's first job was as a messenger for the Air Force. He made forty-five dollars every two weeks. When asked about achieving maturity through the experience, Jeanne laughed and said, "I was awfully young to achieve maturity in married life, or any other kind of life." But life had become a lustrous adventure. "I loved it," she says. "It was the first thing I ever remember being mine."

Solicitous parents hovered about the scene at first. "Of course they thought we were too young," Jeanne explains. "And we were." But Jeanne and Jerry were determined to "go it alone"—all the more because of their youth.

Jerry continued with the Air Force, and through succeeding months he progressed from job to job. He was a messenger, then an underclerk, a laborer (he made more as a laborer than as a white-collar worker), a labor foreman, a storekeeper, and finally a warehouse foreman. The young couple thought that they had arrived. Just a week before their first wedding anniversary, Jerry, Jr., was born. He was a beautiful child.

The first major crisis came with the birth of an heir. The boy's skull was not properly formed, and the doctor warned Jeanne that he might have to operate. If surgery were necessary the child's chances of survival were almost nil. Jeanne wept quietly, night after night. Jerry walked the floor with the tiny bundle of warm flesh in his arms. The parents prayed and dared to hope. At last the doctor said that everything would be all right. An operation would not be necessary.

It was 1943. Jerry was drafted and sent to an army training station. Shortly thereafter he received his discharge. An injured leg, dating back to his boyhood, would not permit the rigors of service in the armed forces. He returned home. Jeanne was overjoyed. They began payments on a new house.

This represents one of the happiest periods of Jeanne's life. Household chores didn't bother her. She loved caring for the baby. Jerry was considerate and helpful. They had time to have "lots of fun together."

While in high school, Jerry had worked with the state employment service as a junior interviewer. His former boss, now a major in the army, wired, asking if Jerry would consider transferring to North Carolina; a civil service position was open in his office. Jerry had been under civil service regulations from the start and met the necessary requirements. He and Jeanne went to the library and scanned books on the East Coast. They asked their friends about it. Light-heartedly they decided to go. Jerry would have to go first and get established, as a second child was due in three months. So off he went, and Jeanne remained behind until she could bring her two tiny children with her.

One of the major factors in their choice was a desire to get away from their parents. Both the Andrews and Schmidt families made themselves too available. Their concern was too obvious. The Schmidts had a tendency to dominate. The Andrews family felt that "the children were so very young." Jeanne and Jerry had made their bed, as one aunt put it, now they must learn to sleep in it. They felt that they had to prove to the world, and to themselves, that they had what it takes to build a successful home. Beginning to realize the nature of the risk that they had taken, they felt that their chances for happiness would be better where they were unknown, and where they could start out as any other young parents. They had to break the leading strings and decisively seize the reigns of their own destiny. This decision, radical as it seemed, was as vigorously maintained by Jeanne as by Jerry.

Jerry left in February. In May a baby girl was born. In July Mrs. Andrews accompanied Jeanne and her two infants on the eastbound train. After two weeks, Mrs. Andrews left for the West again, and the young people were on their own.

The next year was a hard one. Jeanne had no friends. Jerry was working night and day at his job. He became chief clerk, then administrative assistant—and, he was hardly twenty. But they paid the price. Jerry was preoccupied and nervous. Jeanne was lonely and nervous. They had not taken their church responsibilities seriously since their marriage. They were surrounded by the sophistication and moral relativity of a wartime Air Force base and the continual "office party." They drank moderately, adopted the thin veneer of their social surroundings, and concentrated on getting ahead.

Finally they began to awaken. Jerry was considered something of a prodigy but that was an empty satisfaction. They weren't building the kind of home they had dreamed of. They weren't becoming the kind of people they respected. They made two important decisions: (1) they would go to college; and (2) they would return to the life of the church. Jeanne was pathetically eager to do an about-face and move against the currents that had been carrying them in the direction of her sordid childhood memories. She wanted no more of San Pablo, even with silk and tinsel.

In following up their first decision, Jerry wrote several universities, getting information and applying for scholarships. He would major in industrial relations.

With reference to their religious life, they entered whole-heartedly into this new venture. If neighborhood churches were having week-night services, they attended. If Bible conferences were in progress, they attended. They visited the Christian Science church. They read together and talked together. A rather highbrow Calvinistic fundamentalist church nearby had impressed them. The people seemed so secure in their faith. They had an answer for every question. And they seemed radiantly happy! Jeanne and Jerry took the children to that church often. One Sunday they brought a visiting speaker to their home for dinner. He was president of a midwestern Bible college. One of the first things he did upon entering the Andrews home was to single out the Goodspeed translation of the Bible, resting on the mantle, and scornfully note that it was not the "Holy" Bible; only the King James Version was the Holy Bible. Jeanne and Jerry still enjoyed the warm fellowship of the church, but they didn't take its doctrinal affirmations and dogmatic declarations too seriously. More and more they attended the Methodist church downtown. The pastor was a lovable, tenderhearted man with a keen sense of humor. He visited in the Andrews home, expressed interest in the young people's dreams, and made his church available to them. Jeanne and Jerry attended the midweek prayer service downtown. Sunday after Sunday they caught the bus and took the children to Sunday school and church. Sometimes they returned for evening worship. Jerry took the leadership course being offered. One day a Bible appeared on his desk at the office. He was declaring himself, in an adolescent way perhaps, but it was a declaration nonetheless. Something was happening to the Andrews!

One night Jeanne and Jerry returned from church. They put the youngsters to bed and talked about their future. Would it be civil service, or industrial relations, or something else? They got ready for bed and knelt side by side in their bedroom. Each one of them prayed aloud, and they dedicated themselves and their family to the Christian ministry.

The next day Jerry handed in his two-weeks' notice. He didn't know what he was going to do, but he was going to do something. Then Dr. Madden, the minister from the downtown church, came by. He listened as they told him of their decision. He had a plan. Would Jerry consider enrolling in college immediately and accepting a "supply" church appointment at the Annual Conference, just two months away? Would he! The die was cast. Three people stood in the center of a small living room. A bald-headed man with a twinkle in his eye prayed a moving, demanding prayer of consecration. And, as Jeanne remembers the scene, she says that tears of gladness streamed down her cheeks. She and Jerry were twenty, and they were starting their second life together.

Every night Jeanne made a pot of coffee and then sat patiently by as Jerry studied. She was "thrilled" and "excited," yet "dubious"— in fact, "scared to death." This was something so entirely new. She was not sure of her own religious experience. She had had no preparation whatever for this strange and important role, yet she knew that Jerry was right. This was her decision too. And she believed that God would provide. She says, "I knew at that time that whatever I had to do, God would help me." She admits that it was "a little girl attitude," but she is thankful that she had it. Today, as she evaluates this earlier attitude, she says, "When you come right down to it, the parent must let the child make his own way. That's the way it is with God." Today she feels that God helps those who are willing to stand on their own two feet and accept responsibility for themselves and for their actions.

Jerry's parents were both apprehensive and glad. Jeanne's parents couldn't believe it; they just couldn't believe it! Jeanne says, "My whole life was suddenly changed. I would be teaching and singing and speaking." Her first disillusionment came when she discovered she couldn't sing. "I came to see that there were some things even God couldn't do."

When Annual Conference met, Jeanne and Jerry were appointed to a beautiful little town on the Atlantic coast. They would be there four years.

Jerry's predecessor had been a highly trained man; and with the exception of some erratic night-school work in a junior college, Jerry had had no college experience whatever. Even more serious, from Jeanne's standpoint, were the practical considerations of making their new home livable. For six years the parsonage had been minus a woman's touch, since the last two pastors to occupy the house had each been bachelors. The kitchen boasted a two-burner, kerosene stove, an icebox with a twenty-five-pound capacity, and a tiny, stained sink which retreated into the wall beneath a jutting dish cabinet. The linoleum was worn from the floor. The furniture in the rest of the house was ancient and broken. The rugs had holes in them. Jeanne waited until the welcoming official had left. Then she sat down in the middle of the floor and cried. In fact, she says she "bawled." This was the first of many similar trials.

The people in this first church, for the most part, were understanding and sympathetic. They loved Jeanne and her young husband. Several of them made lasting impressions on the mistress of the parsonage. It is interesting to note what characteristics Jeanne singled out as she sought to define these impressions.

There was Mrs. Sanders, "the first true Christian I'd ever known," Jeanne said. Mrs. Sanders was a jovial, motherly woman who, according to her young friend, lived a contagious faith in her daily life.

There was Mary Barker. "She wanted to run everything."

There was Madge O'Brien. "What a woman she was! She could do everything and was a Christian in everything she did."

There were the Fellows. "Their whole life was the church, and each other. They were second parents to me."

There was Mrs. Lambert. "She was the sweetest thing."

There was Mark Culler. "He was boastful and pompous; he lacked love for people."

There were ministers that were impressing Jeanne too.

Dr. Madden (the minister who had been so influential in their lives) : "There's no one like him, anywhere."

Dick Hale: "He was so fatherly."

The Williamses (her husband's district superintendent) : "If our family could be like theirs."

George Clark: "He seemed like a good preacher, but I was easily impressed by what people said about themselves."

Horatio McLean: "We used to laugh at him. He was so arrogant. He was a 'successful' young preacher."

These comments are revealing. They indicate that Jeanne responded to affection and love, and was sensitive to its absence. She was impressed more by goodness than by ability. She still needed to be wanted, to be accepted, to be loved. Her tendency to identify certain persons with family roles also indicates her continuing awareness of a deprivation in early life. The intimate relationships of the ministry would compensate for much which young Mrs. Andrews had never known in the Schmidt home.

Jerry commuted to college every week. Jeanne disliked being alone with the children, but she accepted her aloneness and grew closer to the youngsters. While they were living here their third child, a boy, was born.

Four years quickly slipped by. They were four decisive years, years of uncertainty and growth, years of mixed emotions and increasing confidence. Jeanne taught a children's Sunday school class and was accepted and well liked. She helped organize a "circle" of young matrons, comprised of women who had little interest in the church but who were drawn together through common need. She tried speaking in public on two or three occasions. Each time was a repetition of her pre-examination illness in school. Her inability to cope with this situation disturbed her, but she accepted her limitations. Anyway, her children kept her more than busy.

Jerry completed his college training, and at the end of the fourth year was offered a promotion. Smug Harbor was a city of some six thousand persons. The church there was divided. A procession of thirty-two ministers had served there in thirty-six years. Jeanne and Jerry borrowed the Sanders' truck, packed all of their earthly possessions, and drove southward to their new home.

The tension in the new church was contagious. The people knew that they had a reputation. This put them on the defensive. The church was immersed in its problems, and the new pastor and his wife attempted to minimize the problems and to see the congregation in terms of individual personalities. Statistically, the year was phenomenal, with attendance records broken and nearly one hundred new members received. Old hurts were healed and new leadership was developed. Even so, the Andrews were overjoyed at the end of the year when they learned that a very generous scholarship was being made available to them so that they might go on to seminary. The close personal ties that were notable in their first church were not duplicated in Smug Harbor.

However, Jeanne did make two close friends. Once again she displayed the ability to win the confidence of those who were outside the church. She payed attention to, and seemed genuinely to like, people whom the conventional church members tended to ignore. There was more social stratification in Smug Harbor than Jeanne had previously known. Jeanne seemed poised and at home among the more cultured and well-to-do members, yet she seemed to prefer those with whom she had more in common. She was not a social climber. Perhaps this was because of basic democratic tendencies; perhaps it was because of a continuing sense of insecurity. Culture and relative wealth may have threatened her security in this new world.

While in Smug Harbor the Andrews had their fourth child, a little girl. Their children are healthy except for the anxious beginning of the first child.

The next two years were exciting years for Jeanne. Jerry was in seminary. But their student appointment was just five miles from the school in a lovely suburban section, and the parsonage was next to the church. Jerry's salary did not amount to much, but their scholarship provided an extra hundred dollars each month. Then, too, Jerry accepted as many speaking engagements as he could, and these brought in some remuneration. He participated in an insurance training program and received twenty-five dollars for each lecture. There were other things. Therefore the seminary years were not as uncomfortable for the family as they had anticipated.

Jeanne was introduced to another dimension of her new world. Jerry's school friends were in and out of the house constantly. These were young men who were training for Christian service. They were idealists, and Jeanne was glad to participate in the idealism of campus life.

Their closest friends while in seminary were creative personalities. There were the Fullers. He was an official with the state department of education, and she was a typical southern lady, a woman of rare charm and ability. There were the Smiths. He was an insurance executive, a "boy wonder" in his field. They were well on the way to success in the business world. There were the Michaels. Old Dr. Michael was almost eighty. He had been a minister and a college teacher. He was still an ardent pacifist, a social action devotee, and a member of half a dozen liberal political groups that reflected his social idealism and his political impatience. He was a confirmed optimist. His wife, twenty-five years his junior, was a social worker. She was a delightful person who loved Jeanne for what she was. There was Dr. Joiner, one of Jerry's professors, and his wife. They were a saintlike couple. And Jim and Betty Latt. Jim was a young doctor who had contracted tuberculosis during his training. They were members of Jerry's church. They came to be the closest friends that the Andrews had while in seminary, and theirs was a rewarding friendship. More and more Jeanne felt "safe" with such people. These two years were as much an educational experience for her as they were for Jerry.

What are the most important things in Jeanne's life?

Right now she would place her family first. "The children are really our future." She is attempting to give her children the love and affection that she sorely missed. She admits that she has not been a good mother in all respects. She tends to be impatient. "Parsonage life gets so confused. Sometimes I get pretty cross." Four children demand a lot of work. She seems to be troubled with "nervous headaches" frequently, but the headaches don't come as often as they used to. And, she feels that she is making definite progress. "I'm not nearly as temperamental as I used to be," she says. In spite of her admitted shortcomings, it would seem that Jeanne and her children enjoy an exceptionally fine relationship. She plays with them, shares their interests, talks their language, and they confide in her. There seems to be a lot of teasing and good humor which indicates a wholesome type of communication.

Jeanne is deeply devoted to Jerry. She respects him professionally. She proudly asserts, "Nobody can preach like my husband." Since her educational opportunities have been limited, Jerry has attempted to include her in his studies. They have read good books together and discussed them. "He's helped me so much in explaining things," she says. She feels that he sometimes takes things for granted. "He forgets that I didn't come under the same influences he knew." Sometimes Jerry seems cynical to her, and when she reflects that cynicism it confuses her because she doesn't understand the dynamics that are involved.

Jeanne acknowledges her dependence on Jerry. She believes that this dependence is hurtful. "But," she adds, "I was such a little girl when we were married." Sometimes this dependence puzzles her. "Jerry wants me to learn to make up my own mind and stand on my own feet," she says. Yet he dominates the family. "He has always been 'the king of the roost.' Whatever he did, we followed." Perhaps Jerry has been a father-figure as well as husband and lover to Jeanne. Perhaps she has found longed-for security in this dependence. Even so, it has doubtless impeded her quest for self-fulfillment and maturity.

Religion is another of the most important things in Jeanne's life. She insists that the church is necessary in her life, yet she hates the littleness of people and admits that "most preachers 'leave me cold.'" She dislikes hypocrisy and artificiality and believes that many institutional Christians lack genuineness; their faith lacks relevance.

When asked to explain her beliefs she said, "I can't define things. I couldn't tell anybody what I believe." Then she proceeded slowly and self-consciously to outline her credo.

She began: "I believe that love is the basic religious attitude. Isn't that what Jesus said? Our love for God combines awe, gratitude, and obedience. But that's not enough; we must practice brotherly love too."

"The laws of Christ and the life of Christ are central," she continued. "The Sermon on the Mount is the main thing we have to go by. We try to pattern our lives after his."

When Jerry's father died she stayed with the older Mrs. Andrews for two months. It was then that the value of religion came home to her more than at any other time. "She was an inspiration to everyone in that town who knew and loved them," explains Jeanne. "If someone stopped her on the street to sympathize, she would encourage them. Every time she was the helper; she was the guide." That quiet faith and confidence made a deep impression on Jeanne. She and her mother-in-law are very close now. The old bitterness has passed.

Does she look forward to the future? Very much! "The last twelve years have been full of things I never dreamed of. I have no idea what the future will bring. I can hardly wait for it to get here."

CHAPTER THREE

DEVELOPING PERSONALITY

~~~~~~

This story of Jeanne Andrews, though incomplete in many details, does portray her as a living personality who emerges from an insecure and deprived childhood to a young womanhood that seems to fulfill most of her desires. How does she arrive at this successful position in her world? What causal factors contribute to her development through these twenty-nine years? How shall we understand this progress toward psychological maturity and religious fulfillment?

The answer given will depend upon one's theory of personality. Each reader will observe her from his own perspective, emerging from his background of experience and interpretation. One reader will emphasize the causal factors of biological heredity, as packed in the genes delivering from her ancestors tendencies that were dominant in them, with instinctive cravings to be satisfied by predetermined activities. From this viewpoint one might argue that her happiness as a wife and mother arises from the fulfillment of inherited tendencies as sex and maternal instincts.

Another reader will be impressed by the character-molding forces of environment upon the Schmidt family. The foundation of their security was shattered by the economic depression, which contributed to the failure of business and cast them adrift as migrants seeking temporary jobs wherever such could be found. When they came to San Pablo the local culture was reflected in the behavior of the parents. Jeanne's religious development also varied with environmental opportunities—retarded as a child in a nonreligious home, and ripening as she came to associate with church-going people who provided a religious culture.

A third reader will emphasize the interpersonal relations, and note especially the influence of persons who at one time or another became significant in her life. First, there was her older sister Lila, who stood by her in the crises of childhood and responded to the invitation to apply for baptism. Then there was Jimmy Younger, who invited her to the youth group in his church and introduced her to Jerry Andrews, a boy from a religious home who eventually led her into a religious vocation as a minister's wife. There was Dr. Madden, their pastor, who encouraged them to take the steps toward college and the work of the Christian ministry. Without these persons her life would have been quite different.

And yet she asserted her own individuality in reacting against sex exploits and the kind of home her parents made for her. She aspired to other ideals and decided for herself to associate with religious people in place of the associates chosen by her family. When she and Jerry had at first accepted the moral relativity of the society at the Air Force base, they became dissatisfied with the prevailing mood and decided to turn again to the church and follow a religious vocation. Here is evidence of an inner power of choice that was more decisive than the determinants of environment. A fourth reader might uphold this view.

There will be other ways of looking at personality, but if we take these views as fairly representative we have four typical theories advanced in our time. Each one has sufficient support among contemporary psychologists to consider it a leading school of thought. Each psychology of personality emerges from the systematic analysis of empirical data into a theory which to its adherents appears the most reasonable hypothesis.

If this is so, we may wonder why honest and systematic psychologists come to such different conclusions. To begin with, the data of personality are complex, ambiguous, and open to contradictory interpretations. No investigator would contend that the facts are all in hand, and if incomplete they are inconclusive. To be noted also are methodological differences among investigators, which follow diverging procedures and may thereby arrive at differing conclusions. Again, there is the personal equation to reckon with, as each observer has his particular subjective biases and sees what he reports from the position in which he stands.[1]

Of inescapable significance in every investigation are the premises from which we start. For the premises once admitted are bound to shape the course of whatever argument proceeds from them. Every systematic psychologist will employ a scientific method and will naturally start from presuppositions held in common with other

---

[1] This has been noted by Francis Bacon as the idol of the cave, and by Einstein as the principle of relativity in which the observer is recognized as a variable.

scientists working in related fields. It will be instructive to trace the relationship of the four theories of personality to the sciences from which their presuppositions derive. These four psychologies which we take as representative theories of personality are the following:

1. *Psychoanalysis* as presented by Sigmund Freud has developed from presuppositions of the biological sciences. Steeped in the traditions of mechanistic biology derived from his teachers in Vienna (Meynert, Brücke, Exner), he first assumed that mental processes are determined by neurological reflexes. As he moved into psychology, his motivating system unfolded into an instinct theory of *libido* or dynamic tensions at work unconsciously in all behavior to avoid pain and enjoy pleasure, to fulfill potentialities and satisfy the basic hungers of life.

2. *Field psychology* as represented by Kurt Lewin has developed from presuppositions of the physical and mathematical sciences. He turns to physics for such concepts as vectors and valences in a field of co-existing forces. Topological diagrams are also employed to show dynamic forces operating by interactive processes which comprise a life space in which the individual carries on his drama of inner adaptation to outer environment.

3. *Interpersonal psychology* as represented by Harry S. Sullivan employs presuppositions of the social sciences. Coming to psychiatry from the social sciences, he builds a bridge between them, and outlines a psychology of interpersonal relations as the matrix of personality. The isolated person is sterile, for it is through face-to-face relationships that personality is developed and expressed. In his pursuit of satisfaction and security a person needs to validate with other persons the meaning of his experiences.

4. *Personalistic psychology* as represented by Gordon W. Allport incorporates presuppositions of the ideal sciences. He affirms the uniqueness of the individual in opposition to those who would reduce him to statistical averages and other common denominators. He disclaims the genetic determinism that reduces later developments to earlier motives, showing that personality achieves new centers of integration at progressive levels of conscious choice. His view of personality is open to the insights of the normative sciences of logic, ethics, aesthetics and religion.

It is the task confronting every serious student of personality to comprehend such psychologies with their conflicting claims. Lest in our haste we dispose of theories we do not thoroughly understand, it is well to approach each view expectantly as if we intend to make it our own, giving full and sympathetic consideration to what each psychologist has to say. If the theories prove contradictory indeed, then we would need to accept one by rejecting others. If they should appear to supplement rather than contradict each other we would search for some integration of what is true from each in a new theory seeking larger perspective.

To examine the developing nature of personality we shall call upon these psychologists to instruct us in terms of their investigations. For our purpose it is convenient to view the growth of personality in four successive stages: infancy, childhood, youth, and maturity. As we come to each of these stages in personal development we shall view it according to one psychologist. This does not indicate that the psychologist has been limited to one epoch of development, for each one has considered personality as a whole. Yet by asking each one to view a stage of growth with us, we have opportunity to see the particular tasks of human life at one age, from the standpoint of an observing psychologist.

1. Infancy—According to Freud

To understand the bundle of squirming life delivered from the mother's womb has puzzled the best minds of all time. It is easier to do than to know, and at first the doing may appear more urgent than the knowing. In the first moments of life in this world there are many things to be done for the newborn infant, such as helping him to breathe, tying and severing the umbilical cord, washing and powdering the tender skin, placing him in a warm nest, and preparing for his nourishment and comfort in order to help him grow and feel at home with his humankind. And yet child care requires knowing as much as doing, lest we do the wrong thing.

When we pause to study the tiny infant, we may well begin to wonder. What are you and how did you become so? By careful observation we may study the characteristic activities and behavior patterns from day to day of his growing life. Over a period of months we can also observe changes in bodily structure and weight, as well as demands for nourishment and attention, manifestations of anger and pleasure, focusing of vision and differing responses to the playful or stern tones of the mother's voice. But to put these facts observed into some pattern of meaning we must have a theory.

How do we know what goes on within the infant mind? This is even more baffling than the efforts of you and me to understand each other, for we have a verbal language and other familiar cues by which to comprehend our mutual intentions. To know what the infant wants and what he is striving for calls for insight, i.e., an inner view of what life means to him. To view him as a creature of wants is a theory, to be sure, yet not contradictory to his observed behavior; for he acts as though he wants something and shows satisfaction when he has it. This becomes the hypothesis of Freud.

Sigmund Freud (1856-1939) was the child of the nineteenth century, and came to his medical profession confirmed in the biology of that era. His psychoanalysis, as he said, grew on "a narrowly restricted basis," which was the theory held by his teachers that life is strictly determined by biological preconditions.[2] The young Freud tried sternly to check his speculative interests, but they would not down. The mystery of personality led him from biology to psychology, where he found purpose at the center of his science. By 1900 he had come upon the *wish* as the basic motive force of human life. This he defines as "a current in the apparatus, issuing from unpleasure (*Unlust*) and arriving at pleasure (*Lust*)."[3]

From birth the infant is moved by the wish to turn from discomfort to pleasure. The lust for pleasure Freud named *libido,* and all pleasure-seeking he recognized as erotic. His theory of infant sexuality finds it diffused over the entire body wherever nerve endings are sensitive to pain and pleasure. Is anyone too young to want pleasure instead of pain? Especially in the undisciplined years of infancy the primitive impulses are most regnant. Who does not want to be happy and satisfy the hungers of life? In later years we learn to postpone pleasures and accept pain for a larger good that is worth the cost. But the distant goals are unknown to the infant, who at first lives only in the present and wants what he wants when he wants it.

The infant is born hungry and is naturally oriented to oral satisfactions that predominate in the early period, which Freud termed the oral phase in the developing personality. The satisfaction of his

[2] See Ernest Jones, *The Life and Work of Sigmund Freud* (New York: Basic Books, Inc., 1953), I, 370. As a medical student he refers to old Brücke, his professor of physiology, as "the greatest authority I ever met" (*ibid.,* p. 39). Brücke had pledged, "No other forces than the common physical-chemical ones are active within the organism" (*ibid.,* p. 40).

[3] *Ibid.,* p. 399.

hunger by suckling gives priority to the mouth, and he seeks to incorporate first the nipple, then his thumb and fingers or whatever object he can take into his mouth. There is pleasure also in making babbling sounds with his mouth which later he forms into words in response to words from other persons. The oral phase is one of dependency upon the mother, a close and intimate relationship which he cherishes and may seek to recapture after weening. Later on in life he may have regressive tendencies to return to the comforts of oral dependency.

We have learned from Freud at this point how important are the early satisfactions of the infant to his health and happiness throughout later life. The stern denial of infant wants is yielding to the "demand schedule" to pick up the fretting child for mothering whenever he seems to need attention and affection. For otherwise the infant has "anxious expectation" that becomes chronic insecurity. Infants who are neglected or roughly treated by rejecting mothers become depressed and emotionally unstable. Pediatricians now pay close attention to crying as an indication of discomforts that may disturb the emotional life and imperil healthy relations to other persons. Parents may not be aware of the hostility and anxiety they unconsciously project upon infants. Until they learn to correct their own attitudes, it may not be possible for their children to feel loved and confident that life is good. "Confidence acts as an emotional shelter. It facilitates learning." [4]

This is the time to foster dependence to insure basic security and trust in the growing infant. It is at this time that he is most aware of himself, and unless his hungers are met by others he will turn away from them to autistic or fantasy pleasures. Thumb-sucking and random muscular actions at this age provide needed satisfaction and need not be cause for anxious concern. Overeating in later years or drinking and smoking to excess may be symptoms of deprived affectional relationships, serving as oral substitutes for interpersonal satisfactions.

The period of later infancy Freud named the anal-sadistic phase. With teething the infant shows interest in biting activity accompanied by impulses to hurt the mother, arising from frustrations in satisfying his demands. Toilet training turns attention to the anal region, which

[4] Therese Benedek, "Personality Development," in *Dynamic Psychiatry*, eds. Franz Alexander and Helen Ross (University of Chicago Press, 1952), p. 66.

is also sensitive to pain and pleasure. As voluntary control of the sphincter and urethral muscles is possible by maturation of the nerve system, parents impose new standards of behavior upon the undisciplined pleasure of infancy. If the affectional ties are strong there is sufficient reward in pleasing the mother to compensate for the discomfort of bowel control. To gain the loving approval of the parents is incentive enough to motivate learning even at the expense of instinctual pleasure. But if the affectional ties are not strong enough the infant will show negative and stubborn resistance to suggestion, not only in toilet training but in other activities as well. Aggressive behavior such as breaking a valued object, refusing to obey, or indulging in temper tantrums will indicate the sadistic desire to hurt the parents from whom more love is sought.

And yet these are exploratory adventures for the growing infant, essential to discovering his freedom to be himself and the limits of his freedom. This is the dawning of conscience and social responsibility, when there is new awareness of right and wrong. Parents do well to be tolerant enough in their discipline to give time for the learning of new habits to be established, lest rigid demands and angry retaliation confuse or intimidate the little fellow. To win approval he may then try too hard to "be good," and become compulsive in performing the ritual of conformity, with distressing anxiety whenever a variation occurs in the routine. We may overlook the dangers in the obedient child which are quite as serious as in the stubborn child. Unconditional love is the deepest need of a person at any age, and the infant trying to get along with a family is no exception. Trifling as these daily experiences may seem, they are the stuff of which character is made.

It is in this training period of the second year that the structure of personality is more definitely formed. The infant's demand for instant satisfaction is met by the denials of weening and the delays of bowel control. The pleasure principle by which he governed his first year is countered by the reality principle of what his world demands of him. The psychic economy of this period is complex and precarious.[5] In his oral dependency he was always given to, and what he demanded of his world was usually received. But now he is taken from, and he may well respond in angry hostility when required to give up and yield

<hr>

[5] *Ibid.*, p. 74.

to the wishes of other persons. It need not, however, be a losing game altogether, for the little learner may win new satisfactions to compensate his losses. To win the approval of the mother is a gain worthy of the effort; unless he is already insecure and hopeless due to maternal rejection in unpredictable or punitive moods, in which case he may not readily cope with the new demands. A new sense of mastery may gain him inner satisfaction by which to forego the other pleasures of this dependent luxury.

The emerging of such inner conflicts is basic to the structuring of personality, in the dynamic view of Freud. Three major functions come into play and struggle for ascendancy from later infancy. The libidinous cravings for pleasure are the primitive impulses of life to gratify hungers. With these cravings, which Freud called the *id*, the career of the infant begins, for he knows no other good than to satisfy his needs right now. From these primitive drives life has its dynamic nature, always restlessly striving for means to reduce painful tensions and gratify its ceaseless demands. The id is "a chaos, a cauldron of seething excitement" arising from instinctual tensions and unmet needs.

These instincts fill it [the id] with energy, but it has no organisation and no unified will, only an impulsion to obtain satisfaction for the instinctual needs, in accordance with the pleasure-principle. The laws of logic—above all, the law of contradiction—do not hold for processes in the id. Contradictory impulses exist side by side without neutralising each other or drawing apart; at most they combine in compromise formations under the overpowering economic pressure towards discharging their energy. There is nothing in the id which can be compared to negation, . . . no recognition of the passage of time. . . . Conative impulses which have never got beyond the id, and even impressions which have been pushed down into the id by repression, are virtually immortal and are preserved for whole decades as though they had only recently occurred. . . .
Naturally, the id knows no values, no good and evil, no morality. . . . Instinctual cathexes seeking discharge—that, in our view, is all that the id contains.[6]

But when the pleasure principle comes into conflict with the reality principle by the prohibitions and expectations of the parents, a second

---

[6] Sigmund Freud, *New Introductory Lectures on Psycho-Analysis*, tr. W. J. H. Sprott (London: Hogarth Press, 1933), pp. 98-100. Used by permission of Hogarth Press and Encyclopaedia Britannica. The term *id* (German *Es*) was suggested by Nietzsche and Groddeck.

function begins to operate, which Freud named the *superego*. This censorship of the id impulses represents the authority of older persons, who take their morality seriously enough to impose it upon the child. If the relation of mother to infant has been well established in love and care, the approval of the mother will be desirable to the child and her disapproval intolerably anxious. The unloved child may retreat from such demands to fantasy and autistic pleasures (as masturbation), or respond with stubborn resistance and compulsive rituals of conformity. Learning for him will be difficult due to insecurity and hostility. But the child who is well-loved will accept the restraints and corrections more gracefully for the approval of one he seeks to please and whose affection he has reason to anticipate. In this way he begins to take responsibility to control id impulses by his dawning conscience.

To do so is to exercise a third function, named by Freud the *ego*. When id and superego clash, as in the toilet training, first one and then the other may win out. The satisfaction of soiling may at first be more impelling than that of sphincter control. But the approval of the mother, whose love the child needs, is a counterattraction (cathexis) which may ascend over the primitive impulse. As these desires teeter-totter up and down, the child sits at the fulcrum and discovers he can put his weight on one side or the other. If he resists he is learning to assert his will against another will. If he consents he is learning to put his weight on the side of co-operation and approval. The ego is at the center of growing personality, feeling the pressure of id against the counterpressure of the superego. He can lean either way to express the id impulses or to repress them for the sake of social approval. The ego is the executive who wrestles with the conflicting impulses to decide how he will manage them.

A good deal of this struggle is unconscious, as the organic processes originally were. As a pioneer in opening to psychology the mysteries of the unconscious, Freud learns from analysis of dreams, unwitting mistakes, and free association how extensive and intensive is the interplay of these energies contending with each other. One may gain the impression that the unconscious is a region or battlefield in which armies of impulses clash and strive for ascendancy, in a mechanistic determinism of quantities of blind energy. But as he moves from decade to decade in his successive researches, Freud comes ever more to an ego psychology in which the conscious choices of the ego may have the deciding vote—or be overpowered and yield for the moment to the chaotic impulses of the id on the one hand, or the stern and punitive demands of the superego on the other. (See Fig. I.)

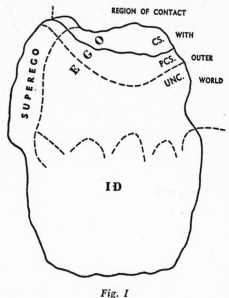

Fig. I
SKETCH OF FREUD'S THEORY [7]

At the center of these ongoing contests of impulses and restraints, the ego marshals defenses to repress the id, or to compromise and compensate for denials by accepting other gains that may seek to avoid punishment from the superego. Character is formed out of these struggles, for as the pleasure principle of the id meets the moral demands of the superego and the reality principle of the ego, the primitive impulses are repressed and overlaid with more acceptable patterns of behavior. These three functions are not separate entities or little men dwelling within one body-mind; they are organizing centers of purpose. They are constellations of wishes and desires that have the continuity and momentum of tendencies or intentions. They form the structural unity-in-conflict of opposing interests as the ego becomes the regulating center of their interaction, seeking to achieve an acceptable balance of inner and outer demands.

[7] Reprinted from *The Structure and Meaning of Psychoanalysis* by William Healy, A. F. Bronner, and A. M. Bowers, by permission of Alfred A. Knopf, Inc. Copyright 1930 by Alfred A. Knopf, Inc.

One can hardly go wrong in regarding the ego as that part of the id which has been modified by its proximity to the external world and the influence that the latter has had on it, and which serves the purpose of receiving stimuli and protecting the organism from them. . . . This relation to the external world is decisive for the ego. The ego has taken over the task of representing the external world for the id, and so of saving it; for the id, blindly striving to gratify its instincts in complete disregard of the superior strength of outside forces, could not otherwise escape annihilation. In the fulfilment of this function, the ego has to observe the external world and preserve a true picture of it in the memory traces left by its perceptions, and, by means of the reality-test, it has to eliminate any element in this picture of the external world which is a contribution from internal sources of excitation. On behalf of the id, the ego controls the path of access to motility, but it interpolates between desire and action the procrastinating factor of thought, during which it makes use of the residues of experience stored up in memory. In this way it dethrones the pleasure-principle, . . . and substitutes for it the reality-principle, which promises greater security and greater success.[8]

Critics of Freud are likely to say that this psychology is reductive in holding the primitive id as determinative, and the work of the ego as merely its agent to gain its ends more cleverly. There are tendencies to be found in his writings that appear to support this criticism. The paragraph quoted above acknowledges the part which the ego may play in the service of the id, and is open to the interpretation that the ego is but a weak pawn devoting its energies to saving the id from destruction. To do this evidently means to save life itself from destruction with all its values, for reckless satisfaction of blind cravings of the id can only be destructive to the larger interests of life, unless controlled and channeled into appropriate fulfillment in healthy and productive ways. This, Freud insists upon in his next paragraph:

What, however, especially marks the ego out in contradistinction to the id, is a tendency to synthesise its contents, to bring together and unify its mental processes, which is entirely absent from the id. . . . The ego advances from the function of perceiving instincts to that of controlling them, but the latter is only achieved through the mental representative of the instinct becoming subordinated to a larger organisation, and finding its place in a coherent unity. In popular language, we may say that the

[8] Freud, *New Introductory Lectures*, pp. 100-101.

ego stands for reason and circumspection, while the id stands for the untamed passions.[9]

Again he cautions against judging too hastily a first attempt at picturing so elusive a complexity as the human mind. He notes that these functions and their differentiations may vary greatly from person to person, and undergo changes in the process of personality development. Finally, in speaking of the therapeutic efforts of psychoanalysis, he says that their aim is "to strengthen the ego, to make it more independent of the super-ego, to widen its field of vision, and so to extend its organisation that it can take over new portions of the id." He then concludes by offering a slogan which has become the motto of psychoanalysis to this day. "Where id was, there shall ego be." [10]

This contest becomes clearer as the little person comes to the age of three, which marks the crossing over from infancy to childhood. This is called by psychoanalysts the oedipal period, because of the typical love triangle in the family of mother, father, and child. In his first year the infant is enfolded in his mother's arms and nourished at her breast in a close relationship. From this intimate relation he receives the sustenance of life, emotionally as well as physically. At first he is scarcely aware of her as a separate object, so dependent is he upon her and so limited in his awareness to his own needs and their satisfaction. Weaning is an unwelcome separation, re-enacting the birth trauma when he was expelled from his fetal home, the womb. This breach of the "we" [11] accentuates his separate existence from the mother, and at the same time his longing to possess her. During the months to follow he gradually discovers that mother has other interests to occupy her attention, rival claims to his own upon her. Sibling rivalry may turn upon a younger baby or older children in the family. It is the father, however, who holds the first claim upon the mother, and the little boy observes the strength with which the father holds the mother in his arms and gathers her affection to himself.

The little boy is likely to feel deprived, first in the weaning, then in the rigors of toilet training, and in time by the rivalry with the father for the affection of the mother. In the sequence of organ pleasures he has been proceeding from the oral and anal to the genital region.

[9] *Ibid.*, pp. 101-2.
[10] *Ibid.*, p. 106.
[11] Fritz Kunkel describes it in his book *In Search of Maturity* (New York: Charles Scribner's Sons, 1943).

When he plays with his penis his mother is likely to reprimand him, giving him the impression that she is rejecting him in that aspect of his being. She removes herself from his libidinal desire and takes the role of an asexual being who does not approve of his interest in sex. He is caught again in the conflict between his id impulses for pleasure and the reality situation in which his mother requires him to renounce the pleasure. In this reinforcement of his superego, he will try to win her approval by denying himself genital pleasure, even as he had in weaning and bowel control.

His father may also threaten him to desist, and set up what Freud called a "castration complex," the fear that he may lose his penis, as his sister seems to have done. His fear then is twofold and may be directed to the father and to the offending organ he may not touch. In the love triangle he comes to recognize his father as his rival for the mother, and in his own weakness to resent the authority by which the father holds the upper hand. In showing hostility toward the father he may be punished and resent the more his inability to succeed in this rivalry. If he identifies with the father and seeks to displace him with the mother, he will be in trouble for taking the masculine role toward his mother as a love object. On the other hand if he identifies with the mother he is denying his male assertiveness and regressing into a dependent infantile attitude to her.

The little girl's development is similar but more complex in the oedipal period. Her genital organ does not obviously come to her attention and her interest in her body remains more diffuse in pleasurable sensations of the skin and muscular co-ordination. Freud accented the importance in the girl of "penis envy"; others note reaction to the favored position of boys socially in our culture. Her psychosexual libido would naturally be directed to the male, he thought. And her interest in the father would involve her in an oedipal triangle similar to the little boy's desire for the mother. But due to her original closeness to the mother the little girl will have more difficulty in attaining heterosexuality. Her conflicting tendencies will be (1) the wish to take the mother's place and be loved by the father, and (2) the wish to be the child and be loved by the mother. The first impulse carries the fear of losing the mother's love, and this may repress her heterosexual development to remain safe with the mother. To evade this dilemma she may identify with the father or brother, as a tomboy who denies feminine impulses by turning to activities in other areas of life. For to have the approval of parents is so important that tabooed impulses will usually be repressed in the following period of latency.

Some of his critics object to Freud's sordid or pathological view of personality motivated by lust for pleasure and conflicting energies. From his psychoanalysis he learned what is no surprise to many parents, that children are not as innocent as they look. But this does not mean that growing persons will be ruled by their "lower impulses." It is in the struggle of the ego to control the primitive id that character is formed and personality developed. Freud insists he does not neglect the "higher moral, spiritual side of human nature." The work of repressing the id impulses is instigated by the moral and aesthetic tendencies of the ego, sustained by authorities who are both admired and feared.

Here we have that higher nature, in this ego-ideal or super-ego, the representative of our relation to our parents. When we were little children we knew these higher natures, we admired and feared them; and later we took them into ourselves.[12]

In the story of Jeanne the record of her infancy is passed over so quickly that many significant details are omitted. But there are clues to indicate the complex emotional struggles within the family constellation. As the third child she always felt rejected by her mother and sensed the mother's jealousy whenever affection was shown her. Consequently, Jeanne was afraid to love her father or receive affection from him. For in the rivalries for attention the parents seemed to prefer each other to the children. Sex interest though manifested by adults was sternly repressed in the children, persisting into adolescence as acute fear.

Jeanne's need for affection is evident at the time of her illness, as well as in her turning to the older sister, Lila, for a substitute mother, and later to teachers and mothers of her friends. Her tomboy play with her brother Delbert served the double purpose of repressing her feminine sex and winning approval from playmates. There was also an outlet for aggressive id impulses in sports approved by her superego and the authorities she feared and admired. Her religious searchings came to meet a deep need in trusting God as a loving Father.

[12] *The Ego and the Id*, p. 47. Used by permission of Hogarth Press and Encyclopaedia Britannica.

2. Childhood—According to Lewin

Toward the end of the third year, infancy passes over into childhood. The exact boundary is neither final nor definite and varies with the child and family as learning and maturing may develop. While yet an infant the little boy or girl is learning to be a child. Nor is he a child all of a sudden, but gradually here and there as he glimpses and ventures his onward course of life. One child may advance in motor co-ordination and skills to maneuver his way around and walk at an early age, while another child may reach out to others in talk with expanding vocabulary and respond to stories and songs with avid interest. The tasks of child life are more intricate and challenging than those of the infant's cozy little world.

As childhood takes up where infancy gives out, so Kurt Lewin (1890-1947) carries on the study of personality where Freud left off. The deeply emotional and circumscribed world of psychoanalysis has much to teach us about the desires, anxieties, and waking capacities of life hungry for love. But Lewin would now have us see the child in a larger world of expanding social interests and activities. The drama of life to Freud is but a repetition of the plot of infancy, striving in ever more devious and subtle ways to satisfy primitive lusts for pleasure. So enduring are the infantile demands and wishes, that for him the growing person ever strives to return or relive those early adventures, to possess the mother or father (or surrogates) and be the favored one whose desires are somehow always to be gratified. This to Lewin is but a fraction of the whole life story.

To understand the child, we need to see him moving out into a widening psychological environment, where he makes his way among a maze of interacting forces and events. He is not motivated alone by the insatiable drives of his biological nature, or the unconscious strivings of libido repeating the historical determinism of his infancy. To the contrary, Lewin will insist that the child is determined by his contemporary environment as he perceives it and participates in it as a young explorer. The past has no influence upon him unless he deals with it as a present experience. There is a "time-depth" in the present where he may recall the previous or anticipate the future, but the present is the center of his focus and the base of his operation.

This larger world in which the child operates is his life space. He has characteristic needs which he wants to gratify in various ways. But in starting to do so he is met by barriers such as a verbal "no," or the physical intervention of a parent which interposes opposition of counterforces around which he will seek a detour. A little boy who is intercepted in his dash for the street where cars are passing by may then turn to his sand box and play with a toy truck, which serves as a substitute value to him. He is setting up a new goal, and when he loads the truck high with blocks he shows preference for a more difficult goal of balancing a stack of blocks to the easier one of placing them on one level. This, Lewin calls the level of aspiration in setting goals.

Conflict situations arise as the child struggles with another child for possession of the toy truck. These conflicts may break out in open hostilities or be worked through peaceably in taking turns, depending upon the atmosphere of the play group which develops from attitudes and procedures of its member adults and children in dealing with each other. Frustration in moving toward goals may lead to hostility, or it may in another situation invite regression, or in a third situation it may stimulate resourceful productivity. In striving for a given goal we may note the relation of the cognitive structure (learning, insight, or roundabout route) to the direction and strength of the psychological forces in power fields.

In this field psychology the individual child is not to be taken in isolation, but rather as a system in tension surrounded by other tension systems of co-existing forces. To study the child we begin with the total situation, which may be fluid and open to change, or rigid and resistant to change when approaching equilibrium. Personality is viewed as an organization of psychic systems disposed to respond to each other. To make them clearer Lewin diagrams these systems as they are related to each other by an oval to be subdivided into regions of dynamic tension. At the center is the inner personal region (I) subdivided into the units more or less accessible, then at the periphery the motor-perceptual region (M) separated by a circular boundary from the environment (E).

The psychical systems of the infant are few in number and relatively undifferentiated. He is not rigidly organized at first, but flexible and mobile. As his personality develops there is a gradual expansion, differentiation, and stabilization of psychic systems by interaction with the environmental field. The life of the growing child is structured first by the family at home. If the parents are rigid and constricting, if they fence him in with stern prohibitions and regulations, the child is likely to develop a rigid set of psychic systems and feel bound compulsively to meet their strict demands invariably. On the other hand,

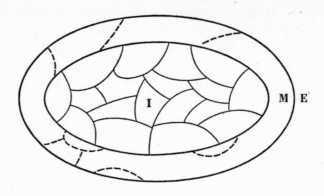

Fig. II
SKETCH OF LEWIN'S THEORY [13]

if parents are more free and easygoing, the child will be more open to change and learning. As he grows older he begins to select his own goals and give new structure to his personality and life space.

Lewin indicates the danger in forcing a child too early into rigid separation of the reality level from the plane of irreality. The life of a child is quite a fantasy world peopled with nursery rhymes, fairy stories, Santa Claus, and fictitious characters of cowboys and adventurers for boys, or dolls and dressing up for girls, where role playing deals with fictions as facts. It would be unfortunate to rob the child of his fantasy world and make him prosaic or restricted in capacity for creative imagination and playful artistry. For if he is stratified so rigidly he will have difficulty in moving from the existing reality to one as yet unreal which may prove more rewarding. All progress is from the real to the ideal, and unless one can move from one plane to another he is incapable of imaginative growth, creative projection toward the not yet real, or the confidence to change for the better.

When a child is in an easy and fluid situation his inner personal region is openly accessible to the outer environment. Under stress, however, the boundaries become defensive walls and the inner regions

[13] From Lewin, *Principles of Topological Psychology*. 1936. McGraw-Hill Book Co. Used by permission.

are more tightly organized against the threat, and consequently less accessible to learning or communication. While under very high tension there may be regression to primitive unification of the inner personal region inaccessible behind a firm defensive hull. A person is in constant interaction with his environment in which other people have a dominant place in affecting him and the structuring of his life space. Yet he is no helpless victim of external forces. He affects them by his behavior too, as he perceives and works with them to move toward his goals.

The field psychologist would view Jeanne's childhood in a different way from the psychoanalyst. He would not deny the importance of her infancy, or the intensity of her need for parental love and approval. But from year to year she was meeting people and confronting new situations in widening fields of activity. By early childhood she was already turning from the unresponsive parents to the other children in the family as her contemporaries with whom to participate in many activities. Then her life space was extended to other communities as the family moved on, with new friends of school and playground. There were barriers to frustrate her in gaining her desires, but she tried out the next best detours toward the goals of her aspiration.

The boundaries of her life space were not so rigid as to cripple initiative. The preoccupation of the parents gave more freedom for the play life of the children to luxuriate. With this freedom Jeanne could indulge her fantasies and pursue the vistas of irreality, to follow the ideal beyond the sober or sordid aspects of reality. There were defensive tactics to fend off the demands and threats of the adult world, and these would trouble her in times of stress as in meeting examinations in school or in public speaking. Yet she was free to select many of her own goals, such as the friends to be with and the church she would attend. In school and youth groups she did win approval, was elected to offices of leadership, and was sought by the boys in adolescent years.

Her life space continued to expand from year to year, as she relied less upon the home circle and more upon the group life of her peers. In each occasion she was concerned about the present more than the past or the future. It was not too difficult to leave the past behind with former associations and to venture forth to the unknown areas and untried fields of marriage, motherhood, and a new vocation with Jerry. These events are far beyond childhood, but they offer further evidence of contemporary causation in a widening field of co-existing forces and events.

With these field concepts Lewin, and the research team which gathered around him, proceeded to social experimentation in natural groups. To study frustration and regression he investigated with Barker and Dembo[14] the behavior of young children (age 28-61 months) in a free play situation as compared with a frustrating situation where attractive toys were visible but out of reach behind a wire netting. Each of the thirty children was first given opportunity to play with the attractive equipment; then it was denied to him. By careful observation the behavior of each child was carefully recorded, such as barrier behavior, escape behavior, substitute behavior, and emotion behavior. Regression was defined as the opposite of development. It manifested a loss in variety of behavior, retreat from extensive areas of activity and interest, reduction of time perspective, and return from organizational dependence to simple dependence. Resourceful development was thereby studied as well as regression in the face of frustration.

Authoritarian and democratic group atmospheres were studied experimentally by Lewin with Lippitt and Escalona.[15] Children of the fifth and sixth grades were formed by random grouping into two clubs of five each. One club was conducted in a democratic style, and the other club conducted by the same leader in an authoritarian style. Total behavior of each group was recorded on a time chart by trained observers and stenographic record. The group goal was to make masks of plaster of Paris, etc., which would belong to the group as a whole.

In the authoritarian atmosphere the leader exerted a strong control of the group, barring members from individual goals and setting his own goals for them. He reduced the space of movement for each member and dominated the interpersonal relationships by dictating the subgroup structure. In the democratic atmosphere the leader recognized individual goals and made them accessible. He presented alternative goals and means of behavior but offered the choice to

[14] Roger Barker, Tamara Dembo, and Kurt Lewin, *Frustration and Regression: An Experiment with Young Children* (Iowa City: University of Iowa Press, 1941).

[15] Kurt Lewin, Ronald Lippitt, and Sibylle Escalona, *Studies in Topological and Vector Psychology* (Iowa City: University of Iowa, 1940), I, 43-195.

members of the group. While he participated with them in group activities, he sought not to control or restrict their freedom but to help them develop overlapping power fields.

The authoritarian experiment resulted in nearly twice as many social actions per unit of time to the leader, but they were responses rather than initiated approaches. The members of this group were more submissive toward the leader, except in demanding attention. They were also more resistant to the leader, ignoring a social approach three times as often as in the democratic group. The children in the democratic group treated the leader more nearly as an equal, initiating approaches to him in less submissive ways. While the authoritarian group became progressively more submissive, the democratic group were more initiating, friendly, and work-minded.

Toward other members in the authoritarian group there was more aggressive and dominating behavior. The democratic members were more objective and friendly in relation to their fellows; they were more open and not so likely to ignore social approaches. The members of the authoritarian group were more "I-centered" and the members of the democratic group were more "we-centered." In the authoritarian group, hostility was twice turned against one member in scapegoating. More conflicts for status occurred than in the democratic group, and the feeling of belonging was less in the authoritarian group. More constructive work was accomplished in the democratic group.

These social experiments show the possibility of studying the child in his total field to follow the dynamic social forces and interactions operating in the situation. They indicate some of the directions in which Lewin seeks to go beyond Freud by a scientific procedure of expanding data and experimental proof in a larger life space where the individual and his environment interact among psychic systems and subsystems. And yet what he gains in breadth may be at the loss of depth, for we miss in the co-existing processes of Lewin the deeper emotional significance of Freud's analysis. Preoccupied as Lewin is with structures and organization, he puts off telling us what is the content of this life he treats mathematically by a "psychological calculus." [16]

[16] Urie Bronfenbrenner, "Toward an Integrated Theory of Personality," in *Perception: An Approach to Personality*, eds. R. R. Blake and G. V. Ramsey (New York: Ronald Press Co., 1951) , pp. 210-16.

Specifically, we miss any reference to the religious factors in growing personality. It is evident that religious associations and experiences were quite decisive in the life of Jeanne. Here she was accepted by a heavenly Father and warmly encouraging friends when she felt rejected by her own parents at home. The religious spirit of love and appreciation for her as a person is what meant most to her in these crucial years of her passage from childhood to adolescence and maturity. Yet Lewin has nothing to say about religious dynamics in developing through childhood. Another field psychologist[17] does acknowledge the effect of church membership, seeing in religion a social force of primary significance. The ultimate reality of God he holds beyond psychological knowledge, but the social reality of God is undeniable. This must be reckoned with in plotting the behavior of religious persons oriented and motivated by such beliefs.

In contrast to Lewin, Freud gives no little attention to religion in personal and social life. To him the religious quest appears as a persistent striving for reconciliation with a father against whom one has rebelled and before whom one stands in the anguish of guilty remorse. From his naturalistic frame of reference he views God as a symbol of the earthly father one has wished to destroy and displace, as Oedipus of Greek legend. And fixating attention upon the neurotic aspects of such guilt, he sees religious striving as a compulsive regression to childish dependence rather than forging ahead in one's own strength to assert the heroic thrust of individuality.

Whether we agree with Freud or not, there is no denying that he took religion seriously. To him religion was a problem, however, more than an answer to the dilemmas of human life. It may have been a problem also to Lewin in the field of group dynamics as a battleline of conflict between religious groups, one of the ever-potential social conflicts to be resolved by scientific analysis and democratic procedures. Honoring their honesty we, too, shall be honest enough to admit that religious loyalties have led to sharp differences and social conflicts. The place of religion in personal-social life is very complex, and we shall need to return to it again. Yet we cannot overlook the importance

[17] J. F. Brown, *Psychology and the Social Order* (New York: McGraw-Hill Book Co., 1936).

that religion may hold for persons, or deny that life is very different with or without religion.

In the next chapter we will continue the study of developing personality by tracing the growth into adolescence according to Sullivan and maturity according to Allport.

CHAPTER FOUR

DEVELOPING PERSONALITY
(cont'd)

~~~~~~

3. *Youth—According to Sullivan*

There is much to learn from field theory about the world in which the child lives, and the intricate design of interacting processes in which he operates. But what of the child himself as an experiencing person? And how does this growing person advance from childhood to adolescent youth? External observations may give a scientific view of co-existing impersonal forces and yet miss the most distinctive qualities of human behavior, the unique and intimate meanings of personal experience. Searching for this we turn to the psychiatrist Harry Stack Sullivan (1892-1949) and his interpersonal theory of personality.

From his first breath the infant has experiences which fluctuate between euphoria (well-being) and tension (distress). The tension of specific needs, as for oxygen and food, calls for satisfaction. Crying may satisfy the need for oxygen by active breathing, and the need for food by bringing the mother to the rescue. As this sequence is repeated he gains foresight into appropriate action to relieve the need tension. To win the response of the mother by crying is already an interpersonal situation, in which the activity of the infant arising from tension of need invites tension in the mothering one experienced as tenderness impelling her to relieve the infant's needs. Such tenderness on the part of the mother to co-operate in caring for the infant, responds to the infant's need for tenderness which is no less important than the need for food.[1]

But if for any reason the mothering person is anxious, a similar tension of anxiety will be induced in the child through empathy. By empathy is meant feeling together a situation by emotional communication. Anxiety is more disturbing than specific needs, or at least

---

[1] Harry S. Sullivan, *The Interpersonal Theory of Psychiatry*, eds. Helen S. Perry and M. L. Gawel (New York: W. W. Norton & Co., Inc., 1953), p. 39. Used by permission.

disturbing in a different and diffused way, such as terror. Other need tensions can be relieved by appropriate action, but there is no specific remedy for anxiety, and the infant has no capacity to act so as to relieve it. On the contrary, anxiety confuses and paralyzes appropriate action, with less foresight and freedom to act effectively. But if the mother ceases to be anxious and communicates confident relaxation, the infant's tensions will subside in interpersonal security. These are the two basic motives of human behavior: to satisfy needs and to gain security from anxiety.

In the interpersonal situation the infant is aware of the nipple-in-lips as a signal for nursing to satisfy his need. As needs are satisfied regularly with tenderness he personifies the good mother. But if there is irregularity or anxiety in satisfying his needs he personifies the bad mother. Later in the training period he is rewarded by additional tenderness as he performs to win approval, and when he displeases the mother he meets forbidding gestures, or disapproval mingled with some degree of anxiety. He begins to personify himself as the *good-me* or the *bad-me*, and when he meets severe anxiety for some behavior as the *not-me*.

From the desirability of being good-me, and the warnings of increasing anxiety, there comes into being the self-system. It is "an organization of educative experience called into being by the necessity to avoid or to minimize incidents of anxiety." [2] This dynamism (enduring pattern) comes to have central importance, as the focal experience referred to as "I" and concerned about how to live with other persons. In learning to decrease anxiety and satisfy needs, recall and foresight both come to function in guiding the behavior of the growing child.

The transition from infancy to childhood is marked by the acquisition of speech, learned at first in imitative play with the persons who are willing to participate, and then as the ability to communicate, which becomes the most important of all human skills. Language notably extends the range and accuracy of learning, and sharpens interpersonal relations by a growing refinement of symbolic meanings to enrich cultural values of living together in social responsiveness. Autistic language may refer to private experience with special meanings to the child in his reverie and fantasy, evading or distorting com-

[2] *Ibid.*, p. 165.

munication. In contrast to this "parataxic" mode of behavior, Sullivan notes the gains of "syntaxic" behavior where the child does communicate and so may validate his own experience by the experience of other persons. Verbalisms may conceal and deceive as security operations to reduce anxiety and avoid punishment. When parents educate by anxiety in giving and withholding approval, the child will learn to conceal as well as reveal, and to hide his anger in secret resentment as well as to aim his behavior to be socially acceptable.

The juvenile period (ages 6 to 9) begins with going to school and learning from other persons in widening associations and activities. The importance of this era can hardly be exaggerated, for it sets the task of becoming a social being, and persons who fail to do so are uncomfortable with their fellows. The limitations of the home environment are now overcome or modified in the school society, in which the juvenile person is able to notice differences among a variety of authority figures and compare his former expectations with the contrasting behavior of his peers and their families. He is freer to observe and choose among these various attitudes and modes of behavior with increasing socialization of his private experience. As he meets a succession of teachers and recreational leaders of limited authority, he comes to acknowledge their differences and accommodate himself to more flexible and less arbitrary possibilities in human behavior. In this process his parents may be "pared down from godlike figures to people," with whom he can live more freely and democratically.

Competition and compromise are basic skills learned in the juvenile era. In our culture competition is a primary value encouraged by the school society in providing activities in which to compete with approval. Yet competition may become destructive in getting the other fellow down, unless there is honest respect for the rights of others. The art of compromise is also to be learned at the same time to counterbalance competition with skill in co-operation with other persons.

The world of the juvenile is so complicated by the presence of other people that he has to give up many of his childhood interests and demands in order to "act right." He thus learns to control his focal awareness to be free from anxiety. What is not approved by other juveniles or adult authorities will be excluded from his conscious awareness. Desires and fantasies of childhood as well as unacceptable memories may be extinguished, and he will recall mainly what seems appropriate to make sense in his contemporary society. It is well to rule out by selective inattention what is not worth bothering about, but it is unfortunate to ignore things that matter as the self-system comes to exert firm control over the content of consciousness.

In learning to substitute socially approved behavior, the juvenile has gained skill in sublimating primitive desires, to more acceptable motives quite as capable of giving satisfactions enhanced by the rewards of successful living. But the juvenile is plagued by ostracism when in-groups segregate him as an outsider, the reasons for which are mysterious and not conducive to self-esteem. Stereotypes are handed on to him by adults and peers as crude and irrational classification of Negroes or Jews, or teachers, or the opposite sex, based not upon reality but prejudice. One's reputation is subject to invidious comparisons, and the juvenile is often taught to disparage others by insecure parents who help him to distort honest judgments and strike at the roots of essential and vital human relations.

The next era of preadolescence (ages 9-10) marks a significant step forward in the need for an intimate relation with a chum or close friend. This new type of interest in another person represents a capacity to love, a sensitivity for what matters to another person. Instead of "What do I do to get what I want?" there appears now "What should I do to contribute to the happiness and feeling of worth-while-ness of my chum?"

Intimacy is that type of situation involving two people which permits validation of all components of personal worth. Validation of personal worth requires a type of relationship which I call collaboration, by which I mean clearly formulated adjustments of one's behavior to the expressed needs of the other person in pursuit of increasingly identical—that is, more and more nearly mutual—satisfactions, and in the maintenance of increasingly similar security operations.[3]

In this way the self-system is more open to influence through new experience. As the preadolescent is now capable of seeing himself through the other's eyes, this development is incredibly important in correcting autistic, fantastic ideas about himself and other persons. If one fails to have an intimate chum at this age, he will be handicapped for carrying on the business of interpersonal relations, and especially with members of his own sex.

The preadolescent relation is primarily a two-group; yet these two

[3] *Ibid.*, p. 246.

71

groups tend to interlock in gangs, which are far more often constructive than delinquent. They further the developing of tender feelings,
and may reverse malevolent tendencies in learning how to be one with
others. When these friendships are intense and durable enough to
know almost everything about each other, they may remedy a morbid
and often illusory feeling of being different. Loneliness is a poignant
sorrow at any age, but its most acute phase is likely to occur in preadolescence and afterward. Then the need for intimacy is urgent, and
when the growing youth is isolated by ostracism or the awkwardness
of growing ahead of or delaying behind his peers, he suffers an almost irreparable loss, which may be disastrous in the timing of his
development.

Early adolescence begins with the eruption of genital potency.
Sullivan does not follow Freud in this theory of infantile sexuality and
would heretofore distinguish boys and girls by gender. But with maturing of capacity for orgasm, comes the awakening of true genital desire.
The need for intimacy has earlier origin, yet is not essentially related
to lust but quite distinct. To make sense of the complexities and difficulties of adolescence and later life, Sullivan would distinguish three
needs intricately combined yet contradictory. These are the needs for
personal security, the need for intimacy, and the need for sex satisfaction.

By this time we can observe a shift in the object of the need for
intimacy from one who is like oneself to someone who is very different,
that is of the opposite sex. This change is naturally influenced by the
appearance of the genital drive. The shift of interest to the other sex
is particularly difficult in the American scene, where so little preparation is made for a fully human relationship with members of the other
sex. Barriers are often set up by the parents, who are reluctant to have
a child grow up and enter upon the adventures of adolescence. Not
only has the genital organ been relegated to the not-me from childhood by prohibitions against touching, but parents are often jealous
of the youth who is seeking to have a personal relation or to act like
an adult in going out on social dates. Ridicule may be used to hold the
adolescent back from this next stage in his development, thus induc-
ing shame and anxiety.

There are painful collisions at this age between one's desire and one's
security, which threaten self-esteem and the feeling of personal worth.
This embarrassment may result in a primary genital phobia which pre-

vents the normal fulfillment of his interest in broadening social experience and ultimately defeats the success of his marriage. Collisions may also arise between the intimacy need and lust, resulting in such awkwardnesses as embarrassment, diffidence, excessive precautions, and swings to the other extreme of bold yet inept approaches to members of the other sex. By reaction to these anxieties he may revert to masturbation or homosexual practices.

Adolescent attempts at heterosexual indulgence may also have painful misfortunes, which are likely to be very expensive to further maturation of personality. Partners may become a prey of guilt, shame, aversion, or revulsion for each other. Preoccupation with lust, whether in act or phantasy, can lead to a serious deterioration of self-respect, due to unpleasant situations, social disapproval, and conflict with one's ideal standards. These problems met so acutely at this age may turn the adolescent to alcohol to get relief from intolerable anxieties, and so deteriorate the self-system as to make the person less competent to protect himself from anxiety.

In this struggle with lust, one may feel pursued by the other sex, or take up the celibate way of life, and become occupied with guarding operations by which to dissociate the offending lust. The isolated adolescent may substitute imaginary companions, who are so ideal as to become a barrier to finding a suitable and durable partner in real life.

And yet the sex desire is a powerful integrating agency when successfully brought into relation with the total needs of personality. The task of adolescence is to achieve a mature integration of these conflicting impulses and needs of the growing personality. To achieve this integration requires a yielding of biological to social and ideal needs to fulfill the mutual expectations of persons in our culture.

The demands of genital desire perform the service of a catalytic agent to challenge the personality in growth toward maturity. To resolve the conflicting interests with satisfaction and security from anxiety, the maturing person will bring sex into its proper place in the larger pattern of human living. As other needs are held in successful balance with sex desire through sublimation, the adolescent youth may discover a wide range of satisfactions and productivity may be achieved. To fail here in these crucial issues is to invite grave disorders in later life.

Society, therefore, joins with the individual in offering educational opportunities, religious and moral standards, and vocational, recreational, and cultural values to enrich and broaden the vital interests of human life. Especially is the growing personality enriched and drawn out by satisfying interpersonal relations to take a mature and responsible role in society. As the partially developed aspects of personality come into proper relation to the whole of life, the maturing youth finds the meaning of love in bringing a sense of worth to another person. Such love is not the entire business of life but through the experience of love one may come to maturity in human relationships.

It is evident that Jeanne had to cope with anxieties in her growing childhood. She remembers her mother as an anxious person, and such anxiety would be communicated to her through empathy in the first months of her life in the Schmidt family. The economic crises and the frequent moving about to find work could only intensify the family insecurity, as indicated by the frequent outbursts of anger and other symptoms of emotional instability. As the parents were preoccupied with their own distresses and deprivations, there was less overflow of affection or confidence to nourish the emotional needs of the children.

In their need for relatedness the children turned to each other and formed a close-knit sustaining group of their own. At school and play other friends shared in group activities and reinforced Jeanne's efforts to form a self-system as a social being. As she was accepted by her peers and elected to a place of leadership, she gained security from her associates, and her parents receded somewhat to average human size; yet even then she was not quite free of anxiety.

The fear of lust hounded her, especially after the threatened attack by the drunken man who followed her into the shed. As she came into adolescence she did make friends with the boys, but was always guarding herself frantically from sex. Her best friend was her brother Delbert, and then his friend Jimmy, who respected her so much he never touched her. It was in the shelter of the church that she felt most secure, where young people could mingle as brothers and sisters and trust one another. When one of these boys tried to take her in his arms she struck him and fled into the house.

Coming to later adolescence she was at war with herself, wanting love yet fearing sex. Then it was that Jerry began to show his devotion to her, and as she trusted him not to exploit her, yet to appreciate her charm, she was able to integrate what had been a frightening conflict.

The possibility of a love able to include sex and dignify it in sacred fulfillment was a new revelation to her. This integration Sullivan finds necessary if the adolescent is to achieve maturity. When Jeanne and Jerry began to grow in this love experience, it became the focal center of life, and nothing could then prevent their decision to marry, though secretly. They were not yet secure enough to face the disapproval of their parents, but as they nourished each other in confident love, they were soon strong enough for open declaration.

To unify the whole of life at mature levels is the aim of religious growth. Sullivan does not speak of religion but it is not to be overlooked as one of the integrating forces of growing personality. The reverent appreciation of person for person is a religious quest for the ultimate worth of life. Who can doubt the significance of religious aspiration in the maturing love of Jerry and Jeanne? The church was their meeting ground and the religious fellowship the beginning of their affection for each other. It is no wonder they sought the blessing of the church for their marriage and eventually their vocation as they came to integrate their impulses into lifelong purposes.

In tracing these developments from childhood through the years of adolescence, we have learned much from Sullivan. He has shown the need for a self-system to integrate the strivings of life and ward off anxieties. But does he tell us how the self is formed, except by the reflected appraisals of others? If that is the whole of it, then the person would be little more than the echo or reflection of the attitudes of others toward him. How shall we then account for the initiative we take to select the stimuli to which we give attention, or to organize impressions into whole meanings, or to gather diverse impulses into choices by which we follow one course of action rather than another?

What goes on between persons has captured the attention of Sullivan. This may result in a peripheral view of personality rather than a central view of the inner development. Allport believes that the inner development is the most distinctive and important aspect of personality. He is not satisfied with explanations of behavior limited to the external influences or reflected appraisals of others. No empty organism, however sensitive to stimuli, would seem adequate to account for the individuality of each person, or the kind of intentional striving that a person demonstrates who organizes his resources and persistently moves toward a self-chosen goal. To understand the motivation of a mature person, he is urging us to seek a more central view of personality.

4. Maturity—According to Allport

In seeking to understand how a person emerges into maturity we turn to Gordon W. Allport (born 1897), whose psychology of personality deals with the upper ranges of human development. He, like Freud, is seeking a central view of personality that will find effective causes of behavior within the dynamic striving of the organism. But he differs sharply from Freud as well as other psychologists who reduce the complex integrations of personality to partial segments. Allport opposes reductionist tactics first in showing that each individual is unique in his pattern of wholeness, and not to be reduced to any least common denominator either by abstract generalizations or statistical coefficients. It is a fallacy of scientism to ignore in a personality whatever is not conveniently reducible to a universal law by which to abstract what is common to all.

Again he opposes the genetic fallacy of reducing the later and higher developments to earlier and simpler patterns of behavior. Other theories of personality may refer every mature motive back to underlying instincts, wishes, or needs which are assumed to be the driving power in all of life. "Thus, the concert artist's devotion to his music might be 'explained' as an extension of his 'self-assertive instinct,' of the 'need for sentience,' or as a symptom of some repressed striving of 'the libido.' " [4] To reduce the whole repertoire of human motives to one or several segmental drives is to oversimplify the dynamic resources of personality. And to set up one unruly impulse to rule over a multitude of other impulses is so arbitary and irrational as to lead to confusion rather than clarification.

What is most significant about a human personality is the amazing capacity to outgrow himself again and again in his progress toward maturity. The interests of early infancy are limited to the most elemental needs of security and satisfaction of hunger. But soon the range of awareness expands and new interests become goals for restless and insistent striving. Each new experience awakens heretofore unrecognized possibilities for exploratory outreach and the exercise of

[4] Allport, *op. cit.*, p. 192.

potentialities. So prolific are these awakening interests in the successive stages of a growing person moving through the years of infancy, childhood, and adolescence, that the crucial problem is how to integrate them into harmonious unity.

To make room for these enlarging and changing patterns of interest and striving, Allport is seeking a theory of personality that is open and flexible to growth rather than rigid and constricted to instinctual drives or animal models of learning. A personalistic psychology finds the meaning of behavior in the whole personality with its unique system of motives at the highest contemporary stage of development. As the person advances from one stage to another in his development, he acts from new motives that are autonomous in their own right and not determined by earlier ones. This living from the present level of development he calls the functional autonomy of motives.

The dynamic psychology proposed here regards adult motives as infinitely varied, and as self-sustaining, *contemporary* systems, growing out of antecedent systems, but functionally independent of them. Just as a child gradually repudiates his dependence on his parents, develops a will of his own, becomes self-active and self-determining, and outlives his parents, so it is with motives. Each motive has a definite point of origin which may lie in the hypothetical instincts, or, more likely, in the organic tensions and diffuse irritability described in Chapter IV. Theoretically all adult purposes can be traced back to these seed-forms in infancy. But as the individual matures the bond is broken. The tie is historical, not functional.[5]

Maturity is no static goal that can be dated by chronological age, or crossed like a threshold from one room to another, after which the door is closed with no return. Persons achieve maturity at different ages and by unique integrations or styles of life. Maturing is a dynamic process of growing capacities to realize the whole meaning of one's life in the present, and yet to continue growing in the direction of future goals. A mature person acknowledges his past but is not determined by bondage to it. He accepts the present for what it means but is not satisfied to settle down with no more adventures. He plans for the future and reckons the time required for the unfolding of such purposes, but he does not deny the good of the present in overanxiety about future goals. Past, present, and future are held together in the

5 *Ibid.*, p. 194.

77

larger perspectives of maturity. From this view Gordon W. Allport entitles his Yale lectures on personality, *Becoming*.[6]

The enemy of maturity is arrest. Every immaturity, whether emotional or intellectual, social or religious, is a case of arrested development. Premature fixation defeats growth by insecurity that fears to take the next step, as for instance, the overdependence of a child upon his parents. When growth toward a healthy self-reliance is arrested, an adult may be overanxious about the approval of others and unable to make his own decisions successfully. Again, a child may be unable to postpone his demand for satisfaction of desire, and this tendency may continue as immaturity in the adult. But a mature person orients his desires toward long-range goals and learns to defer his demands to fulfill an ongoing purpose of more enduring values.

The task of maturity is to achieve an inner unity by which to guide the far-flung and often conflicting interests of human life. Allport calls this central unity of personality the *proprium*. "The proprium includes all aspects of personality that make for inward unity." [7] Peripheral motives at rudimentary levels of becoming consist of impulses and drives for immediate satisfaction and tension reduction. But with the developing of the ego to co-ordinate impulses in the direction of long-range goals, the person operates from a new system of motives. Propriate striving for a long-range goal seeks to maintain rather than to reduce the tension.

This is demonstrated in Roald Amundsen, who from the age of fifteen gave himself passionately to the vocation of polar exploration. Obstacles confronted his progress at every step, and he was often tempted to give up and reduce the tension. But he faithfully continued his preparations and efforts until he reached the North Pole. Then instead of giving up when that goal was won, he undertook a successful expedition to the South Pole; and after that he flew over the North Pole, in the face of repeated difficulties and deprivations as fatigue, hunger, ridicule, and danger. When finally he met his death in seeking to rescue another explorer, he was even then unswerving in the course he had pursued by an undiminished inner unity. Such motivation is not the unity of repose but of continuous striving for goals which give a person something greater than himself to live for.

[6] *Becoming: Basic Considerations for a Psychology of Personality* (New Haven, Conn.: Yale University Press, 1955).

[7] *Ibid.*, p. 40.

Conscience is an important function in the growth of mature personality. At first the child is subject to external sanctions of parents and other authorities whom he is constrained to obey to reduce anxiety and have their approval. But in the process of maturing, the external sanctions yield to internal standards, and the "must" is replaced by the "ought." Self-guidance emerges from the inner unity by which one prefers to live according to a self-concept that he is able to respect as decent and worthy. Conscience may be arrested in its development and become an untrustworthy guide for conduct. Religious sentiments may also be immature and juvenile, unless they continue to grow in response to new and relevant experiences which are integrated into enlarging appreciations and relationships.

In striving for maturity, Allport notes three primary avenues of development open to the growing person. First, there is the avenue of widening interests by which one may extend the range and enrich the meanings and values of his life as an expanding self. Falling in love is such a self-extension in which previously unrelated dispositions are now integrated into a personalized devotion to another person. Interests once remote are now incorporated to become a vital part of himself.

A second avenue of maturing is the ability to see oneself more objectively, with insight and detachment. For a person to see himself as others see him and to find his place in the larger scheme of things as one who is significant yet not self-centered, is to be mature in his attitudes toward others as well as himself. A sense of humor is an important asset in this effort to relieve rigid constraints and perceive life suddenly in a new perspective.

A third characteristic of maturity is the avenue of integration by which the diverse interests of our kaleidoscopic existence may be brought into essential unity. In this effort a unifying philosophy of life, whether religious or not, may be a source of coherent meaning. Immature religious sentiments are likely to be segmental rather than unifying, and criticism of religion is usually directed upon its immature forms. But mature religious experience is concerned with the central and permanent values of life, through which to come into a unifying wholeness.

Religion is the search for a value underlying *all* things, and as such is the most comprehensive of all the possible philosophies of life. A deeply

79

moving religious experience is not readily forgotten, but is likely to remain as a focus of thought and desire. Many lives have no such focus; for them religion is an indifferent matter, or else a purely formal and compartmental interest. But the authentically religious personality unites the tangible present with some comprehensive view of the world that makes this tangible present intelligible and acceptable to him. Psychotherapy recognizes this integrative function of religion in personality, soundness of mind being aided by the possession of a completely embracing theory of life.[8]

Maturity is not to arrive at a final goal where we settle down with accumulated possessions to defend. It is no sedentary life where after the struggles of youth we retire to spend the rest of our years in motionless repose. The enemy of maturity, as Allport shows, is arrest at any stage in a person's venture to fulfill his potentialities. Persons may seize upon religion as a system of infallible dogmas, or an established tradition not to be changed, or an institution like a fortress to prevent the crossing of boundaries. But mature religious devotion is not so bound to the past; it is an ongoing quest to enlarge and complete the presently known and attained. It is a way of life to follow as a pilgrimage, a journey without end. This unfaltering search for the ultimate in value and integration is what Allport finds in religion:

A man's religion is the audacious bid he makes to bind himself to creation and to the Creator. It is his ultimate attempt to enlarge and to complete his own personality by finding the supreme context in which he rightly belongs.[9]

As Jeanne and Jerry took the vows of marriage they were groping for a new and central meaning for their lives. Not yet graduated from high school each one was dependent upon his parental family. But when they completed high school they announced their marriage and established their own home, in which to live their life and support themselves as an independent family. The coming of a baby was a major responsibility, and in the first crisis of the baby's health they both prayed earnestly seeking the healing of God. They came to see that maturity is more than a struggle to be independent: it is the reaching out to larger resources by interdependent relationships.

With their work and the round of social activities, they found life

---

[8] Allport, *Personality*, p. 226.

[9] *The Individual and His Religion: A Psychological Interpretation* (New York: The Macmillan Co., 1950), p. 142.

in the East busy enough. Yet they felt empty somehow and unsatisfied at the center of life, until they recalled what religion had once meant to them and turned again to the Bible and the religious fellowship. In their searching for a larger purpose by which to live, they felt that God had a work for them to do, and together they dedicated themselves to the vocation of the Christian ministry. At the age of twenty, they decided to start a new life. Jerry resigned from civil service to go to college and then to theological school. While in school he served as the pastor first of one church and then another.

To them, religion was a search, as Allport would say, for a value underlying all things, which gave central meaning to their living as "a completely embracing theory of life." In this venture they had come upon an ongoing purpose that challenged their best efforts with no prospect of dwindling or running out. In these efforts they were not alone but sustained by a sense that God was with them to uphold and guide them. They were also sustained by the loyal devotion of other religious persons who believed in them and were ready to work along with them in these mutual responsibilities.

As they continue in this Christian vocation they do not hesitate to acknowledge their own inadequacies but they are determined to keep on growing in religious devotion and faithful service to other persons. It is again, as Allport would say, an ultimate attempt to enlarge and complete their personalities "by finding the supreme context" in which they may truly belong. In this context they believe that love is the basic religious attitude. To experience God as love was to them a creative energy available to share in family living and extend to others in a loving community.

In Chapters III and IV we have traced the course of developing personality according to four psychological theories, which represent contemporary thinking upon the subject. The student of personality will want to consult the original sources and consider the evidence submitted as well as the critical appraisal which each view brings to bear upon the others. We have taken only the first steps in our journey, yet we may already have some sense of how personality develops. These views will come before us again as we continue to explore the religious aspects of personality.

In the next chapter we will turn from these theories to a concrete life situation to see what life means to another growing person. The young woman who records her life story is also interested in a psychological understanding of these events as they come to focus in her own experience. In consenting to our reading of this autobiography, she invites our study with her of the causal factors which have contributed to the religious personality she is now becoming.

CHAPTER FIVE

DOROTHY STRONG

~~~~~~

My father was proud of the ancestry he gave his children and would often speak of it to visitors in the home. His family could be traced to the days of the early settlers, and even now the family name is familiar to students of early American history. Education was of great importance to his family. Most of the women were teachers, and the men either teachers or preachers. The family church had for several generations been Congregational. The homes of the older members of the family are furnished with relics of the early days; their attics, filled with trunkfuls of ancient books and clothing and many curious antiques, were fascinating places to play on rainy summer afternoons.

My mother, on the other hand, was a third generation German, and her parents were solid farm folk of the Free Methodist faith. Daddy's mother and aunts never let him forget that he had married beneath him, culturally speaking.

As a child I was very conscious of attitudes of rejection toward Mother and myself. When I was old enough to understand, Mother explained to me that separation between them was pending until she learned that I was on the way, and hence the much desired divorce was never effected until years later. Naturally enough, since I was the preventive factor in the situation, I was conscious, as much as she, of being rejected; and Mother's "in-laws" became my "in-laws" too.

Mother was confined most of the time to the home. An improperly set bone in her foot left her somewhat crippled and subject to considerable pain. She was unable at this time to walk very far, and since we lived over a mile from church and school, she seldom attended those places. The car was never hers to drive and Dad never took her out. He would be gone for days at a time visiting his mother or conducting athletic trips with the school teams. I wasn't very old before I began to realize that there were other women who figured in his

83

life. Occasionally one of them would come to the house and then mother would be extremely sick for several days.

Mother scarcely had decent clothes to wear. The clothes she had were given her by her sisters. She never attended a school function in which I participated until I graduated from the eighth grade, and then there had been a terrible quarrel, I remembered as I tried to hold back the tears while marching with the other graduates. Yet, both parents kept this well concealed. When people were around on infrequent occasions, Dad was nothing but the considerate husband to a crippled wife, and she would smile and say she would love to go but really wasn't physically able, or she didn't want to leave the children.

There is a brother seven and a half years younger than I. There was another child who died at birth as a result of a quarrel between my parents. Mother was injured, since Dad never hesitated to use physical means to enforce his own wishes; premature labor was induced and the child was not able to survive.

In addition to the frequent presence of Dad's mother (his parents were divorced), there was also a great uncle, afflicted with epilepsy, who was slowly dying with cancer. He was bedridden and Mother had the complete care of him. The horrible cries of pain and seizure that escaped his lips have left a vivid memory. Once, in a fit, he took a knife to mother. I jumped and sat on his chest while mother wrenched the knife away. He was a powerful man, 280 pounds and well over six feet tall; the two of us held him down until daylight, a period of about four hours, until I dared leave her long enough to go next door to phone the doctor.

After his death, Mother's parents came to live with us. That was a pleasant interlude, for Mother's mother was the one person my Dad seemed to respect and he was much kinder when she was around. She relieved Mother of much of the drudgery of the housework which was so difficult for her. Grandpa was blind, but he could carve wonderful objects from wood. He would tell stories by the hour, and when he wanted to go out for a walk or hike the mile and a half to town, he took me along to help him cross the streets. I loved my grandparents dearly. Before they came to live with us, while Grandpa still had his sight and worked the farm, my summers were spent with them. There were five cousins, a girl and four boys; and of course what we six couldn't think of doing, wasn't worth doing anyway. There wasn't a foot of the house, barn, orchard, or pasture we didn't know by heart. On Saturdays we climbed onto the wagon and rode to town with the rest of the family, happily sucking on the sweets Grandpa provided us. On Sundays the team was hitched to the buggy and away we rode to the big old red brick Methodist church downtown.

Those months spent on the farm are the fondest memories from my childhood. The freedom, the closeness to nature, the abundance of living creatures, left a deep impression. I had a little pet woolly lamb who tagged me all over the farm and even gamboled after me over the fields when I wandered off to search for flowers. As an adult sheep he was kept in a pasture by himself except at mating time. Many times a day I would straddle the gate to his field and call him. Over the hill he would come, and even if I didn't have a sugar cube or a salt lick, he would nuzzle my fingers and let me scratch his dirty, woolly head.

Other memories centered around the fluffy little chicks and duck-lings that inhabit a farm. I would sit down in their midst and try to catch them, and then, after succeeding in getting a skirt full, would watch them escape, peeping or quacking to their mothers. I loved to feed the chickens and usually went with Grandma to help feed them and gather the eggs. One day, Grandma announced we were going to have a chicken dinner and sent Grandpa out to behead one of the white cluckers. I followed after and horrified watched the creature flapping its wings even after the head was gone. I didn't eat any chicken that day or ever again if I could help it. I don't remember the exact thought processes that went on, but when I learned that mutton and chops were once a woolly lamb like my pet, when I realized that meat was something that had been killed to provide food, I refused to eat flesh food of any kind. Nor would I drink milk for some time. That was a source of considerable concern to my parents. But I solved that problem; when they persisted in forcing me to eat what had become distasteful to me, I persisted in regurgitating into my plate until they ceased and no more was said about it. I have seldom eaten meat in my life nor do I know how to cook it.

The same thought process concerning meat also extended into the region of wearing apparel. My mother gave away a coat trimmed with fur which had been purchased for me. I couldn't wear it.

Aside from the farm experience the only other contemporary event which affected me directly in the early years was the depression. My parents were constantly concerned over finances, although later evidence revealed that money which should have gone for necessities was spent on my father's special, private interests. As a family group, we did not do things together. If Dad was dissatisfied with what Mother prepared for supper, he would storm out to buy a meal, but he seldom took the family. On the few occasions that we were included, there was a noticeable unwillingness on his part and we weren't allowed to order much to eat.

My father was a religious searcher and during the years when the family circle was still unbroken, he ran the gamut from metaphysical philosophy to conservative legalism, finally ending his quest in the dim limbo of agnosticism. The family was expected to concur with his beliefs, accepting and rejecting as he directed. After their marriage my parents had divided their interests between the Congregational and Methodist churches, attending one on one Sunday and the other the following. They took equal parts in the activities of the two churches. They were finally asked to leave the Methodist Church because of this division of affiliations.

Dad was superintendent of a high school at the time and highly progressive in his educational policies. Mother was then the home economics instructor. Their religious activities were devoted to the Congregational Church until again they were asked to cease their affiliation both in the church and in the school because of tendencies and policies that were too liberal for the community. Both parents became embittered. Shortly, they moved to another state and Dad entered graduate study. Religious topics were never mentioned in the home nor do I ever remember attending church except, as previously mentioned, during the summer with my grandparents. One winter, when I was about five, some of my friends took me to a nearby Episcopalian church until my father found it out and forbade me ever to enter one again.

Shortly after this, Dad sank his religious interests into a metaphysical organization, the Rosicrucians. He and Mother would be closeted in his study for hours, my brother and I forbidden to enter. Once when both parents were on the first floor, we slipped into the study, which was on the second floor, and looked around. There were mirrors, and candles and strange metal objects. Somewhat frightened by these, plus the danger of being caught, we left the room still unsatisfied as to what really went on.

For some reason unknown to us, Dad abandoned his Rosicrucian activities and again affiliated with the Congregational Church. This church was without leadership and Dad became youth director as well as Sunday morning speaker along with his teaching program in the high school. Mother seldom attended church, but I usually went to Sunday school and came home to help her afterwards. We occasionally had young people at the house and for a time our home was a little happier. When out of the classroom Dad spent most of his time at the church; but his disposition was better and when he was at home, though usually in his study, he was easier to get along with.

This continued for about two years until Dad became disturbed over details of church administration and turned in his resignation. I continued to attend for a time but found it discouraging to come home on Sunday noon to find my parents quarreling, or to be asked to help with some household activity that I did not think ought to be done on that day.

From this point Dad gradually swung his interests to a conservative and legalistic church and made its tenets binding on the whole family in a very unpleasant manner. Not for long, however. About the time I finished high school, Dad was seeking to complete his doctorate at the University of ———— where he had become interested in higher criticism. He lost his faith in his church and has remained an agnostic to the present time.

I was seldom allowed to play with other children and when the occasion did arise I didn't know how to play. Their games frightened me. I couldn't compete and was terrified by the tales that were told of the "boogie man" hiding under the bed, etc. I was terribly afraid of the dark and, along with not eating well, slept poorly, frequently plagued by nightmares. I started school at six, but was ill so much I couldn't attend regularly. Finally the doctor advised my parents to move from the city to a small community where I would be away from the noise of the city and would have plenty of opportunity to be out of doors.

The move to a sparsely populated area was accomplished. We had a house and many field and preserve areas where I would roam with my dog for hours at a time. For many years the family lived in the same place, Dad teaching in the public schools, and I, although often lonely, becoming well acquainted with the surrounding countryside. There was one place in particular that was my favorite retreat, a tiny peninsula of land jutting out into the river. Surrounded by weeping willows, it was secluded, lovely, and easily accessible. When free from school on week ends and in the summer time, I would pack a lunch, take some books, and spend the whole day there, reading, thinking, watching the life along the water's edge. I would often wonder what life was all about and wanted very much to do something of real worth for unhappy youngsters like myself. I used to pray for release, for happiness, for a reason to live, and found comfort in the quiet beauty around me.

School days were even more frustrating than were the early years at home. I was absent more than present due to "illness." It seemed as though I was always behind the rest of the class and was publicly referred to as dull and slow to learn. There was one teacher in particular who made a class issue of that fact and had the rest of the children poke their fingers at me because I couldn't learn fractions. My escape was into a dream world of my own imagination where there were many playmates. At about the age of eight a second escape was found in books. They were the one thing I had plenty of and my father never hesitated to buy me more whenever I asked. Scott, Dickens, Shakespeare, and other classical writers were familiar to me even before entering high school.

There was continued rejection from my father connected, I felt, with my slowness in school. I froze when people would speak to me and couldn't utter a sound. If I did speak words would come out in an unintelligible mass, so laughter was the result. It was the same with music. When I was alone, playing the piano or violin was no problem; I enjoyed practicing, but as soon as someone other than my mother entered the room, it seemed as though bands of steel were snapped around my fingers and I was unable to produce anything. My father constantly harped at me about this and threatened all sorts of dire results.

My main pleasures were in the avenues of escape—imagination, reading, roaming the countryside. I was not comfortable with my own sex; I had never learned how to play their games and my clothes were a constant source of frustration to me. I remember a cousin remarking once that I had no personality whatsoever and never would marry. Another remark, made by a teacher, disturbed me. In class one afternoon this particular instructor handed a child a glass of water and bid her stick her finger in the water, then withdraw it. The child obeyed, whereupon the teacher said, "That is the hole you will leave in the world when you die." What, then, was the use of even continuing to live? I contemplated suicide, even going so far as to wonder what kitchen cleanser would do if taken internally, and finally settled for aspirin tablets, which fortunately only made me sleepy.

Ideas of what I was going to do in life centered around intellectual and social success. I decided not to marry (I was sure I would never be asked). In addition, my knowledge of sex was nil, and such questions as where I came from and how I got here were immediately hushed up with threats of punishment. I was very concerned over menstruation but was afraid to ask questions. I distinctly remember my mother telling me that men were wicked and demanding and I should never have anything to do with them.

Yet, the few social contacts that I did have were with boys my own age. I found more acceptance with them than with girls and learned to climb trees, bat a ball, and play cops and robbers with the rest of them. Dolls I seldom if ever touched. Stuffed animals I was very fond of and as a child played with them much more than with any other toys.

I was forced to wear long pigtails, corrective shoes, and cotton dresses when the other girls all had short curls, skirts and blouses, and moccasins. I never could have a new dress—it was stupid to want those things. My mother did her best to make a few things over for me but I still was in for plenty of teasing by girls who thought my clothes were funny and my hair style old-fashioned.

Conditions brightened somewhat upon my entry into the sixth grade. The homeroom teacher gave me vocal instruction and included me in a couple of musical groups. For the first time I could do something that warranted a little appreciation, and I didn't hear so many remarks about my clothes. For one public appearance I wore a dark velvet dress when the other girls were in pastels and organdy. The discomfort was partially deadened by the feeling of accomplishment over the success of the group singing. Once I was chosen to be the Indian princess in a musical production because I was the only girl with long braids. Momentarily I was rewarded.

In the eighth grade I learned that another way to get attention was through good grades. Night after night I would carry my books home and study until early morning. My father was delighted; kids that age didn't need so much sleep anyway, he would say, and he encouraged me to sit up all the later. Of course that would eventually lead to illness and I would be out of school, but I managed to maintain a high enough average to satisfy him. Mother helped me with my assignments when Dad wasn't around and would sit up with me making something over for me to wear.

I was finding increasing satisfaction in playing with my brother. When we got home from school (he had started in the first grade at the age of five) we would go to my room and play until we heard Dad's car drive in. We used to find especial satisfaction in the game of Authors. Why, I have never been able to figure out. There was a woods behind the house and sometimes we would escape out there and play battle or cops and robbers with the older boys who were there. My brother felt as rejected as I and would often discuss our dislike of Dad and wish Mother would leave him and take us with her.

High school opened up new interests. I had learned that long hours of studying brought A's, which gained a smile from Dad and an occasional new outfit. Further, I found that joining every club for which I was eligible furnished an excuse to put off returning home from school. I even sneaked in a few movies with the money I earned baby sitting (if Dad didn't get it away from me). Dates and shows were strictly forbidden and once I got home I had to stay there.

Dramatics and debate work were sources of endless satisfaction. In the former I could get out of myself and be someone else. I would try out either for highly comic parts or the melodramatic in which I could emotionalize the deep feelings within. Debate was wonderful because I had male companionship and sneak dates as well as the distinction of being the only girl on the squad. A few minor successes were found in some plays that I wrote which were locally produced. A job as secretary to the Dean of Women further showed me my own capabilities and helped me to begin to feel accepted in my own social group. I was able to buy myself a few clothes and dress like the other girls.

At seventeen I began dating regularly, much against my parents' wishes, but I no longer paid any attention to them. When my first "boy friend" was killed over Germany during the early days of the war it was quite a shock to me. It was not that I was in love, because I wasn't and knew it; it was that I experienced death from a new angle. Before, death had seemed a release; now it was a robber, taking away someone of whom I was very fond. Our last discussion together had been a serious one. We were at a night club, and about ten o'clock

Ken called a taxi, saying that he was taking me home, that I was too clean a girl to be in such a place. We were some five miles from my home. Upon returning to the house we sat on the front steps and talked—about life in general. Ken wasn't sure what he wanted to do in life, nor was I, unless it was to teach. Ken spoke of his religious longings, of his desire for something tangible to believe in, his desire for a true knowledge of God and of a faith to live by. We both agreed to begin church attendance again; perhaps we would find some answers, something that would give a purpose to life. Ken left shortly after this and I never saw or heard from him again. When news of his death came, it left me dry-eyed but aching within. How I hoped he had found the answers for which he searched!

It was after Ken left that I began to face squarely the problem of a religious faith. I knew the round of ceaseless activity in which I had engaged was an escape. It would have to end sometime, and what would I have? I was depressed when alone, and thought again of taking my own life; it would certainly solve my problems and would be a means of revenge on the people I hated. Or would it? Something held me back. Perhaps there was a reason to live.

My first knowledge of God had come as a small child. I can remember one afternoon rummaging through a closet and, discovering a box of pictures and cards, lugging them into the next room where Mother was ironing and asking her to tell me what they were.

One card in particular attracted me—a beautiful nature scene bearing the caption "God is love." I asked questions but Mother was unable to answer. Shortly after that I remember waking in the night crying. Both parents came. I told them I was afraid and wanted to pray and asked them to show me how. Their reply was that praying was something that could not be taught, I would have to learn it myself. The next morning, escaping to the yard, I looked up into the heavens to watch the moving clouds and ever-changing patches of blue and white, and I cried out some childish equivalent to "God, I want to know more about you; I want to know more of your love. Teach me."

Looking back, it is evident how God answered that prayer. After that early request I prayed regularly for a time, asking mostly for protection and freedom from fear and greater knowledge of the Divine Being.

It was probably a decade later that similar desires for communion swept over me again—longings for righteousness and a reaching upward to God. I went to the library, checked out a New Testament in a modern version, and read parts of it over and over again. Rom. 6:23 disturbed me. I was frustrated with guilt because of hatred for my father, and these guilt feelings added to my feelings of rejection and were responsible for much of the mental anguish I suffered.

When I found relief in the round of ceaseless activities of high-school life, religion and God were gradually pushed into the background. Religion seemed to add to my problems and, in addition, church life was very unsatisfying. One Sunday evening (after my father had retired from his activities as youth leader) we were gathered in the chapel for a brief devotional. Hymns were chosen at random by members of the group. A number was called by one of the young persons—"Rock of Ages." The minister arose and asked that we not sing that hymn or any other that pertained to the blood of Jesus. They were old-fashioned and outdated. Jesus was simply another person, and ideas connecting salvation with his blood had no place in modern life. Such ideas were not to be propounded in his church any further. This concerned me—Was the church simply another organization like the school? At the fellowship hour after the devotional service, a local jeweler spoke, discussing various jewels and precious stones, their uses and settings. That was one of the last times I ever attended church there. My questions were not being answered; my longings were not being satisfied. The wearing of jewelry, I felt, had little to do with the great questions and problems with which my inner being wrestled.

One evening at about this same time, the choir had gathered at the minister's home for rehearsal. Afterwards we were served some kind of punch in beer mugs. Liquor was not unfamiliar to me. It was used in my own home. There was a wine cabinet in the basement and beer in the refrigerator, but that was not to my liking. It somehow didn't seem right to me. I had read in the writings of Paul that our bodies were the temple of the Holy Ghost. How, then, could human beings willfully defile themselves with such habits as drinking, smoking, and dancing? How could I feel a desire for display by wearing jewelry? How could I waste precious time in the playing of pointless games which seemed to foster unpleasant attitudes and to promote intemperance in habits of sleep? Such thoughts I kept to myself, in fact pushed them from my mind. If the church condoned such things, why should I suffer feelings of guilt for engaging in the accepted social activities of my age group? Church attendance ceased altogether and life was full of school and good times.

Then, after Ken left, I withdrew from social activities abruptly and completely, reading more than ever and thinking more than ever, trying to find answers to some of the problems that perplexed me. Vocationally I was undecided, having considered, at one time or another, teaching, social work, and writing. Many of the problems existing locally fired me to express myself on paper. I was deeply disturbed by the racial problems existing in the community. There had been fist fights between the white boys and the colored boys at high school because of segregation. That wasn't right! One of the loveliest girls in my class was not invited to parties because she was Jewish. That hurt! Another girl whom I had known for years was alienated because she had borne an illegitimate child, yet she was lonesome and bewildered and heartbroken. She needed friendship. Still another girl whose parents had only recently come to America was often ridiculed because of her poor clothing and her speech. Was that what she had come to America for? I identified myself with these individuals, trying to give them what I could of companionship, and yet feeling alienated even as they were.

One night, out of the depths of my own troubled conscience, sleep being denied me, I began to express in writing the conflicts within. Every spare moment I wrote until my play was finished. The manuscript was placed in the hands of a sympathetic teacher, who a few days later called me to her room and said she had found a producer who would give me two hundred dollars for the script. I was more deeply troubled than ever, for the play had been an expression of rebellion against society and it did not contain the right solution. Something within forced me to take back the manuscript. That night, late, I slipped from the house and went to one of my favorite spots in the corner of the yard. It was late spring; on one side of me was a bed of lilies and over my head a blooming lilac spread its fragrant boughs. I sank to the ground and tried to think my way through my confusion. How could happiness be found in a world where there was so much unhappiness? Was there anything good in all the evil around? Would the war really solve anything? It would probably determine who would be boss for another few years, and then another war would set up a new leader. The center of the turmoil concerned myself, however. The play I had written ridiculed the very ideals I was beginning to formulate as my own. Yet another lancet twisted its way into my tortured mind.

For months I had not prayed; I had been trying desperately to shut God from my mind. My father had discussed with me some of the problems presented by the higher critics. Doubts crept into my thinking, coupled with the disillusionment I had experienced in the role of the church. Reading I had done in psychology had also played its part, for the psychologists' explanation of prayer had taken from it much of its sweetness. Perhaps man would be better without religion, without God. Yet, if man was master of his own soul, he was certainly doing a poor job of it. In between the shreds of cynicism there still remained wisps of guilt. I could continue in the same paths no longer, but where was I to turn?

For some weeks I had shelved in a far corner of my mind a knowledge of a church that observed the seventh-day Sabbath. How strange! I thought at first, until suddenly it occurred to me that the Bible did speak of the seventh day in connection with Sabbath keeping in both the Old and New Testaments. Certainly Saturday was the seventh day on our calendars, but what about the biblical calendars? Modern methods of time keeping differed from the ancient. Besides, how reliable was the Bible? Nevertheless I read on the problem and, to my surprise, found that history affirmed the keeping of a seventh-day Sabbath, and that Jesus himself had said, "If ye love me, keep my commandments." Intellectually I had recognized the validity of the claim but was unwilling to do anything about it.

With such a mass of confused thoughts racing through my mind, I tried that night to pray, tried to find peace within; but there was no response. I felt a physical heaviness and the night seemed darker than any night had ever seemed before. I huddled close to the ground seeking warmth, and finally out of my misery came the words, "Jesus, show me thyself; have thine own way; I will keep thy commandments; I will observe thy Sabbath." Peace came; the weight was gone from my body, and the sky was dotted with stars. I do not know how long I remained there, but when I finally arose and went back to the house my decision was made. I had experienced God; I knew he existed regardless of what the higher critics or the psychologists or the ministers said. My life was dedicated to his service, and I began attending the Seventh-day Adventist Church.

But one's problems are not solved in a night, and finding a faith in

God was only a step; many more needed to be made. I was still confused and afraid of failure, loss of friends, and marriage, and I was still terribly lonely. Three favored teachers at high school were abruptly fired. A committee of students, I among them, went to the school board with a protest. We were somewhat coldly received and told to return to our classes and to say nothing more about the incident; from then on we were being closely watched. It just so happened that we had unwittingly stumbled into a ticklish political situation. My father, as an officer in the local teachers union, was appointed as one of the investigators. Because of the outcome of the investigation, plus the fact that I was the daughter of one who played prominently in the outcome, I was advised to change schools at the beginning of my senior year.

Looking back I am sure the providence of God played heavily in succeeding events. The only place I could attend was a Seventh-day Adventist academy about six miles from our home. Somewhat reluctantly I enrolled. Reluctance soon changed to acceptance and support. Seventh-day Adventists, fundamental and evangelical, practice a simple theology which has its roots in an intellectual as well as experiential acceptance of Jesus as Saviour and Lord of life. The services of the church are characterized not by emotionalized preaching and response, but by a reasonable and logical presentation of what is required of the Christian. Along with the doctrine of original sin they teach the great worth of the individual for whom Jesus died. That worth may be realized through acceptance and a daily consecration to his cause. Repentance and acceptance of Jesus as Saviour is only a beginning of a life that must be sanctified by obedience to the commandments of God and devotion to the needs of humanity.

Now, at last, life was becoming meaningful. The many new friends I made and the helpful understanding of Christian teachers, together with a new religious concept, did much to heal my inner pain. I wanted to be of as much help to others as others had been to me. The problems at home didn't seem to matter as much any more. My new attitudes led to an open break with my father. On the night of my graduation from high school, he stormed that I had disobeyed him for the last time, that he hated me and my church.

I was eighteen, tired of the conflict, the restriction, the inconsistencies. When my father gave me ten dollars and bade me leave the house, I packed my suitcases and left for another city some distance away.

Mother was very understanding, saying she did not blame me a bit and making our parting as easy as possible. My brother, then eleven years of age, was the one who really took it hard.

At eighteen, a naïve young lady, with only ten dollars in her pocket and in a strange city miles from anything she had ever known before, might easily get into difficulties. What took place that summer is a story in itself, but somehow by the time autumn came, there was enough money to go to college. By working full-time during summers and part-time during the school year, I completed college in the usual four years. Dormitory life taught me how to get along with my own sex. I finally learned the methods of procreation and that the feelings I was experiencing physically were perfectly normal. I began to see a purpose to all life; I wanted to experience rather than to escape, to realize that there were other people with problems far worse than mine. The state of mind at which I finally arrived—wherein I could accept my unhappy childhood with a minimum of resentment, could feel genuine pity for my father, and could be thankful for the problems that had been mine because they led me to a deeper understanding of other people—came as a result of a winter spent in the home of a faculty member.

One of the speech instructors and his wife were particularly intuitive individuals. Untrained in psychology per se, they practiced its principles, seemingly by nature. During a brief illness of mine, the wife insisted I stay at their home. She apparently recognized the emotional elements in my physical complaints and she and her husband gradually drew from me my story, the things I had been ashamed and afraid to tell anyone. Living in a happy home situation, I gained from them what my parents had been unable to give. There was someone to discuss my problems with and a place where I was encouraged to bring my friends; my financial burden was somewhat lessened; dating was encouraged and plenty of stress placed on the need for social life. At the same time I felt wanted and needed because I did my share of the housework and helped look after two small children in the home. Life became rich, full of opportunity and interesting people.

The next year I slipped even more easily into the flow of school life. Realization of success came to me in the moment I was presented as the newly elected president of the largest social organization on the campus. My fears of not being accepted were gone.

Vocationally, I still wasn't sure what I wanted to do in life. I had chosen an English major but didn't enjoy my classes. During my sophomore year I was editor of the school paper. A large comfortable office was provided and I spent as many as forty hours a week there, using it for study and committee meetings as well as editorial purposes. It was a busy place and often crowded with staff members. Students dropped by to see if they could help, or maybe to use one of the typewriters, or just to chat. It wasn't long until some of them came more and more frequently. They wanted to talk. They had problems, deep disturbing ones to them—problems concerning broken homes, or love affairs, or difficulty with school subjects. Some of them were concerned with their relationship to God, all the many frustrations that college students face. Regular appointments had to be made and soon even faculty members were asking me to see certain individuals.

I felt hopelessly inadequate in the face of all this, and yet I could feel with so many of my fellow students—I had been through it too. Some of the girls would come to my room in the dorm at one and two o'clock in the morning, saying they could not sleep and had to talk. My roommate would often get up and prepare a snack while we were talking. I felt there was little I could do for any of the students except listen to them and pray with them and try to encourage them when they seemed to need it. I reduced the number of my classes until I was taking only three and was barely earning C's in them.

At midterm of that year I knew what I wanted. Going to the registrar's office, I made a request for a change of course from English to religion and philosophy. There was considerable opposition to this from the administration. They felt I was making a mistake, that my abilities lay in other areas, but I persisted.

It was not an easy schedule; there were deficiencies to be made up, a thesis to be written before a degree could be conferred, field work to fit into an already overloaded program. But to me it was worth the effort. I realized that in this area I could find some of the answers which would help me to be more effective with other people, as well as a better person myself. Many of the classes were of inestimable value to me and have been increasingly so in the years since. Philosophy of religion was the most difficult, and yet the most challenging, course included in the curriculum. It gave me the intellectual basis for my faith. Several classes in Old Testament were of equal value. The instructor for these courses was the man who later produced *The Mysterious Numbers of the Hebrew Kings,* which contains the key to the chronology of the kings of Israel and Judah. Receiving his doctorate from a school of higher criticism and yet retaining his own fundamentalist faith, this instructor conducted classes which were of vital interest. He challenged us with the higher critical points of view and then gave us his answers to them as a foundation for building our own. Additional classes in textual criticism were of equal value.

A second deeply religious experience took place between my junior and senior years in college. I was employed by the denomination in a city some two hundred miles from the campus in one of our Bible correspondence schools. Late one afternoon the office phone rang. The leader of the youth group who had the meeting for that night had suddenly become ill. Would I take over? With the help of the office force, a program was hastily organized. The "minutemen" did a beautiful job. The benediction was in the form of a prayer song:

> If I have wounded any soul today,
> If I have caused one foot to go astray,
> If I have walked in my own willful way—
> Dear Lord, forgive!

These words conveyed a new meaning to me. Mentally reviewing the day's activities, I knew there could be no "if" in my prayer. A broader concept of sin was born for me that evening. Sin was not only an outward act, but also an inner one, centering in the desires, motives, and thoughts of life.

I seemed always to be able to pray more effectively when out of doors. When my life is troubled with great problems and issues, communion is sweeter in some quiet spot in nature. Such an experience was a little difficult since I was living on a main thoroughfare in a busy city; but returning to my apartment, I opened wide one of the windows and, kneeling where I could see the stars and feel the night breeze, I talked with God. With my confession came the realization that I was failing in the very thing God wanted me to do in life; i.e., in loving people, understanding them, feeling with them, counseling them. True, I was doing plenty of counseling in my work, but I was conscience stricken over my impatience, my mental categorizing of people into the worthy and unworthy, the manner in which I had used particular instances to satisfy my own ego, my self-pity because of an unhappy childhood. Insight regarding self was developing, and with it a new understanding of the love of God. The fullness of life can be realized only through responding to his great love. Whatever means I used in life to earn a living would be secondary to the primary goal of being available to those who wished counsel and help.

It was in April of my senior year in college that Amos and I began to recognize the serious elements developing out of our campus friendship. I was afraid of marriage. There had been several other proposals throughout my years at college, and although I thought a great deal of the young men involved, I was frightened by their apparently serious intentions and usually broke dating relations with them almost immediately. I had already committed myself to a job in Washington, D.C., when Amos expressed his deep interest in me one night in June. I realized I cared too much to say no, yet I was afraid, and a little skeptical of the integrity of men. Amos was kind and understanding and I soon learned my fears were groundless. Love and appreciation for my husband have deepened through the years we've been married. His love and understanding of me, his solicitous care for my needs, his devotion to his life's work, his singleness of purpose, and his deep religious experience, leave me daily grateful to the God who brought our lives together.

Home life has followed anything but the pattern usually anticipated. One or both of us have been in school and/or working the entire time. Parental opposition was severe at first but has lessened with time. Moving two thousand miles away gave us an opportunity to adjust to each other and to solve our problems ourselves without interference. We have had problems, never between ourselves but always of external origin. They have served as a means of drawing us even closer together, and the companionship we share is indeed rich. I feel privileged to make a home for one I love and who loves so deeply in return. Though others are frequently in our home, we have followed the practice of maintaining a retreat in some easily accessible place where we can rest and meditate and enjoy a little time alone together.

We came to California in 1948 and for the first two years lived in a small town in the Sacramento Valley. It was difficult to find work, and what I did find was not too pleasant. Moving to San Francisco I entered the area of medical social work but was severely handicapped by the failure of associates on the hospital staff to realize its potential. The three of us in the social work area were constantly being cut off from valuable sources of aid to the patient. More than that, we were not given the status or the salary that the position deserved, and, with high tuition, the salary meant a lot to us.

Out of this situation, plus the desire to narrow the intellectual gap between Amos and me, came the decision to return to school. This I finally did, entering the area of speech. I chose this area for a number of reasons, primarily for the opportunities it presented for counseling, both with students in a school situation and even more so in clinical work.

I do not recall that my faith in God has been shaken since the conversion experience at seventeen, but faith in my church and in myself has been shaken many times. The concern of church leaders for the observance of the letter of the law, with little regard for the psychology behind people's actions, is disturbing to me. Another distressing thing is the cruelty and thoughtlessness of people who are supposedly controlled by the bonds of Christian love. At times it is difficult for me to forgive what people do to one another. Then when I get to know them better, and realize what is behind their actions, I understand and am sorry for my own attitude.

The thought has occurred to me at times that we might have more mature Christians without a definite church organization; yet I see the need for identification with a religious group. The diversity of denominations in our country is a blessing, for as long as there are many we will enjoy religious freedom; but should there be only a few, religious conflict or the dangers of a union of church and state might follow. Yet, to whatever persuasion we may belong, we are still children of the same God, members of the same human family. Although I believe individual church identity should be maintained on the basis of personal conviction, I also believe in a fellowship. Our service, our contribution to life, should not be to one church group only but to all, so that the full potential of each human life may be realized, that in sharing we give and receive in ever increasing measure. Although on a week end we may go our separate ways to the church of our choice, in a wider sense, the whole world is our church and all its inhabitants our brothers and sisters.

There are many incidents of my past life which have been unpleasant; yet from them have come the goals and aspirations, the philosophy of life, which I now hold. The rejection I experienced at home and school made me more responsive to the love manifested toward me by others during college days. My earlier identification with nature has continued to the present time; here I find escape, strength, and a sense of divine presence. The need for a father-figure was filled by the faculty member in whose home I lived for a time. The Christian living of that family led me into a deeper understanding of God; the transference was culminated when this particular instructor performed the marriage ceremony uniting Amos and me.

Deep-seated feelings of guilt sprang both from being rejected and also from the hatred and resentment I harbored against not only my father but any who seemed authoritarian and arbitrary. These feelings have been the most difficult for me to overcome (they still exist), and only in a relationship with a loving and forgiving God do I find peace. It is very difficult for me to talk with other people concerning myself. In fact, these pages contain more than I have ever expressed to anyone. This reticence again springs from the early feelings that no one was interested in me. Perhaps other individuals in a like situation might have found some value other than religion. For me, however, it was the only thing that could heal and re-create.

My interests in the area of speech may well have sprung originally from a desire to emulate my adopted father-figure. Yet I feel sure my present interest has transcended that, for it provides an avenue of helping people even as I have been helped. The only true values in life lie not in the accumulation of material goods, but in the friend-ships we build, in the strength and faith we can pass on to our fellow human beings and receive in return, and in a living of the great com-mandment.

CHAPTER SIX

THE LONELY PERSON

~~~~~~

1. Who Is Lonely?

Dorothy Strong was a lonely child. Her first recorded memory was a feeling of rejection by her father and his family. It was a vicarious rejection which she shared with her mother, and yet she was told that she was the cause of unhappiness to both parents in holding them together contrary to their desire. She was thereby to feel separation from both parents as the unwelcome child who was the instrument of their sorrow and the unwilling victim of their emotional storms and bitter quarrels.

What could she do to right these wrongs and correct the intolerable situation? She could cling to the mother in frantic dependence, but the mother was too anxious herself to sustain the burden and became a semi-invalid. By emotional contagion the mother's anxieties induced anxiety in the child; and, finding no protection against them, Dorothy, too, sought escape and found refuge in illness. When she turned to the father for comfort she was alternately favored and rejected, in a state of constant insecurity, trying desperately to please yet failing so often that she could not approach him with confidence but froze in terror. And the violence of the dying uncle frightened her the more.

To find playmates might provide a happy release from the tensions. But she was forbidden to play with other children and when the occasion permitted she did not know how to play and their games frightened her. She was seven and a half years old before a brother was born, and not until he was five did he fulfill her need for a playmate. At school, not learning to feel at home among her schoolmates, she was ill at ease and was often kept at home by illness.

There were delightful interludes when she came to visit her grandparents and the five cousins, with whom life was more jolly. But these vacations always came to an end and she was again subjected to the unsolved tensions that blocked and intimidated her. Consequently she turned to solitude as a relief from the frustrations of anxious social relations, and found in nature a peace and acceptance she had missed at home. Dumb animals helped to satisfy her need for quiet affection, and she cherished them more than the humankind who afflicted her.

Books were another source of solitude, and the hours she spent in reading provided much of the satisfaction denied to her elsewhere. Drawing a Bible from the library she found it both encouraging and disturbing. Reaching out to God in prayer she aspired to a religious experience that would provide the answer to her searchings. In these ways she explored the resources of solitude and came to find them not empty but enriching.

Out of her loneliness then came the first cure for the distress of feeling lonely. Yet solitude was not enough to heal her lonely anxiety. For life was incomplete and fragmentary for Dorothy in her isolation. It was rather a foil to be used in the practice of more successful interchange with other persons. It was a restful surcease from unbearable conflict, but not the solution. By such a private life she was saved from the anguish of public disgrace and failure, until she could gather inner resources to rise and meet the anxious situations more bravely.

The road to emotional health was uncertain and long; she could not be expected to find it alone. She was blessed by the kindly grandparents who gave her their approval and affection. She was helped along the way by a brother and by the cousins and playmates she came to enjoy and trust. She was reinforced by the gains of well-earned successes in school and college, the recognition given her by classmates and teachers, and the growing appreciation of the friends who came to find her trustworthy and resourceful. Life turned again from solitude to a succession of meetings with other persons who opened new vistas and joined in larger experiences of value and meaning.

It is easy to be lonely. It is the natural state of man, as inevitable as the succession of night and day. At night one may feel his loneliness acutely when the lights go out and the door is closed; then he must endure his separation as best he can. It is no wonder that children are afraid of the dark and wail bitterly when excluded from the warm circle of light where other members of the family are together. When at length one passes over the dark threshold to slumber, he is farther removed in the island of unconsciousness from his kindred except for the imagery of fleeting dreams. Roused again by the morning light he goes forth to greet other persons who will rescue him from loneliness for a while as he enters with them into the interests and activities of the day.

As I meditate upon our human adventure from this New Hampshire hillside, the mood of loneliness is all-pervading. The hills across the valley are shrouded in mist blotting out the mountain peaks beyond. No human sounds reach my ears; only the twitter of birds fills the vast silence of the landscape. Grasses sway in the wind, dotted with hardhack and blueberry bushes; then I see the pines and birches standing tall among the crowding maple trees. Looking out from the cabin window I see a stone wall standing forth as a stalwart monument to the pioneers who cleared the land two hundred years ago. Two empty cellar holes testify to the labors of courageous families who built a home in the wilderness, and, when fire demolished it, moved across the lane to build another, which in time was also consumed in flames.

Why did these rugged men and women come to this abandoned farm and why did they depart? They were free men who declared their independence by daring the perils of long, snowbound winters, contenting themselves with the sparse living they could wrest from nature with their own hands. They bound themselves together in newborn villages, where neighbors could lend and borrow from each other and could lift to heaven the white spire of a church in which they might worship as one people. Next to that they built a little school and a town hall; here they could learn how to read and write and conduct their community life in democratic order.

Down the road a short way is old man Clough's place, where the curtain falls on the drama of another homestead. Everyone had left the place when we first came ten years ago except old man Clough, who lived alone in the stately home, too feeble to farm his acres and too poor to hire anyone. He eked out a precarious existence in defiant loneliness until he sickened and was carried to the hospital up the river to die. Now the house has fallen in and the flattened barns are overgrown with weeds. The deserted farm is a mute tribute to man's heroic adventure, before the earth and its relentless vegetation closed in around the last remains.

Historians may trace many reasons for the departure of those men and women from the farms of these hills lying so bright and peaceful in the sun. It was no doubt a part of the general migration in recent history from rural to urban centers of population, a movement in which economic and sociological conditions will not be overlooked. It may well be, however, that the reasons of the heart are deeper than economic factors, important as they are. If we could but know the emotional struggles of these children of the pioneers, it would draw us together in closer understanding and sympathy. From the inner view, we may well believe that they departed because of intolerable loneliness.

Now that we have huddled ourselves together as most of us have in our midcentury, how has our loneliness been cured by the throngs of city life? Here we are seldom out of sight or sound of our human kind. Most of us work in organized groups of colaborers where our tasks are fitted into larger patterns of assembly-line production. Eating is a social event in which we gather together around a family table, or choose a restaurant where others are eating too. Religious aspirations may be observed in private, but churches are maintained by the united desires of many persons to have public worship together as a congregation. With radio and television at arm's length, no one need be alone, when the turn of a knob brings into the room a whole company of voices or a troupe of exciting entertainers.

Yet in reality we are as lonely as ever. No place can be lonelier than a crowd, in which no one seems to know us and appreciate our worth. David Riesman, in *The Lonely Crowd*,[1] so characterizes the middle-class urban society of our time, in which persons flock together to escape their loneliness. Success is typified by the approval of one's peers, and every effort is made to sensitize children to the opinions of others. This kind of other-directed living may not actually cure loneliness, but it does represent a frantic effort to do so.

Rollo May has analyzed this situation in his perceptive book *Man's Search for Himself*.[2] In considering the inner problems that most concern people in our time, he comes to focus upon emptiness and loneliness. "We are the hollow men," as T. S. Eliot says,[3] not knowing what we want, uncertain even of what we feel as we reflect like mirrors the expectations of others, able to respond but not to choose, with no decisive center of inner motivation. Without inner resources to cope with the anxious confusions of living, we turn eagerly, often desperately, to other persons for the support we need. And our persistent anxiety is

[1] New Haven, Conn.: Yale University Press, 1950.
[2] New York: W. W. Norton & Co., Inc., 1953.
[3] From "The Hollow Men."

the threat of being left out or excluded. So we try to keep "dated up" with social events lest we fall into the vacuum of isolation.

To the hasty glance it may appear that some of us are popular and busy with an endless round of social activities, while others are shut out to a lonely life due to social ineptitude and failure to "adjust." Dividing the sheep from the goats may be a pleasant device to simplify the complexities of living and consign oneself to the company of the spotless good people or the spotted bad people.

But closer inspection will reveal that every person is lonely. The busy person may put on a show of feverish success by plunging himself compulsively into the social whirl. In this way he may conceal from others, and even himself, the void within, until some failure or dismay brings sharply to focus the hidden loneliness that drives him to his social pursuits. By contrast, the secluded person is one who is more open to admit his dissatisfaction with the social scene, or less willing to undergo the strain of keeping up with its demands. He may not feel free to talk with others openly about his feelings, taking his reprisals in cynical and sarcastic attitudes toward the social joys of others. But to himself he may admit the futility of keeping up with the pretenses of the ever-busy social bee, and well know the poignant sorrow of lonely separation.

This is clearly seen by Anne Frank at the age of fourteen, two years after going into hiding with her family and another family during the Nazi occupation of Amsterdam. Looking back to her former life she writes in her diary these observations:

If I think now of my life in 1942, it all seems so unreal. It was quite a different Anne who enjoyed that heavenly existence from the Anne who has grown wise within these walls. Yes, it was a heavenly life. Boy friends at every turn, about twenty friends and acquaintances of my own age, the darling of nearly all the teachers, spoiled from top to toe by Mummy and Daddy, lots of sweets, enough pocket money, what more could one want? . . .

Yet I wasn't entirely happy in 1942 in spite of everything; I often felt deserted, but because I was on the go the whole day long, I didn't think about it and enjoyed myself as much as I could. Consciously or unconsciously, I tried to drive away the emptiness I felt with jokes and pranks. Now I think seriously about life and what I have to do. One period of my life is over forever. The carefree schooldays are gone, never to return.

I don't even long for them any more; I have outgrown them, I can't just only enjoy myself as my serious side is always there.

I look upon my life up till the New Year, as it were, through a powerful magnifying glass. The sunny life at home, then coming here in 1942, the sudden change, the quarrels, the bickerings. I couldn't understand it, I was taken by surprise, and the only way I could keep up some bearing was by being impertinent.

The first half of 1943: my fits of crying, the loneliness, how I slowly began to see all my faults and shortcomings, which are so great and which seemed much greater then. During the day I deliberately talked about anything and everything that was farthest from my thoughts, tried to draw [Daddy] to me; but couldn't. Alone I had to face the difficult task of changing myself, to stop the everlasting reproaches, which were so oppressive and which reduced me to such terrible despondency.

Things improved slightly in the second half of the year, I became a young woman and was treated more like a grownup. I started to think, and write stories, and came to the conclusion that the others no longer had the right to throw me about like an india-rubber ball. I wanted to change in accordance with my own desires. But *one* thing that struck me even more was when I realized that even Daddy would never become my confidant over everything. I didn't want to trust anyone but myself anymore. . . .

He who has courage and faith will never perish in misery!

Yours, Anne

To see the folly of fleeing into social gaiety to escape oneself may be the first step in coming to terms with loneliness.

2. *The Awful Dilemma*

The lonely person is *I* aware of my separation. This awareness does not dawn upon me all at once, but emerges into consciousness gradually through a series of eventful experiences. The first is birth, when the new life is expelled from the womb where every need was constantly supplied, into a larger world where supply is not equal to demand. Among the discomforts of the larger world of delays and deprivations is the distress of being alone. From this loneliness one is rescued from time to time by the mother, who takes him in her arms and enfolds him in the warm affection of her love. The baby is not prepared as yet to endure the experience of being alone. He retires in sleep to the unconscious peace that recalls his intra-uterine bliss, wherein he may rest from the sufferings of conscious existence. He awakens to suffer again the pangs of loneliness and to cry for enfolding arms of reunification.

Each step in growing up separates him farther from the mother and

107

requires him to regulate his own life and behavior. He is no longer dealt with as a helpless infant to be cared for in every need, but as a responsible person to do for himself what others have done for him. He is subject now to disapproval if he disappoints the expectations of others. Emotional separation is too intolerable to endure, as Sullivan has shown, and to avoid that distress the child represses his contrary impulses to gain the coveted approval from his parents. He stifles his individuality to hold the love he is so dependent upon.

This is the awful dilemma confronting every growing person. Shall I assert my independence at the risk of disapproval and emotional separation? Or shall I submit as a dependent child who surrenders my individuality to gain the security of emotional approval? The awesome character of this dilemma is the urgency of these contradictory demands which each person has to face. No one can be a person in the mature sense unless he is free to assert his individuality. Yet to assert one's individuality is to separate oneself from the sustaining relationship and to endure the distress of standing alone. The price of independence is loneliness. The price of dependence is surrender of individuality. The cost of either alternative is too great to bear. If the dilemma is insoluble and inescapable, then we are left in despair.

Anne Frank wrestled with this dilemma in her efforts to grow up from childhood into womanhood. After two years in hiding from the Nazi persecutors who eventually sent her to death in a concentration camp, she began to feel love toward Peter the son of the other family crowded into their "Secret Annex." He was living in the attic and invited her upstairs for companionship; here they sat in each other's arms and talked over the life they were trying to live under the limitations of such restraining confinement. To be honest rather than underhanded, Anne felt she should tell her father of this experience. Her father advised her to be cautious and not permit such intimacies with Peter. But feeling it was her decision to make, she wrote a letter, in which she sought to declare her independence, and put it in her father's coat pocket:

"I believe, Daddy, that you expect a declaration from me, so I will give it to you. You are disappointed in me, as you had expected more reserve from me, and I suppose you want me to be just as a fourteen-year-old should be. But that's where you're mistaken!

"Since we've been here, from July 1942 until a few weeks ago, I can assure you that I haven't had any easy time. If you only knew how I cried in the evenings, how unhappy I was, how lonely I felt, then you would understand that I want to go upstairs!

"I have now reached the stage that I can live entirely on my own, without Mummy's support or anyone else's for that matter. But it hasn't just happened in a night; it's been a bitter, hard struggle and I've shed many a tear, before I became as independent as I am now. You can laugh at me and not believe me, but that can't harm me. I know that I'm a separate individual and I don't feel in the least bit responsible to any of you. I am only telling you this because I thought that otherwise you might think that I was underhand, but I don't have to give an account of my deeds to anyone but myself.

"When I was in difficulties you all closed your eyes and stopped up your ears and didn't help me; on the contrary, I received nothing but warnings not to be so boisterous. I was only boisterous so as not to be miserable all the time. I was reckless so as not to hear the persistent voice within me continually. I played a comedy for a year and a half, day in, day out, I never grumbled, never lost my cue, nothing like that—and now, now the battle is over. I have won! I am independent both in mind and body. I don't need a mother any more, for all this conflict has made me strong.

"And now, now that I'm on top of it, now that I know that I've fought the battle, now I want to be able to go on in my own way too, the way that I think is right. You can't and mustn't regard me as fourteen, for all these troubles have made me older; I shall not be sorry for what I have done, but shall act as I think I can. You can't coax me into not going upstairs; *either* you forbid it, *or* you trust me through thick and thin, but then leave me in peace as well!"

Yours, Anne

This was a brave declaration, and she meant it with all her conscious ability to decide for herself. She felt the time had come to renounce the dependence of childhood, and was taking her courage in her hands to define her clean break with parental authority. But the issue was not to be so quickly settled by open declaration. Her father was very upset and challenged her right to be so independent. She was then impaled on both horns of the dilemma, wanting to keep an approving relation with her parents and at the same time to be free to make her own independent decisions. One has to yield to the other, as she writes in her diary two days later:

Daddy and I had a long talk yesterday afternoon, I cried terribly and he joined in. Do you know what he said to me, Kitty? "I have received many letters in my life, but this is certainly the most unpleasant! You, Anne, who have received such love from your parents, you, who have parents who are always ready to help you, who have always defended you whatever it might be, can you talk of feeling no responsibility toward us? You feel wronged and deserted; no, Anne, you have done us a great injustice!

"Perhaps you didn't mean it like that, but it is what you wrote; no, Anne, we haven't deserved such a reproach as this!"

Oh, I have failed miserably; this is certainly the worst thing I've ever done in my life. I was only trying to show off with my crying and my tears, just trying to appear big, so that he would respect me. Certainly, I have had a lot of unhappiness, but to accuse the good [Daddy], who has done and still does do everything for me—no, that was too low for words.

It's right that for once I've been taken down from my inaccessible pedestal, that my pride has been shaken a bit, for I was becoming much too taken up with myself again. What Miss Anne does is by no means always right! Anyone who can cause such unhappiness to someone else, someone he professes to love, and on purpose, too, is low, very low!

And the way Daddy has forgiven me makes me feel more than ever ashamed of myself, he is going to throw the letter in the fire and is so sweet to me now, just as if he had done something wrong. No, Anne, you still have a tremendous lot to learn, begin by doing that first, instead of looking down on others and accusing them!

I have had a lot of sorrow, but who hasn't at my age? I have played the clown a lot too, but I was hardly conscious of it; I felt lonely, but hardly ever in despair! I ought to be deeply ashamed of myself, and indeed I am.

What is done cannot be undone, but one can prevent it happening again. I want to start from the beginning again and it can't be difficult, now that I have Peter. With him to support me, I can and will!

I'm not alone any more; he loves me. I love him, I have my books, my storybook and my diary. I'm not so frightfully ugly, not utterly stupid, have a cheerful temperament and want to have a good character!

Yes, Anne, you've felt deeply that your letter was too hard and that it was untrue. To think that you were even proud of it! I will take Daddy as my example, and I *will* improve.

Yours, Anne

The heart-broken penitence is genuine. She does not want to hurt her parents who have done so much for her. The brave declaration of independence has backfired, and she now sees herself as a harsh, ungrateful person whose pride has betrayed her into this terrible mistake, of which she is miserably ashamed. To her sorrow she learns she is not self-sufficient, nor can she go her own way alone regardless of how her actions may affect others. She is responsible to her parents for their happiness and will try to be more like them. Her independence falls from its high pedestal and she must begin again as a dependent child who has yet much to learn from her parents. But she is not wholly discouraged for she has Peter, who respects her as an equal, and her sister Margot, who understands how she feels.

After two months she returns to the question again with a somewhat calmer perspective to re-examine herself in relation to her parents. In this entry she wants to give full credit to them for their kindness to her, yet she does not see how they can do for her now what she has come to realize she will have to do for herself:

Now I want to come to the chapter of "Daddy and Mummy don't understand me." Daddy and Mummy have always thoroughly spoiled me, were sweet to me, defended me, and have done all that parents could do. And yet I've felt so terribly lonely for a long time, so left out, so neglected, and misunderstood. Daddy tried all he could to check my rebellious spirit, but it was no use, I have cured myself, by seeing for myself what was wrong in my behavior and keeping it before my eyes.

How is it that Daddy was never any support to me in my struggle, why did he completely miss the mark when he wanted to offer me a helping hand? Daddy tried the wrong methods, he always talked to me as a child who was going through difficult phases. . . . [He] always takes up the older, fatherly attitude, tells me that he too has had similar passing tendencies. But still he's not able to feel with me like a friend, however hard he tries. These things have made me never mention my views on life nor my well-considered theories to anyone but my diary and, occasionally, to Margot. I concealed from Daddy everything that perturbed me; I never shared my ideals with him. I was aware of the fact that I was pushing him away from me.

I couldn't do anything else. I have acted entirely according to my feelings, but I have acted in the way that was best for my peace of mind. Because I should completely lose my repose and self-confidence, which I have built up so shakily, if, at this stage, I were to accept criticisms of my half-completed task. . . .

"For in its innermost depths youth is lonelier than old age." I read this saying in some book and I've always remembered it, and found it to be true. . . . Older people have formed their opinions about everything, and

111

don't waver before they act. It's twice as hard for us young ones to hold our ground, and maintain our opinions, in a time when all ideas are being shattered and destroyed, when people are showing their worst side, and do not know whether to believe in truth and right and God. . . .

It's a real wonder I haven't dropped all my ideals, because they seem so absurd and impossible to carry out. Yet I keep them, because in spite of everything I still believe that people are really good at heart. I simply can't build up my hopes on a foundation consisting of confusion, misery, and death. I see the world gradually being turned into a wilderness, I hear the ever approaching thunder, which will destroy us too, I can feel the sufferings of millions and yet, if I look up into the heavens, I think that it will all come right, that this cruelty too will end, and that peace and tranquillity will return again.

In the meantime, I must uphold my ideals, for perhaps the time will come when I shall be able to carry them out.

Yours, Anne

The awful dilemma of human life is the choice between relation and separation. The choice is forced upon us by the very nature of human existence, which requires both to fulfill our destiny. This dilemma threatens us because either alternative presents an unwelcome choice. We are caught in a life situation so complex that our fate is to desire and fear both options, each of which appears inescapable.

It is this complexity in the human dilemma that makes our choice so difficult and disturbing. Yet each person will have to choose for himself. To surrender my choice to others is after all my choice. Whatever I do is a selection of this in preference to that course of action. Even to do nothing is deciding not to act in this time and place. The necessity of choice is a strange paradox at the root of our dilemma. The external observer is naturally impressed by the necessity of external events to the extent perhaps that he will deny the effective power of choice. But this is to miss the inner necessity by which a person is continually choosing how to respond to these events. And his inner responses are decisive enough to make the real difference between persons and things. Persons respond in unpredictable ways because they exercise unique choices among given alternatives.

A person is lonely at the center of his being because he is a person. It is his awareness of his uniqueness that presents the dilemma of relation versus separation. One might argue that social patterns decide who is lonely by the proximity and accessibility to other people. But it would be too superficial to insist that no one has a right to be lonely in a congested city with so many people around him. For loneliness is an inner feeling best known to the person who feels that way, not a spatial arrangement of objects but a psychic experience of a subject who decides for himself whether he is lonely. A person, as we have seen in the first chapter, is the inner center of conscious experience. A personality may stand alone, but only a person can feel lonely and decide whether to relate or separate himself.

To understand what it means to be a person we turn to the sciences of the inner life—psychology and religion. Each discipline offers a way of life to follow in its characteristic approach to the subject. The urgency of the dilemma calls for choices which every person must make for himself if he is to cope with the problem of his loneliness. How will psychology and religion guide him at the point of such a decision?

3. A Psychological Answer

Psychology recognizes that the lonely person has to live with himself. If he is the one to decide, he will need to become the court of final appeal. However much he may differ with others he will want above all to make peace with himself. Conflicts are to be expected and divisions are bound to arise, but they can be tolerated if one has achieved integrity. Psychologists do not hesitate to disagree over many intricate details of theory and method in their search for a more accurate understanding of personality. But in general most psychologists appear to agree that each person should fulfill his potentialities in a mature integration of his own personality.

The following exposition may not satisfy any one psychologist as an exact description of what he is trying to say. It is not presented as *the* psychological answer, but only as *a* psychological answer to suggest a possible way out of the dilemma confronting us.

In his struggle to grow up, the person will have to undergo one separation after another. He will suffer no little anxiety in going through these distressing experiences, but they are not to be avoided or postponed if he is to fulfill his destiny as a growing person. He had better learn to like it as best he can and tolerate the anxiety as the price of achieving his independence. He will be misunderstood and pursued by his parents, who will try to hold him to them in a dependent relation long after he has outgrown childhood. This tendency of parents to overprotect children and keep them dependent, one psychologist has called "momism," insisting it has weakened the character of our manhood. There is no need to react by heaping abuse upon parents who are only following their natural impulses or good intentions to do their utmost for their children. But the growing person will have to sever the psychological umbilical cord [4] that ties him to his parents and take courage to assert his freedom to live his own life.

It will not be easy to achieve personal independence, and one must prepare for a long struggle rather than a quick victory. For even after the parents have relinquished their external controls, their demands and expectations will continue to guide our choices. Because we have loved and admired them we take them as our models. Even in our revolt against their domination we aim to displace them by succeeding to their position of authority. If their authority is to be overthrown, we see ourselves as standing in their place and exercising the same authority they once held over us. As growing persons we introject their ideals into ourselves, and then proceed to rule our own impulses by this inner authority we set up as our conscience.

The struggle against external authority is now internalized as conflicts within the personality. Freud, as noted in Chapter III, indicated three levels in which these contests rage within personality. The amoral and irrational impulses emerge from the primitive id. When these reckless id impulses get us into trouble with our society, the executive ego seeks to hold the wild impulses in check by repressive and sublimating measures. The ideal by which these impulses are disciplined becomes the superego censoring natural behavior by the standards of ideal authorities now enshrined within ourselves.

Consequently a person may not be able to enjoy the freedom he has won at such cost. Having broken with the authorities of the past, he continues in servile bondage to their image, which he has set up as his own conscience. Aggressive hostility, which we first turned against the parents and external authorities, is now turned in upon himself in contests between the upsurging impulses and the restricting pressures of the punishing conscience. He is beset with guilt feelings and self-rejection on account of his aggressive impulses. He develops inner

[4] May, *op. cit.*, p. 121.

tensions that interfere with his work and his rest, or break forth in emotional eruptions and psychosomatic symptoms. He may need to undergo psychotherapy to gain release from these tensions, and to work through psychic conflicts to a state of peace and efficiency that is free from interlocking anxieties and compulsive striving.

In all this we are counseled by psychologists not to give up the struggle for mature independence by turning to easy solutions and deceptive half-way measures. To be trapped by neurotic anxiety is to lose the momentum of growth and to surrender in the face of difficulties before maturity is won. It is better to move ahead in spite of anxiety, not recklessly, but steadily advancing beyond the fixations and regressions of childish dependence. One is not to yield his initiative to other authorities, known or unknown who tell him what to do, lest he be a hollow shell like a mirror or radar, reflecting only the opinions of others with no creative purpose of his own. Let every person decide for himself to affirm his own individuality and respect the right of others to do likewise. For there is a positive core of potential goodness in everyone, which if freed from stultifying pressures will assert the undeniable capacity to grow and actualize the inherent nobility one seeks to develop.

This psychological answer we may call the goal of *heroic independence*. Confronting the dilemma of relation or separation, our psychologist would choose the pain of separation rather than the comfort of relation. He would consider obligation to grow as the primary ought of human life, essential to the fulfillment of one's potentialities in moving on toward maturity. As the mark of immaturity is dependence, he would find it possible to mature only by asserting one's independence at any cost. The pain of growing up is not to be evaded in the illusive hope that an easier way might appear. Freedom will offer its own rewards to compensate for the losses one may suffer. Therefore, the psychologist concludes, let us seize the nettle firmly without complaining and take up with unfaltering courage the responsibility of asserting a mature independence.

Such a view of man is egocentric in the best sense of the term. The independent person may be lonely and suffer anxiety in the stress of growing toward maturity. He will, like Anne, be grateful to parents and friends who have nourished his growing life but will no longer be dependent upon them to uphold his ideals or regulate his behavior. He will accept responsibility for himself, whatever the cost, and live his life outward from an inner center of initiative and decision. He need not boast of mastering his fate, but he will see to it that he is captain of his soul.

4. A Religious Answer

There is truth in what the psychologist has said, and courage in the high resolve to make the most of one's potentialities by responsible decisions to grow at the cost of suffering. But it may not be the whole truth as he presents it, nor is courage the only virtue needed as we wrestle with our destiny. Another approach to the dilemma of man is worth considering, as seen in religious perspective. How would a religious man reply to the question before us? As we listen to this religious answer we may not identify the speaker as any one of the great theologians quoted by followers of a religious way of life. But he may well represent a religious viewpoint in some circles of the faithful.

The great illusion is the self-sufficiency of this finite creature we know as man. It is true that a person should do what he can to develop his potentialities, but it is an error for him to suppose that he can be independent. Without resources beyond his own he cannot live at all. He is dependent not only as a little child but throughout his entire life upon oxygen to breathe, food and liquid to nourish and replenish the cells, and temperature appropriate to maintain the living organism. A Harvard University scientist calculated 214 specific items that must be present in proper proportion on our planet for life to exist here at all.[5]

In addition to these physical conditions we are dependent upon other persons for interests to stimulate learning, emotional support to provide security and confidence, ideals and values to appreciate, ideas and inventions to explore and develop, law and social traditions to guide community life. Human culture is not the creation of a self-sufficient man but the long achievement of co-operative enterprises in which many persons depend upon each other. In growing up one may become less dependent than the helplessness of infancy, and more independent in the responsible decisions of maturity. This is the partial truth in what the psychologist contends, but it becomes misleading if it passes for the whole truth in proclaiming *my* independence as one who can stand alone in splendid isolation.

[5] L. J. Henderson, *The Fitness of the Environment* (New York: The Macmillan Co., 1913).

The danger of self-sufficiency, as of any false claim, is the deception into which we are led. To believe that I am independent leads me to act as if I can be sufficient to myself, which comes to unhappy consequences. If I feel self-sufficient why do I need to learn or to ask anything of others, or to maintain good relationships with other persons who are nonessential to my success? If I feel so independent why bother with community life in this individualistic paradise, where others may amuse me but cannot be expected to need me any more than I need them?

Theologians have a word for this belief in one's own sufficiency; they call it pride. To them it holds a special danger so insidious it may undermine a man's stability without his knowing it. If one presumes too much upon self-sufficiency, he is blind to his inadequacies and acts heedlessly in a vain conceit that justifies the proverb "Pride goes before a fall." To become independent does present a heroic face, but beneath the mask is the deception to feel more sufficient than in fact one is or can be. And to deceive oneself about his independence is to rely on empty gestures that belie the real situation and betray him into eventual defeat.

The virtue most needed when courage betrays us to reckless assumptions is humility. If pride is deceptive let us look at the reality of the human situation and acknowledge the truth of our finite insufficiency. We are dependent creatures and will always need humility if we are to learn the truth or grow into larger fulfillment of our potentialities. There is no disgrace about childhood with its immaturity if one has the humility to learn and the willingness to grow. Whoever will not become as a little child shall not enter the kingdom of God, said Jesus (Mark 10:13-16). Childlikeness promises growth when one is willing to admit he is not sufficient, but is ready to participate with others in larger co-operation and coeducation.

A truly religious person is ready to acknowledge the fact of his dependence, not to perpetuate the weakness of childhood, but to extend the area of growth. The psychologist is rightly opposed to fixation, in which a person ties himself to one stage of development and fails to move beyond it. But there is merit in a temporary regression to childlikeness, as when one becomes a student of a teacher or a patient in psychoanalysis, entering a dependent relationship to learn and outgrow his fixations. The evil which the psychologist decries in dependence is fixation, and the good which religion seeks through dependence is growth.

The aim of religious discipline might be called *creative dependence*. The intention is not to stifle one's freedom but to exercise it through enlarging relationships. A religious person, in the true sense, is not one who accepts his limitations in weak resignation, or nurses a martyr complex by insisting his sufferings are the crown of enduring to the end the person he was at the beginning. Rather, he is one who is devoted to the cause of eternal growth and willing to suffer in order to fulfill a greater destiny. He is not content to dwell in the little dependence of his childhood when he submitted helplessly to his parents with little or no responsibility to do his part. A religious person will renew his youth by penitent humility and press on to the goal of mature responsibility through all of his relationships.

Confronting the dilemma of relation versus separation, the religious person will choose the way of relationship. If he cannot honestly see himself as sufficient enough to go it alone, he will openly acknowledge his dependence upon the relationships by which he is able to live. Not only will he affirm his dependence upon his relationships, but also his responsibility to uphold and develop these relationships to the fullest extent. He will not rely forever upon the first relationships of his infant life in the confines of his local family, but will extend his relations outward to the universal family where all persons are children of one Father in a greater family. "Who are my mother and my brothers? . . . Whoever does the will of God is my brother, and sister, and mother." (Mark 3:33-35.)

To do this is to extend a mutual dependence of giving and receiving through expanding interdependence. The religious vocation will have to face separations in foregoing the old security with its bondage to the inertia of the past. Every creative religious leader has forsaken old and comfortable ways for new and daring departures in the pioneering enterprise of following a heavenly vision. He may stand alone against the smug and powerful majority and assert a fearless independence from the stifling tradition of established institutions. Yet he draws strength to defy resistant authorities by the discovery that he is not alone, that if God is with him his resources are stronger than the resources of those who oppose him. This was the experience of the Hebrew prophets as well as of Jesus who said: "The hour is coming, indeed it has come, when you will be scattered, every man to his home, and will leave me alone; yet I am not alone, for the Father is with me" (John 16:32).

It has been demonstrated time and again that those who depend sufficiently upon God have not had to rely weakly upon human authorities. They have often shown a kind of boldness that astonishes the cautious politicians, who may be overawed by public opinion or deterred by a paralyzing fear of what people will think of them. Their sense of greater dependence upon heavenly resources has saved them from crippling anxieties and made them independent of earthly threats and fears. To be free from these local intimidations of parents and petty officers who may oppress the growing person is the aim of the psychologist. But he who stands alone is weak if he is truly alone; and his fight for freedom will either be too violent and sudden, or too brief and vacillating to repose in sufficient strength. To achieve freedom in the larger sense of unflinching responsibility to uphold the freedom of all—this will require sustaining relationships deeper than the divisive forces of separation.

The religious aim is to develop these sustaining relationships to the largest possible extent. This will be seen as the basic need if a person is to grow, and the inescapable responsibility if he is to do his part in helping other persons to grow. In the opening chapter, the person was defined as one who seeks values through all his relationships. This quest for enlarging values in all relationships is the vocation of religion, and to that cause of eternal growth all of its resources are devoted.

Psychoses in mental illness have been called private religions, pursuing compulsive rituals and dogmas that have special meaning to one but are not recognized by others. It would be more accurate to call them magic or demonology, as these are private systems for avoiding anticipated evils. Religion is a public and social enterprise in which a group moves out together in search of values. Religion is essentially a universal outreach to all relationships; and in spite of reactionary sects who may take exclusive attitudes, the genius of the religious life is its openness to broadening interests and associations. It is this universalizing movement that gives religion its most characteristic influence upon the history of civilization. Though often closed in by narrow and intolerant dogmatism, so prevalent in human prejudice whether secular or sacred, the main thrust of the religious vocation is to achieve ever more inclusive values. This we see in the religious maturing of Dorothy Strong as she seeks to serve a widening circle of friends in outgoing, affectionate relationships.

It may be noted that psychology is also exploring the meaning of interpersonal relations, with no less effect than religion; and furthermore, that a balance is needed between relation and separation, which psychology and religion may better seek together than in rival camps of suspicion and opposition. This kind of collaboration is not to be rejected as beyond the realm of possibility; in fact this book is one more attempt to achieve a working partnership between the two. In chapters to follow, these possibilities will be explored further.

The lonely person will continue to wrestle with the dilemma of relation versus separation, suffering the anxiety yet initiating the steps to work through to larger integration within and around himself. A psychologist may accent separation as the basic drive of the growing person, to which his relationships are to be subordinated. A religious person may emphasize relatedness as the basic direction of his growth, to which his separatist strivings are to be subordinated and by which they are to be fulfilled. The psychologist is concerned about local relationships as they serve his goal of heroic independence. The religious person is concerned about his ultimate relationships to God and the eternal purpose in universal dimensions.

Have we set these viewpoints of psychology and religion too sharply in opposition to each other? It is evident to many psychologists that isolation cripples a growing personality, that healthy relationships are essential if one is to fulfill his largest potentialities. To many theologians the need for separation has also been evident if a person is to stand on his own feet and be true to his religious convictions. What we oppose in the heat of argument is often an extreme and exaggerated position not intended by the one to whom it is attributed. To insist on absolute dependence is just as reckless as to strike out for absolute independence. Each must have its limits, and the need of a growing person is for a measure of independence in open, not stifling, relationships.

We seem to be converging upon the mediating position of interdependence. Does this wipe out the distinction between the work of psychology and religion? Not at all, for each has its own unique perspective from which to focus upon personality. The psychologist intentionally and rigorously limits his field of operations to the boundaries of a natural science. To attain maximum precision and predictability he turns his focus upon the human scene as a system of natural events. As a person he may wonder about the beyond, but as a scientist he decides not to look over the fence, to restrict his attention faithfully to the field of man in limited context.

The religious seeker is engaged in a wider exploration which aims at universal perspective. He is also finite in his starting point as a human thinker, but he desires to see the meaning of his life in the largest context possible. He will be grateful for every fact uncovered by the natural sciences, but he is trying to put the details together into whole meanings. He may be a scientist himself when he goes to his laboratory, but he is also a person with family, community, and cosmic relationships. To explore these other connections beyond the limits of his science he must become a philosopher of sorts, who asks persistent questions about the larger meaning of all things taken together. Searching for ultimate being he considers the purpose of God as creator of life. He is concerned to find the answer to his seeking, a response from beyond to him as a person with a destiny and a destination.

In Part I we have been trying to see what it means to be a person. We have sensed the intricate complexity of the life processes involved in personality, and have traced the stages of its development according to four theories of contemporary psychologists. At the center of personality we have found the lonely person who struggles as best he can with the awful dilemma of relation and separation. In Part II we will consider what it means for this lonely person to be religious. To what will he relate himself? In what context will he free himself and dedicate his energies?

PART II

To Be Religious

CHAPTER SEVEN

CONDITIONS OF
RELIGIOUS GROWTH

~~~~~~

1. Basic Relationships

Each for himself will decide how to manage relation and separation. To be a person is to be one. This we seek by separation to know ourselves more inwardly, to bring self-conscious awareness to sharper focus, to sense how it feels to be a person and what it means to be an individual distinct from the mass. Yet to be one is to seek the relations of wholeness. A finite person is forever incomplete and needing to be related to that which is beyond himself. He will find himself in the courage of going apart to wrestle with his destiny alone, and the humility of coming into relation with other persons to search together for the values of life in community. A person may be lonely in either condition, but his opportunity to grow in perception of the meaning of life is enhanced by both experiences.

The religious quest follows such a pattern in moving alternately from solitude to community. William Ernest Hocking,[1] in his study of religious experience, has called this the "law of alternation," as the devoted seeker moves back and forth from inner solitude of meditation and prayer to outgoing meeting with others in fellowship and service. It is characteristic for the great religious soul, as Jesus or Gandhi, to go apart for hours of silence, wherein the meaning and purpose of life is clarified and the inner resources of the spirit are renewed. Yet this is done, not as a final retreat from the noisy confusion of the city, but rather as a preparation by which to return with new vision and strength to the responsibilities of social life.

The need for solitude is often overlooked in the congested living of our day, and it may be scorned by the busybody as unhealthy in-

[1] *The Meaning of God in Human Experience* (New Haven, Conn.: Yale University Press, 1912).

troversion to be condemned as "escapism." But the uses of solitude could be explored more thoroughly before discarding it so hastily. If one is to think calmly or see clearly in true perspective, there is need to stand apart for another view of the situation confronting us, where one can be himself more honestly and decide for himself more truly. The lonely person may be able to see quite distinctly what a crowd may overlook in the mad rush of keeping up with the majority. Dorothy Strong was more capable of thinking and deciding for herself in moments of solitude.

It may be that one is related even in solitude, and more deeply perhaps than in the thronging crowd. Social relations are often external or casual, but in prayer one may meet God in a profound experience of communion. If this is what happens in prayer it is more than auto-suggestion or talking to oneself; it is what the theologians mean by confrontation, a living, dynamic encounter of person with person. To a religious seeker this may be the most significant relationship of life, the central reality amid the illusory and transient *maya* of external appearance, the revelation of truth and the resource of spirit by which to live creatively. Apparently alone one is not alone; externally withdrawn one is engaging in the most intense kind of interaction; audibly silent one may be moved by eloquent communication. Centered in this relationship one may come to other persons in a new and vital appreciation.

The cure for loneliness is not social activity, for one may keep very busy in a social whirl of goingness as frantic as it is futile. To be up and doing can be as empty as the activity of a squirrel in a treadmill cage, racing on in circles of frenzy without getting anywhere. To go through the motions without the genuine emotions of friendship is a hollow deception that fails to deceive. To advise a lonely person to join up and get into the swim of social activities may not satisfy his needs, which is for a deeper sense of being wanted and needed in a mutuality of caring enough to rejoice and weep with each other. It is not the number of social contacts and events that fulfill the hunger of loneliness, but the kind of response that is given by one person to another, indicating that one is appreciated for what he is and loved for his intrinsic worth.

What every person needs in order to heal the wounds of loneliness are basic relationships that hold the vital significance of mutual esteem

126

and affectionate concern.[2] Most of our social contacts are momentary and superficial, especially in the anonymity of urban life, in which one serves or is served by strangers and there is no recognition of each other as a person. Unless one has been loved he is incapable of loving other persons. The most significant relationships begin in the loving family where one is held in the warm and sustaining affection of father and mother, brother and sister. If we learn in the family to give and receive personal regard, we go forth to find other persons with whom to share the meaning and value of life in responsive appreciation.

Is it not surprising to discover how defensive and competitive most of us are in our society? Seeing other persons as rivals we guard what we say lest we betray our inner feelings or reveal attitudes that others may ridicule or hold against us. To play safe with other persons who might disapprove or be offended, we talk of the weather and such inconsequential topics as will not reveal our true feelings. Trying to conform to empty conventionalities we hide our deeper selves behind a defensive mask to keep up the appearances. Small wonder that we are lonely when we hold each other at a safe distance by such maneuvers without permitting the real person in me to meet the real person in you. Distrust holds us back and keeps us apart when we hunger to know and be known; yet we hide behind our defenses and guard every entrance as if to ward off the enemies we fear others will be.

Separated by such lonely defenses we confine ourselves to prisons of living death. For separation is exactly what death means to a living person. One by one, our best friends depart until eventually all relationships are severed by death. Each separation is a tragic loss, foretelling the final and complete loss of all values. Confronting these losses, every person is afflicted with a basic anxiety which Tillich calls the threat of nonbeing.[3] To cope with the threat of these progressive deprivations, one needs a courage arising from enduring relationships, which uphold us in spite of the shocks and losses of human existence.

How can we restore what is lost in the attritions of separation? The answer would seem to emerge from relatedness which can survive the losses and sustain the lonely person in a tide of ongoing life values. When friends depart and we are separated from those we love, there

---

[2] This is shown by Ina May Greer in her consideration of *Loneliness* (Department of Social Service, 1 Joy Street, Boston, Mass.), published first as "Token Relationship: A Study of Counterfeit Interaction," *Journal of Pastoral Care*, I (Winter, 1947), 1-5.

[3] *Op. cit.*

must be counteraction of some kind to reverse the trend and link us in vital connections to a living wholeness. If religion is that life-giving resource which binds us together (as the Latin *religio* seems to mean), it is not surprising to find men turning to religion at time of loss when the threat of nonbeing calls for the courage to affirm the larger unity of Being.

Basic relationships are the vitalizing context in which we find life at once stimulating and sustaining. Interpersonal relations offer resources to fulfill the needs of wholeness not possible in isolation or empty, impersonal association. The human quest is not primarily to reduce tensions (as Freud, Lewin, and Sullivan are inclined to see it), but actually to maintain the tensions that keep us moving on toward ideal goals (as Allport demonstrates). Not all relationships are equally significant, many are remote and indifferent to the inner concerns of the growing person. But every person hungers for relationships signifi-cant enough to invite his devotion and central enough to orient his striving.

Here we find the first condition of religious growth. For religion is the search for meaningful relationships. To know a secure and satisfying relation with someone who loves is to have a basic pattern for religious experiences of faith and love. In such a trustworthy relation at home or elsewhere, a growing person can learn to trust God as creator and sustainer of life in every faithful relationship where love is manifest. In being so loved one can learn to give love and devotion to another person and come to devote himself in worship to the ultimate love of God. Without such a basic relationship a person is crippled in his capacity to trust and love.

And yet in the dynamic striving of life toward goals, there is con-stant interaction between negative lack and positive fulfillment. A negative denial may serve as a persistent motive to seek what will satisfy the need. This is obvious enough in the efforts of an organism to satisfy hunger and thirst. What is not always obvious but nonetheless determinative is the seeking of human life for basic relationships. We have seen in the life stories of Jeanne and Dorothy how their religious quest moved from less to more faithful and loving relationships. If a person is deprived or disappointed in one relationship, he is likely to seek the more ardently for another significant relationship. There are instances in pathological characters when a person has been disappointed beyond the point of returning hope, and becomes a chronic aggressor or a mute and withdrawn schizophrenic.

Nevertheless the desire for a basic relationship remains a primary need of human life. And this need is a dynamic condition of religious growth. "When my father and my mother forsake me, then the Lord will take me up." (Ps. 27:10 K.J.V.) To some extent every finite person is deprived of the wholeness for which he longs. The relationships of family and associates are good so far as they satisfy basic needs, but they do not prove constant enough to satiate or extinguish these human needs. For every relationship is variable and unpredictable to a degree where good is mingled with evil, and the satisfaction blends with dissatisfaction. From the complex of these contradictory experiences the religious seeker is striving for a more complete relationship —intimate enough to meet the need for love, and ultimate enough to provide a trustworthy basis for self-giving devotion in the eternal faithfulness of God.

2. Empathy and Identification

Why is a basic relationship so urgently needed? To cure the wound of separation in which the lonely person suffers a loss of value. There are two ways in which we depend upon each other for our values. First, the value which I place upon myself is a reflection of the appraisals of other persons. From early infancy one is aware of the approval or disapproval of the mother by tones of the voice, gentle caressing, and affectionate care in response to cries of hunger, discomfort, and loneliness. Such empathic communication is learned before language and continues throughout life as each person searches for signs of approval and responds to cues of emotional attitudes manifest by other persons. To feel rejected or excluded is a tragic sorrow, as a person is reduced in value and deprived of a sense of worth. A basic relationship is therefore satisfying insofar as it reinforces a person's ability to value himself acceptingly rather than rejectingly. This was a distressing anxiety for Dorothy in her childhood, as she felt rejected first by her father and then by her playmates. Her summer visits with her grandparents were the more satisfying because she was accepted by them with approval as a person of worth.

Another gain in such relationships is the increase of values by sharing them mutually with other persons. To seek the approval of another person and find him valuing what I value is a reinforcing experience that confirms my own appraisals. We enjoy eating with other persons around a table because together we enhance the joy of satisfying our hunger. The participation of each eater with zestful attack upon the food, the smacking of lips, and favorable comments upon the flavor contribute to the value of the common experience, what Sullivan calls a consensual validation. A successful dinner party appeals to the visual sense in colorful decorations, to the auditory sense in the repartee of conversation, as well as to the taste and olfactory senses, as a common enterprise in which the sense of worth is validated by mutual agreement.

To feel what another feels is to enrich the emotional life by the diversity of vivid contrasts and the unity of converging experiences. This is what we mean by empathy—to enter another person's experience to comprehend what life means to him in his living adventure. By such imaginative projection one crosses over from his lonely isolation to join with another person in sharing a mutual experience. A relationship then becomes meaningful in feeling with another person his experience, and perceiving its value or disvalue. A two-year-old boy pointed to a bandage on my finger and said, "Hurt," in a whimpering tone of voice that clearly indicated even at this age how he was able to have empathy by recalling a similar experience of his own, and so to enter into the joys and sorrows of others.

At the turn of the century, social psychologists were stressing imitation as the basis of learning. Then came the experimental psychologists to show the association of stimuli and responses in conditioning. Yet these concepts give but an external and mechanical view which may characterize animal better than human learning. The inner dynamic of learning is more aptly described by Freud as a process of identification.

At first, according to Freud, it is the child's primitive impulse to possess the love-object, the mother or father for himself. In his desire to possess the mother, the little boy finds he cannot have her all to himself because the father has a claim upon her. How can he resolve this conflict? By identifying himself with the father to become as the father. This is an act of introjection whereby the growing person takes into himself the admired parent as the model or ideal of what he wants to become. This introjected ideal becomes his superego, the internalized authority by which he seeks to regulate his conduct and become the person he longs to be. The cathexis or dynamic relationship to the father or mother is taken into his own person as the ego-ideal by which to repress and sublimate his impulses into moral behavior.

How are these capacities essential to religious growth? If religion is a search for value through relationships, then, to be religious, a person must develop a sensitivity to meaning and value in relationships. Empathy and identification are such abilities to experience the emotional value of a relationship. Otherwise a relationship will be external as to a physical thing, say a pencil, which one uses until the lead is gone and then throws away. But an interpersonal relation has intrinsic value to be cherished as unique and irreplaceable. A person-to-person relationship offers the privilege of sharing experiences of mutual value for the sake of what they mean to each together.

To Freud, identification is the basis of both morality and religion. The development of a social sense is representative of the most important events both to the individual person and the human race. The formation of individual character and the achievement of civilization are the product of identification, the process in which primitive impulses are sublimated and reconstructed into the higher love of person for person in spiritual and intrinsic valuation. Objects desired are thus personalized, and external relations are internalized to become the moral conscience and religious aspiration. What was longing for the father becomes theistic religion of a heavenly Father. What was rivalry with the brother becomes identification of interest and co-operation to uphold a common code of moral conduct.

Psycho-analysis has been reproached time after time with ignoring the higher, moral, spiritual side of human nature. The reproach is doubly unjust, both historically and methodologically. For, in the first place, we have from the very beginning attributed the function of instigating repression to the moral and aesthetic tendencies in the ego, and secondly, there has been a general refusal to recognize that psycho-analytic research could not produce a complete and finished body of doctrine, like a philosophical system, ready-made, but had to find its way step by step along the path towards understanding the intricacies of the mind by making an analytic dissection of both normal and abnormal phenomena. . . .

It is easy to show that the ego-ideal answers in every way to what is expected of the higher nature of man. In so far as it is a substitute for the longing for a father, it contains the germ from which all religions have evolved. The self-judgement which declares that the ego falls short of its ideal produces the sense of worthlessness with which the religious believer attests his longing. As a child grows up, the office of father is carried on by masters [teachers] and by others in authority; the power of their injunctions and prohibitions remains vested in the ego-ideal and continues in the form of conscience, to exercise the censorship of morals. The tension between the demands of conscience and the actual attainments of the ego is experienced as a sense of guilt. Social feelings rest on the foundation of identifications with others, on the basis of an ego-ideal in common with them.[4]

As a very young child, Dorothy identified with her mother in feeling rejected by the father and his relatives. As the mother retreated into invalidism, Dorothy identified with her mother again in the frequent illnesses that kept her home from school. In college she found a substitute father in the speech professor and identified with him in choosing the vocation of a teacher of speech. In her religious desire to give her life in service to others who are in need, she was moved by empathy to share their feelings and enter into a common concern with them. Her religious development was aided by empathy and identification, which brought her from isolation into significant relationships.

There can be no doubt that these capacities make a person more open to suffering, more sensitive to the tragic sorrows that afflict human life. But only so is it possible to be fully human and know the whole breadth and depth of emotional experiences. The great religions demonstrate a compassion to enter vicariously into the suffering of others, to bear their burdens and do to others as to oneself. Such religion does not operate by hedonistic motives nor promise to save from pain and sorrow in this life. Religious devotion is a historic refutation of hedonism in demonstrating the appeal to humble folk as well as martyrs of the willingness to renounce immediate pleasures for spiritual values of another kind.

Though Freud was apparently unfriendly to religion as an "obsessional neurosis" and a regressive longing for dependence, he was obviously referring to neurotic and immature religious motives. Even the stanchest defenders of religion would agree that some people are religious from immature motives, such as an obsessional preoccupation with anxieties or the desire to escape suffering. Actually Freud classified religion with the arts and social gains of civilization, as achievements in controlling and rising above (sublimating) the primitive demands of the id. He does allow hedonistic motives for the id which knows no

[4] *The Ego and the Id,* pp. 46-49.

other good than pleasure. But in the development of the ego-ideal through identification with the highest and best, a person moves "beyond the pleasure principle," to guide his conduct by the ideal principles. In so doing he becomes a responsible and conscientious member of society, who renounces pleasures insofar as they conflict with other values. This is the behavior characteristic of a mature religious person.

The disciple who seeks to grow in religious maturity by identification with Jesus is introduced to the Father with whom Jesus identifies himself. When Philip said, "Show us the Father, and we shall be satisfied," Jesus replied: "He who has seen me has seen the Father. . . . I am in the Father and the Father in me." (John 14:8-11.)

Such empathy and identification can heal the wound of lonely separation by a basic relationship as intimate and abiding as it is satisfying and stimulating. When a religious person seeks primarily to satisfy the need for comfort or pleasure, his motives are immature. But when he seeks primarily to grow through enlarging relationships in responsible living, his religious motives are maturing.

3. Communication of Meaning

Granted that religion may enrich the emotional life through experiences of empathy and identification, what if it is a fiction of the mind? This was evidently the contention of Freud in his essay *The Future of an Illusion*. Will this mean that religious growth follows error rather than truth? Freud might seem to mean this in saying that what science could not give he would not seek elsewhere.[5]

But on the contrary he insists that an illusion need not be false. It may be an experience that does not raise the question of truth as in the myth that is valid in artistry by the irresistible appeal of its beauty. Santayana defines religion as the poetry in which we believe. A belief may be unproved scientifically, and yet it need not be false but rather beyond the reach of logical proof. Theologians are likely to agree that we cannot prove the existence of God, for he does not fit into the finite categories of human logic. Scientists are likewise agreed that not final certainty but a degree of probability is the conclusion of their utmost labors to demonstrate and prove.

It should be acknowledged that religious seekers have labored as earnestly for the truth as scientists. When they differ in their view of

[5] *The Future of an Illusion,* tr. W. D. Robson-Scott (London: Hogarth Press, 1928).

the truth it is urgent for all concerned to re-examine their evidence and their inferences. It would be dogmatic to contend that truth resides only with us, whether our claim be scientific or religious. For such dogmatism is not in keeping with the humility and the questing spirit of the true seeker, either religious or scientific. In such humility each will be eager to learn from the other, even though they may speak a different language. And the language is important for it may either confuse or clarify the understanding of truth. Violent disagreements often indicate a problem of communication.

Communication of meaning is another condition of religious growth. Possibilities of learning are strictly limited without the ability to communicate. This fact was dramatized by Helen Keller, who was isolated in the lonely darkness of a blind-deaf person until, with her teacher, she came upon a code by which they could communicate. Then a whole new world was opened to her as she learned to give and receive messages through this narrow channel of communication.

When the infant learns to talk he moves rapidly into new areas of experience which he is now able to share with other persons. In bilingual families a child may learn more than one language by which to give and receive meanings. Actually there was nonverbal communication going on from the time of his first cry and the response of a mothering person. Nonverbal communication does not yield to language, but rather continues to expand alongside language by a growing repertoire of cries and signs. All of the senses participate in recognizing cues, first the elemental senses of touch, taste, and smell; then the more complex relating senses of sound and sight. And yet no experiences after the first hours of infancy can be sensory, pure and simple. For memories and associations soon come into play, by which cues are grasped or prehended, related to other impressions, and integrated by interpretation into meaning. Extrasensory perception goes on continually as long as a person is conscious, and probably in ways of which he is not conscious at the time. For perception utilizing sense data is always more than sensation; it is apprehension of meaning.

It is sometimes opined that science is more trustworthy than religion because it limits the evidence to sense data. Comte became the father of positivism in conferring upon these procedures the honorific title of "the positive sciences." [6] But this was a false assumption from the

[6] Auguste Comte (1798-1857).

start, as Comte and every positivist interprets whatever data he chooses to deal with in nonsensual integrations of meaning. Meaning is not in fact a sense experience, but a relating perception of abstract generalizations inferred from the data. In the refinements of physical and mathematical sciences, the concepts worked with are as intangible and nonmaterial as the concepts of theology. Physicists, who diagram forces and cling to the particle as the last vestige of sense data, are ready to admit that these are but crutches for the imagination.

Lewin in his field theory was free to acknowledge that these devices were used for convenience in the effort to communicate meaning. To reason together about any subject, even to perceive together, will require the use of symbols, whatever they may be, that are agreed upon by the co-workers as a common language referring to designated meanings.

The symbols of a religion need not be the same as those employed by a science. But to communicate we shall need to agree upon the meaning of the symbols used in our conversation, or else resort to a babel of confusion. To grasp the meanings of any discourse fluently, one must practice with the symbols until they become facile tools for the understanding. This is quite evident in learning a foreign language, and yet we may reject another's theory offhand as unintelligible if we are unwilling to learn the meaning of his symbols. Those who find a religious symbolism unintelligible may have prevented their own understanding by not accepting the discipline required to learn the meaning of symbols.

Lewin warns against crippling the power of imagination, a capacity essential to creative arts and sciences, by too sharp and rigid boundaries between the levels of reality and irreality. A growing child may be punished for delving into fantasy when his parents expected him to deal only in reality percepts. The Santa Claus myth is a fantasy, to be sure, in which families participate to their mutual delight in the playful, joyous spirit of the Christmas season. Who can measure how much generous giving and receiving of tokens of affection and esteem, how much unselfish effort to make others happy and to fulfill the responsible devotion of kindly interest and thoughtful remembrance, come as the bright fruit of this rewarding fantasy. To expose the fantasy in the name of reality, and declare, "There is no Santa Claus," does violence to the whole truth for the sake of a partial truth of literalism. Not only the children are disappointed, but everyone who participates in the fantasy is cheated by the denial of reality to the spirit of generous giving for the happiness of others. And everyone is poorer by denying the joy of giving, as Dickens portrayed in his story of Old Scrooge. The trappings of Santa Claus are fictitious and dispensable, but the spirit of generous giving was historical in Christian saints who remembered the children with gifts. At any rate the reality is present in every parent or friend who offers a gift in the spirit of love and kindness to another.

A religious person is one who is able to realize spiritual values. In learning to deal with the realities of the spirit he will find symbols helpful in one way or another. Words are symbols and they will have their place in the communication of religious meaning. Other symbols may take form in architecture and traditional designs, in sculpture and paintings, in music and dramatic ritual, or in silence and meditation with its rich imagery. As in every creative quest, free reign will be given to the awakening imagination. And yet there will be need for discipline as well to follow through from fragmentary and fleeting impressions to integrated and consecutive experiences of meaning. Jesus taught his disciples at first in the picturesque symbols of parables, but eventually by the example of his own life, which has become the great symbol for all who follow him.

To grow spiritually calls for appropriate nourishment as urgently as food is needed for organic growth. Religious growth is nourished by meanings perceived even more than by impressions sensed. The sense impression is a valuable aid, to be sure, when not mistaken for an end in itself. The realities of the spirit are best nourished by growing appreciation for unseen yet vividly experienced values of unselfish love, patience in adversity, and faith to rise courageously above doubt and fear in belonging to a larger relationship. The symbol is the outward and visible sign of an inward and spiritual grace by which we perceive our relatedness to a living tissue of loving concern, the family of God.

If this larger relationship is to be real, the growing person will experience communication. Symbols will suggest associations with other experiences and will communicate meanings that are tied together by linkages of living tradition and revitalizing continuity. Yet symbols are abstract even in their most concrete form, and are powerless apart from the living connection of meanings shared with other persons. Communication in the most alive and growing sense is person-to-person conversation. We learn more from persons than things because they respond from moment to moment with ever new perceptions. They speak and invite a response; they listen and try to comprehend what we mean.

Religious growth is fostered best through the mutual discovery of teaching and learning. As another person communicates his perceptions to me, and I seek to see and understand what he sees and means, we stand together at a threshold of learning. To transmit literal information by rote, as the names of the books of the Bible, does not lead to creative learning, unless two persons find the joy of sharing a meaning significant for their living in the exciting moments they cherish together. It is when two or more persons make a mutual discovery in communicating each to the other a vital meaning that learning is most effective.

We recognize the communication of such meaning as a condition of religious growth. When Jeanne saw her sister Lila at the altar she was startled and concerned about her own religious life. But the opposition of the parents blocked open communication at that time. Later when she attended the youth fellowship with Jimmy Younger she found a congenial group willing to communicate religious meanings with each other. Reinforced by the growing affection of Jerry Andrews, she was able with him to discover the joy of a religious devotion and the ongoing purpose of a Christian vocation. As they participated with other Christians in a loving community, she entered with growing confidence into the mutual discovery of vitally contagious faith and love.

4. Reverence and Devotion

The capacity for reverence and devotion is another condition of religious growth. During the impressionable years of her childhood Jeanne lived among irreverent people in San Pablo. In those years of the depression when her father failed in business, the family suffered more than economic losses. The bitter quarreling of her parents, the drinking bouts, and the sex exploits indicate spiritual losses as well. The foundation of security upon which they were dwelling caved in, and their whole system of values tumbled down. They had relied upon the sober virtues which were their heritage from devout parents in a moral society. They assumed that if you are honest and hardworking, if you deny yourself to save and serve others faithfully, you will receive just rewards for your labor and frugality. When these expectations were disappointed, their spiritual security came down in ruins also. In despair and defiance they said, "What's the use of trying to uphold these values? We will seek our pleasure and forget the rest."

Irreverence is the denial of value by attitudes of distrust and defiance, or mockery and careless neglect, until the entire system of values suffers depreciation. As this occurred in the Schmidt family, they found life less valuable and consequently lived more recklessly. How was Jeanne able to develop reverence in these circumstances?

Reverence is the affirmation of value by attitudes of trust and approval until the entire system of values grows in appreciation. Jeanne suffered with her family the losses in economic and moral security. But she reacted differently to those losses. As a child she did not participate in the exploits and because of them suffered the more. Seeing the situation differently through her suffering as a neglected child, she was the more determined to find values she could affirm. With Lila and the other children she clung to what stability could be had and responded to the faith manifest by church members who held firmly to a system of values. As she came into the youth fellowship and learned to know the Youngers and the Andrewses, she participated with them in reverent experiences of worship and trust, with growing capacity to affirm and appreciate the meaning of a religious devotion.

A study was conducted by Braden at Northwestern University, in which more than two thousand people were asked why they were religious (if they were). Of all the answers given, the one most frequently offered was that "religion gives meaning to life." [7] In the midst of economic insecurity and losses in other values, life may appear meaningless. The need to find meaning and enduring value in the face of separation and loss is one of the most persistent searchings of the human spirit. To discover an order of spiritual values that will not fail when other goods decline is the basic difference between confidence and despair. Some larger meaning such as the faith of religious affirmation is urgent if we are to hold life together in the depletions and destructions around us. This is what Jeanne

[7] Charles S. Braden, "Why People Are Religious—A Study in Religious Motivation," *The Journal of Bible and Religion,* XV (January, 1947), 38-45.

was seeking and what she was able to find in a growing capacity for reverence and devotion.

Albert Schweitzer has been distressed by the contempt for life in our world, manifest in the neglect of its value through careless indifference, exploitation, war, and the prostitution of science to massive destruction. In searching for a cure to this acute illness in our civilization, he finds it in reverence for life. When this is lacking every person is afraid and causes fear by distrust of others. Reverence is a disposition to appreciate the good in all life and to affirm the will-to-live in others as much as in oneself. This capacity to feel deeply the worth of life, to cherish and uphold that which is good, to sense gratitude in the whole meaning of existence—this is to be religious.

All vital religious feeling flows from this attitude of reverence. "In reverence for life religious feeling lies before us in its most elemental and profound form." It is not concerned to explain the objective world, but to accept and affirm it. Here knowledge passes over into experience. "My life bears its meaning in itself. And this meaning is to be found in living out the highest and most worthy idea which my will-to-live can furnish." By reverence I sense value in my own life and all other life. To reverence life is to experience the original and eternal, forward-thrusting will. To feel this mysterious impulse is to live my life in God and to give myself out for other life.

All spiritual life for Schweitzer meets us within the natural life. Reverence for life, therefore, is directed to the natural as well; and the stronger the reverence for the natural the more it cherishes the spiritual. Jesus, in the parable of the lost sheep, values not merely the soul but the whole animal. Reverence for life brings us into a spiritual relation with the world, and gives meaning to existence by raising the natural to a spiritual relation by resignation. True resignation is a feeling of subordination to the course of a larger purpose which enables one to affirm his own existence and win his way toward inner freedom from external fortunes, with strength to deal with them as a deeper and more inward person.

As a being in an active relation to the world he comes into a spiritual relation with it by not living for himself alone, but feeling himself one with all life that comes within his reach. He will feel all life's experiences as his own, he will give it all the help that he possibly can, and will feel

139

all the saving and promotion of life that he has been able to effect as the deepest happiness that can ever fall to his lot.

Let a man once begin to think about the mystery of his life and the links which connect him with the life that fills the world, and he cannot but bring to bear upon his own life and all other life that comes within his reach the principle of Reverence for Life . . . expressed in action. Existence will thereby become harder for him in every respect than it would be if he lived for himself, but at the same time it will be richer, more beautiful, and happier. It will become, instead of mere living, a real experience of life.[8]

Reverence for life does not allow me to appropriate my own happiness. At moments when I should like to enjoy myself without a care, it brings before me thoughts of the misery I have seen and surmised. It refuses to allow me to banish my uneasiness. Just as the wave has no existence of its own, but is part of the continual movement of the ocean, thus I also am destined never to experience my life as self-contained, but always as part of the experience which is going on around me.[9]

Reverence is, therefore, more than pleasure or ego-satisfaction. It is devotion to life beyond my own, arising from a sense of awe that life is so much greater than I, and a sense of ought that commits me to give my life in outgoing service to other life. This view of life Schweitzer calls ethical mysticism and finds it the basic motivation of religion and ethics, demonstrated in his own life mission of mercy on the Ogowe River in French Equatorial Africa.

Without reverence religious experience would be unknown. It is the unbroken thread binding together all the ethical religions of mankind. To miss the authentic note of reverence is to misconstrue the meaning of religion and mistake it for scheming magic or groveling superstition. When a stranger to religion who has not known the meaning of reverence undertakes to describe religious devotion, he is very likely to offer a grotesque portrayal, as misleading as a crude fetish or hideous idol of an evil spirit. Psychological explanations of religion may try to explain it away as nothing but fear or obsession or frantic and inappropriate efforts to appease guilt and anxiety. And so it may be to those who find nothing more in it.

But to reduce reverence to fear, or religious devotion to a com-

[8] Albert Schweitzer, *Out of My Life and Thought,* p. 268. Used by permission of Henry Holt and Company.

[9] Albert Schweitzer, *The Philosophy of Civilization,* Part II: *Civilization and Ethics.* Copyright 1929 by The Macmillan Co. Used by permission of The Macmillan Co. and A. & C. Black.

pulsion ritual, is to throw out the baby with the bath water, and to miss the vital essence of the living religious person. The living experience is compounded of higher aspirations and deeper emotions not reducible to segmental drives or fragmentary wishes. Otto, in his study of religious emotion, was unable to reduce it to a feeling of dependence or any other facile oversimplification. He found it necessary to arrive at a larger concept, the *numinous,* to integrate the religious experience as a sense of tremendous mystery and awful fascination in meeting the Wholly Other.[10] There is more to hope in approaching religious experience as a tremendous mystery than to reduce it merely to this reflex or that reaction. For the greatness of religion, as of every outreaching experience, is its capacity to outgrow primitive origins and attain ever higher levels of motivation.

This is well demonstrated by Allport in his functional autonomy of motives. As a religious person matures he grows in ability to see himself in relation to other persons, and to extend himself in self-giving devotion to others. In seeking value through all relations he devotes himself to what is ultimate and permanent or central in the nature of things.[11] Religious motives are not well explained as pushed from behind by instincts or unconscious complexes. They are better explained as intentions which move consciously toward a goal of higher value. When Thomas a Kempis prayed, "For my whole desire sigheth after Thee," he was giving classic utterance to a religious intention both comprehensive and integral. In such devotion there is a way of integrating conflicting impulses into one purpose, as with Paul in deciding: "This one thing I do, forgetting those things which are behind, and reaching forth unto those things which are before, I press toward the mark for the prize of the high calling of God in Christ Jesus" (Phil. 3:13-14 K.J.V.).

For some, the religious sentiment may be rudimentary and even peripheral to the central concerns of life, in which case it will not exert great influence or move one very deeply. But when reverence is sincere and genuine it will hold central meaning and motivate a person or a community in attitudes and deeds of faithful devotion. As Allport says of religious seeking:

[10] Rudolph Otto. *The Idea of the Holy,* tr. J. W. Harvey (New York: Oxford University Press, 1923).

[11] *The Individual and His Religion,* pp. 56, 124-42.

It is the portion of personality that arises at the core of the life and is directed toward the infinite. . . . It is his ultimate attempt to enlarge and to complete his own personality by finding the supreme context in which he rightly belongs.[12]

So it is to find God and enter into communion with the supreme context of religious living.

In this chapter we have explored some of the conditions of religious growth, and the study is by no means exhaustive. A beginning was made, however, in considering the importance of basic relationships, empathy and identification, communication of meaning, reverence and devotion. In the next chapter we will follow the course of religious growth in the life of an Egyptian who was born into a Coptic Christian family.

[12] *Ibid.*, p. 112. See also Howard Thurman, *The Creative Encounter* (New York: Harper & Brothers, 1954).

CHAPTER EIGHT

TALAT KHALIL

In Assiut, the capital of Upper Egypt, there was in the second half of the nineteenth century a very religious weaver, who devoted his life to the Coptic Church and to his large family of four sons and six daughters. The old man weaved flax in his home, where there were four looms. The daughters would help him, but the sons went to school.

The eldest son Attallah (God's Gift) completed his primary education in the Coptic school, and secured a job in the post office. The second son Botros (Peter) became a banker. Some bad friends encouraged him to drink alcohol. He became addicted to it and died while he was still a young man. The third son Aziz (Dear) became a lawyer.

Unfortunately, the fourth son Mosaad (Happy) suffered from brain injury and never developed mentally beyond the age of seven. Being as religious as his parents, he devoted his youth to the Coptic Church. Every Saturday he would clean the church. On Sundays he would light the one thousand candles of the five big chandeliers, and, after the service, extinguish them one by one, very carefully and patiently, with a small hollow conical instrument. Mosaad loved Allah and wanted to do something for him in his temple. When he was thirty years of age, Mosaad died with an internal disease which the doctors could not diagnose. God loved him so much that he invited him to heaven and released him from lighting the chandeliers.

When Attallah was thirty-three years of age he wanted to marry. His mother told him about several Christian families who had daughters. She took him with her and visited those families, but their girls did not appeal to him. At last, he went to the El Zayat family, where Shafika (Kind) brought him a cold drink of rose syrup on a silver plate.

He loved Shafika. She was thirteen years of age, with jet black hair, dark brown eyes, lovely, silky white skin, and a warm, attractive smile.

He fell in love with her, and put a gold coin on the silver plate. This was a custom of announcing engagement. He also gave her mother fifty golden sterlings, and she bought the furniture for four rooms and provided Shafika with golden bracelets, earrings, rings, necklaces, trousseau, and all an Egyptian bride needed for her wedding day.

On a rainy day three months later, they married. There is a superstition in Egypt that marriage on a rainy day means a happy marriage; and it happened to be so. They were the best of comrades in the sad and happy adventures of life. For thirty years they were an ideal couple, who devoted to each other love, respect, sincerity, and admiration. They enjoyed family happiness, because as children both of them experienced a happy home life with their religious parents. He was a prince of poise, sitting on the throne of peace and wisdom. She is the most generous person I have even seen. She always gives and never takes. If she has a dollar which she needs badly, and anyone asks her for it, she wholeheartedly gives it away. She is an angel without wings.

Five years after her marriage, Shafika gave birth to her first child Nasief (Just). On the fourteenth day of August, 1909, he was dethroned by the second son. According to the cultural tradition, seven days after his birth, the parents invited all the children of relatives and neighbors for a party. They put the babe in a cradle full of nuts and candies. Near him there was an earthen pitcher dressed like a boy with jewelry around the neck. On a table were three lighted candles and under each a label with a name written on it. The names were Efat (Puritan), Fahmy (Intelligence), and Talat (Supreme). The babe must be given the name under the candle that burned the longest. Late in the night, Talat was the name shown under the dim light of the last candle.

Talat was not a lusty child. He had spells of illness. He was less than the average in stature and weight; moreover, he was an anemic case. With the care of his parents and the family doctor, the feeble, delicate child lived, and passed the danger of death in the early days of his childhood. That child was I, growing in the nourishing love of my family.

Nasief, the elder son, was not jealous of me. Each day, the kind mother devoted a long time to be spent exclusively with Nasief. She never nagged him with a continuous torrent of "don'ts." She was very cautious not to make comparisons between him and me that were unfavorable to him. Moreover, there were no interparental tensions.

144

As a natural consequence of all this prudence, Nasief and I became very loving brothers. He was the ace of my play group; and still, he is my best friend. He is, constantly, more than a brother.

When I was five years of age, my parents sent me to the one-room school of the deacon of the Coptic Church. He was a blind man, who knew by heart all the rituals of the church. In his school there were thirty pupils of different ages, ranging from five to twelve. The blind, corpulent, and robust deacon used to teach us hymns and lessons in religion. His collaborator taught us reading, writing, and arithmetic. We never used exercise books; our papers were slates, and our pencils were chalk.

A year later I was promoted to the Coptic pre-elementary school, where I spent one year. Then I entered the Gamalia Government School in the first grade.

The school was located in one of the historic districts of Cairo. Its building was an old mosque erected in the sixteenth century by El Mamalik, who governed Egypt at that time. Every noon the muezzin would go up the minaret and call the people for prayer. Whenever I heard his musical calling tune I was exceedingly pleased, because it was the time for the bell to ring for lunch. I would run to the shop in front of the school to eat *tamia,* the Egyptian national food, which is made of fried, soaked ground beans. At the end of the school day Nasief and I would walk home. It was a long walk, a one-hour walk, but our little feet never felt tired; we were saturated in love and happiness. And there in the home we found always our kind and charming mother awaiting us with the holy kiss.

Five years later, Nasief and I were graduated from Gamalia School. Being older than I by three years, he was not accepted in Tewfikieh Secondary School, which I joined, as it was for younger students. It was the first time we had parted in our academic career. It was a shock for him more than for me. As a result, he had an emotional block which hindered him a while in secondary education. Later on he was successful in his studies and graduated from the University of Cairo as an accountant. Now he holds a good position in the Ministry of Supply.

Nasief and I began religious training before the birth of our parents. Our grandfathers, the weaver and the old oil merchant, were both very religious. Our father was sincerely religious. Our mother is a saint in the dust frame of a human being. Our parental aunt is a

Coptic nun, who used to take us with her to church every day before we knew how to talk or walk. The regularity and repetition of the family religious experiences cultivated in our souls the love of God, people, and church. Our dependable, trustworthy environment secured us a sound basis for religious life.

Our environment was full of affection, gentleness, and kindness. God was first known to us in the love of our parents, relatives, friends, and all the people. We learned religion by observation. We developed a sense of values by sensing what our parents held worthy. Our parents showed attitudes of reverence, devotion, and gratitude to God; and hence we were deeply impressed. The moral and religious traits they wanted us to have, we took as the ripe, ready fruit from the vine of their living example. We just repeated what they did. Their emotions of harmony, faith, courage, poise, peace, love, and wisdom became ours. It was a natural effect, for emotions are contagious.

Constantly, we felt God was present among us as a member of the family. The motto of our father was "God is with us"; and we never believed the contrary. For the family, prayer was as natural as conversation. Our father taught us to remember Jesus whenever we put a piece of bread in our mouths. He taught us the silent prayer. It is still my favorite aspect of life. I practice it when I walk, swim, work, or eat; I discontinue it only when I am asleep. It has become the background from which my life projects.

When I was thirteen years of age, the husband of one of my paternal aunts died, leaving her and a twelve-year-old daughter with no money at all. In Egypt, the tradition is that a widow never marries again; if she does, she will be looked down upon. Meanwhile, the avenues of work are not wide open for women, as it is here in America. Naturally, we welcomed our aunt and her daughter Nargis (Narcissus) to make their home with us.

Nargis was in the fifth grade and I helped her with her studies. She was an industrious and studious girl. Both of us stayed up late studying our lessons. As every day passed I discovered some new trait in her personality to hold in common between her and me.

One night, after finishing our studies, we put out the oil lamp; and there were the moonbeams with which we refreshed our minds and washed our fatigue. We felt the mystic rays spreading silently over our bodies, spirits, and souls. I ran past the rim of these feelings to the real paradise of life when I revealed to her my love and devotion.

146

The moonbeams of our newly born love penetrated deep into the bottom of our hearts, and since that night the silvery ties of unity have entangled us in a golden ring of beauty, charm, and magic. After that silent night we became two nightingales just wavering the wings of happiness and singing the melodies of bliss. We were Adam and Eve in the paradise of life. I sowed in her heart the seeds of attachment, affection, and devotion, and I irrigated them with the flood of my love.

Nargis became my courtship partner without the knowledge of my family. According to the Egyptian cultural tradition, courtship is entirely forbidden. Egyptians do not believe that the courtship period is a selective factor in aiding the participants to determine whom they should and whom they should not marry. They do not believe that courtship partners mature in ideas and attitudes in the direction of adult perspective. They do not believe that during adolescent and postadolescent development, courtship serves as a resource for emotional release, wherein the emotions and activities of the courtship partners are channeled into desirable rather than undesirable forms of behavior. Facing all these heavy chains of tradition, Nargis and I kept our love a deep secret in our hearts.

Nargis and I were both religious. Our childhood religious experience was enriched by deeper reverence and satisfaction in communion with God. Church symbols, traditions, and fellowship became meaningful and inviting. Worship became a vivid reality. There were no doubts or revolts in our religion because our Coptic Church never taught us the narrow, inflexible teachings, which were incapable of expansion and harmony with mature experience.

By that time, I started to think about a vocation. The calling was medicine, the noblest profession on earth. I wanted to be a doctor and to treat the patients of the Egyptian villages free. Medicine is needed badly in my country among the poor peasants. I was longing earnestly to spend all my life among the poor, healing their diseases, uplifting their souls, and helping them to develop better conditions of living.

When I was sixteen years of age, I graduated from the secondary school and entered Cairo University, in the school of medicine. I was very happy, for the way to the poor became near.

Three years later, my father died. His government pension was not enough to keep us, a family of seven. I left the school of medicine and secured a job in the Egyptian government in order to help in rearing my two younger brothers and two sisters. All my hopes had collapsed. I could not think of marriage, and Nargis went to Upper Egypt, where her mother persuaded her to marry. Thus our adolescent, charming love came to a bitter, sad end.

In this very minute, when I remembered this holy love of adolescence, I found myself composing the following Arabic poem:

Fain enti aseiki,
Damee Hanani.
Lamma enti Sebteni,
Hayaya Wadani.

Where are you? To overflow thee
With my tears of kindness.
Since you left me,
I bade farewell to happiness.

Through the years of my adulthood I have built mansions of wisdom in the unfading garden of religion, which is resplendent with blossoms of soul qualities. It took me years and years to know myself and understand my abilities. I controlled anger, hatred, and flesh desires. I knew my limitations and welcomed reality as a sincere friend; hence I lived cheerfully.

First and foremost, I tried to be a joyous person and satisfy my needs for health, happiness, prosperity, and wisdom at the same time. I became immune against sadness. Nothing could blight my smiles. Grim death, disease, or failure could not daunt me. Disaster would not touch my happiness, for I have found the unconquerable, unchangeable, ever new bliss of God. To be really happy, man must find what cannot be lost at all. I have found this in God, so I am happy forever. Finding him, I find through him all things I crave. I am free and happy. The truth made me free, and the love of God, people, and nature made me happy.

I do believe that God lives in every cell of my body, so I must keep this temple in the best state of health, strength, and purity. I have found this can easily be done through athletics. Consequently, I devote my leisure time to swimming. I became a world champion in long-distance swimming. I hold a world record of swimming forty-one hours continuously in the Mediterranean Sea. I swam the longest course of eighty miles in the English Channel in twenty-seven hours and thirteen minutes.

I devoted the rest of my leisure time to writing. I wrote, in the Egyptian newspapers and magazines, articles on social reform and personal hygiene. I have translated four books of fiction from English to Arabic, and all were published. In 1948 my first book of poetry was published. I gave it the title *My Days*. The manuscript of my second book, *On The Waves,* was completed when I was in England pursuing my academic studies, but publishing an Arabic book in England is beyond the scope of practicability.

In my government career I held important posts. For ten years I was the inspector of chambers of commerce. Then I was promoted to the position of Secretary of the Research Institute. One year later I was appointed the Secretary of the Ministry of Supply. After two years I was given the post of Director of Press and Translation Administration.

By that time I decided to be more useful for humanity. I felt that my mission was in the field of psychotherapy. I applied for study leave and was granted four years. Then I left for England, where I joined Reading University. There I studied philosophy under the guidance of Professor Hodges and psychology under the guidance of Professor Oldfield. After that I came to America with the aim of finishing my studies in clinical psychology.

My purpose and goal of life is to write books in Arabic for the man in the street, for the people of the Middle East, to teach them the art of happiness. The art of happiness cannot be mastered without psychology and religion.

CHAPTER NINE

ADVENTURES OF A RELIGIOUS PERSON

~~~~~~~~~~~~~~~~~~~~~~~~~~~~~~~~

1. The Emerging Self

It is the privilege of a person to have religious adventures. Until one becomes a person he is not capable of religious experience. A psychologist who was interested in a comparative study of child development took into his home a baby chimpanzee and raised him as a companion with his infant son. For the first few months they developed in similar ways, but after the first year differences began to appear, and the human child moved out into interests and capacities not shared by the chimpanzee. The most distinctive capacity which a human being develops in his second year is self-consciousness, the capacity to be aware of himself as a person.[1] This we find to be an essential condition of religious experience.

It may be that animals have a feeling of dependence and show devotion to a master. Such a relationship may approach one component of religious experience in a rudimentary sense, as "response to a Sustainer of Values."[2] But the full meaning of religious experience is only possible for a self-conscious person, who is aware of himself in relation to another person. To know that I am valued as a person of unique worth by another person is likely to be my most significant discovery. From this epochal revelation will come my awareness of personal identity, of moral responsibility, and of religious reverence. As a person of value I become responsive to values and responsible to realize them in widening context. In so doing, the person becomes a valuer responding to other valuers.

To be religious is a person-to-person experience. The response of one person to another is radically different from his behavior toward a thing. I will use a thing as a tool for some purpose, such as a chisel

---

[1] Rollo May, *op. cit.*

[2] Paul E. Johnson, *Psychology of Religion* (New York and Nashville: Abingdon Press, 1945), p. 29.

to shape a piece of wood to fit into a fireside bench. When the bench is finished it may have a number of practical uses, and also a rugged beauty which I may admire as the product of handcraft art. And yet whatever its use and however admired, it is still an inert thing to serve as an instrument for some person who uses it for his own sake. My relation to a thing has been called the *I-It* relationship.[3] A thing may be manipulated according to the desire of the owner because it is a thing.

But a person is not rightly to be manipulated or exploited, because he is a unique and creative center of experience and value. He is not one of the interchangeable parts on the assembly line of mass production. He is irreplaceable as a person who puts his experiences together in patterns of meaning and nuances of qualitative worth. A person is to be treated with respect for his feelings, because he is capable of joy and sorrow in the sensitivities and appraisals of self-consciousness. If I truly comprehend from my own experience what it means to be a person, and realize that another person is conscious of himself in equivalent though distinctive ways, will I not take him seriously enough to consider what life means to him? For he is likewise a center of reference in sensing the meaning of our relatedness. In relation to another person I may experience an *I-Thou* relationship.

Religious experience may well be seen as a relationship of I and Thou. It is not open to a thing or to anyone whose attitudes are oriented primarily to things. Religion is the antithesis of materialism, which holds physical objects in ascendant value. A religious view, whether of one's own life or the universe at large, is oriented to persons as counting more than things. And yet no person can be religious alone, however rich may be the ecstasy or despair of his isolation. Authentic religion, wherever we find it, is rather a relationship in which one person responds reverently to another person. Religion is "personal co-operation with a trusted Creator of Values." [4]

In his poetic account of his childhood, Talat Khalil affirms the basic relationships of his close-knit family as the matrix of his self-consciousness. Seven days after his birth the relatives were invited to a party in his honor, at which time his name was chosen by the ceremony of the burning candles. Thus he was given a name by which

---

[3] Martin Buber, *I and Thou*, tr. R. G. Smith (Edinburgh: T. & T. Clark, 1937); *Between Man and Man*, tr. R. G. Smith (New York: The Macmillan Company, 1948).

[4] Johnson, *op. cit.*, p. 30.

to identify him as a unique personality, and to focus the varied experiences and relationships of life in one individuality. He was sustained in his own value by the care and loving attentions given to him in the shared life of the family. His mother Shafika, whose name means "kind," is remembered for her warm, attractive smile, as the most generous of persons, who always gives and never takes. His father Attallah, whose name means "God's gift," is recalled as "a prince of poise" on a "throne of peace and wisdom."

And yet the boy's self-awareness arose in a larger context than his family alone. The candle ceremony symbolized an overarching destiny in which the name was chosen by the candle which burned the longest, as if a divine Providence participated in a choice too important in its far-reaching consequences for the parents alone to decide. If the father was a gift of God, the son would be also in the devout religious gratitude his family felt at the joy and wonder of childbirth. This was no casual event of trivial moment, but the creative act of God imparting to this new child a value of eternal significance.

It was natural for this emerging self to be a religious person. As Talat says, his religious preparation began before the birth of his parents. His grandparents were sincerely religious and they passed on this heritage to his religious father. His mother was "a saint in the dust frame of a human being," and his aunt a Coptic nun who took him to church before he could talk or walk. His environment was trustworthy and formed a secure basis for religious faith, in a home atmosphere of affection, gentleness, and kindness. God was first known to him in the love of parents and relatives. A system of values was developed by sensing what the parents held worthy, as well as by attitudes of reverence and devotion to God, "present among us as a member of the family." Prayer was as natural as conversation, and the children were taught to remember Jesus whenever a piece of bread was put in the mouth. Silent prayer has become the background for the whole of life, for all of Talat's decisions and activities.

The ultimate devotion of a religious person arises from faith in a Creator of Values. Beginning in the inner circle of the immediate family, the religious spirit extends to other persons, and eventually to the ultimate Being who creates persons and values. Theologians and philosophers will debate whether or not God is a person. But if we come to this question psychologically in seeking to understand the meaning of religious experience, the answer is clear. The basic motive of the religious quest is to find a person-to-person relationship of faithful love. To interpret this quest according to the evidence of most religious experience, is to perceive a religious person responding to God as the ultimate person who creates values.

2. The Struggle for Freedom

In a family of such mutual appreciation and affection it will not be easy for Talat to win his freedom. He will be able to affirm himself, but as his family approves and wants him to be. His system of values and especially his view of himself will be (as Sullivan would say) reflected appraisals of what other persons think of him. The stronger the ties of family affection the more effort will be required to stand alone and be himself. He was drawn to his older brother Nasief almost as closely as to the parents; the boys were constantly playing and going to school together, a walk of one hour, "but our little feet never felt tired; we were saturated with love and happiness." When they had to go to different schools they were heartbroken by the shock of separation, but Nasief continued to be his best friend.

These separations were not of his own choosing, and like most children leaving the home for play and school, he found that the first steps on the road toward independence were difficult. But as the little person learns to take these steps successfully and to manage his separations without dire consequences, he is rewarded by new adventures and growing confidence in himself. At the age of thirteen when his cousin Nargis came to live with them, Talat tasted the forbidden fruit of romantic love, contrary to the customs of his people. In affirming their own desires these young people were taking further steps toward independence. Yet they were bound in the "heavy chains of tradition," and were unable to declare their love openly but felt they had to keep their love a deep secret in their hearts. As much as they longed to marry, they could not seem to break these chains of tradition, or to speak out to their families to assert their wishes or claim for themselves what they most desired. Nargis was taken away by her mother and persuaded to marry another man, a blow from which Talat did not recover to enter into a marriage of his own.

Again he asserted his freedom, and this time openly, to choose the vocation of medicine. But three years later his father died, and he had to leave medical school to return home and take his father's place in supporting his mother with two younger brothers and two sisters. It was many years later when he was finally able to gain that freedom from his beloved family to go abroad for vocational study. In the meantime he worked hard and achieved well in government service, in athletic contests, and in literary pursuits. But he had to forego his two deepest desires, to marry Nargis and to become a doctor of medicine, by reason of the unbreakable loyalty to his family.

We can see in this struggle for freedom an acute religious dilemma. The religious family which he loved so much had given him the values he cherished most. From them he had learned the joy of faithful love and the beauty of religious devotion. Their religious values had become his own and they had enriched his life beyond measure. He was indebted to them for the incomparable treasures of a well-ordered life of peace and harmony, ideal aspiration and honest fulfillment, knowledge of God as a loving Father who cares for his children, the mutual response of gratitude and appreciation, the awakening challenge of worship in the symbolism of the Coptic Church, the solace of meditation, and the exalted communion of prayer. He owed to them the very texture of his spiritual life, the sense of eternal destiny and personal worth, the growing responsibility to love and serve his fellow men beyond the walls of home. He may well have felt with Lincoln, "All that I am or hope to be, I owe to my angel mother" —and to the family which had nourished these values so meaningful for growing life. And yet he was chained by this very family and bound to deny himself the freedom to fulfill desires of his own.

What is his religious duty here? Is it more religious to remain obedient to the wishes of his family, or to break the bonds and become a free person in his own right? The religious tradition which nourished him would counsel obedience to parents and the authorities of the church in holy submission. And yet in his love for Nargis he found a new religious ecstasy of romantic love contrary to the authoritarian tradition, by which two adolescent individuals could affirm, though secretly, forbidden values of their own choosing. "We were Adam and Eve in the paradise of life," facing exactly the same dilemma as that first pair of lovers in the Garden of Eden, wondering whether to obey or to enjoy the fruit of their own choice. They cherished in secret a freedom to choose their own heaven on earth. They were both religious and their love was a new and exciting religious discovery. But there were "no doubt or revolts in our religion," and eventually the tradition won out.

But the dilemma persists. Is obedience to authoritarian tradition more religious than to affirm one's own discovery of personal value? We have faced this question before in Chapter VI, to see that the struggle is not merely one of the lonely person standing against the external authorities of his world. It is actually a running combat of two tendencies within the person himself, whether to be dependent or independent. We have considered the heroic independence sought by a psychologist and the creative dependence of a religious seeker as each has stated his case. Are we then to choose one and renounce the other?

The crucial choice is not to affirm or deny oneself altogether, but how to affirm and how to deny. For any life, whether psychologically or religiously oriented, to have a coherent meaning will require both affirmation and denial. To say Yes or No impulsively or indiscriminately will result in chaos rather than order and meaning. To make any sense at all out of living we have to live according to some reasonable plan. Then we will affirm and deny on purpose according to principle rather than whim or impulse. This is not to deny every impulse, but to affirm such impulses as contribute to the larger meaning for which we live. Self-denial is not an end in itself, but a means to some value the self can affirm.

How to be independent and *how* to be dependent is what in truth we want to know. For every person will be seeking some integration of both tendencies. To ask if it is more religious to be dependent than independent is a null question that has no answer. To sharpen the issue and find intelligible meaning, we must turn from hasty generalizations to concrete situations. Then we shall have to forego the easy deception of simple answers and undertake the discipline of more refined analysis of particulars. The essential condition of organic life is interdependence. Every life is separate in its individuality and yet related as an organism within and beyond oneself.

David Riesman[5] and his research associates have made a provocative study of the changing American character. In reviewing the history of Western society he finds the people of the Middle Ages directed by tradition. American pioneers broke with traditions that dominated Europeans and guided their lives by inner direction. Contemporary Americans in middle-class urban society appear to be other-directed.

[5] In *The Lonely Crowd*.

With mass media of communication, they are tuned to the suggestions that come from others and govern their style of life accordingly. Driven by urgent need for approval, they make every effort to be sensitive to what others say or think, and to conform to the signals received from public opinion. Popularity is the goal of the other-directed man, who responds like a radar to stimuli from without rather than to his own experience within. He looks to the "good guys" and best people to guide him in all he does and seeks to become.

In this manner of speaking we might note that Talat was tradition-directed, for the chains of his religious and social traditions were too heavy to break, and he bore them with noble patience and gratitude to achieve a creative life within the limitations they set for him. Dorothy might appear as an inner-directed person who found in solitude and prayer a personal center of direction contrary to the views of her family in the question of eating meat, of her teacher in the decision not to publish the play she had written, and of her minister and peers as to the purpose of a youth group in the church. Jeanne may be viewed as other-directed in her response to Jerry and other religious persons who so enriched her life.

At this point we are aware of two observations. First, religious people do not classify as one type, but if one appears tradition-directed, another may be inner-directed, while yet another may be other-directed. It would not be true to claim that religious persons are all of one kind, e.g., ruled by authoritarian tradition, in contrast to a modern atheist who is inner-directed, or a social scientist who may be other-directed by a popular wave of secular cynicism. Such hasty generalizations confuse instead of clarifying why people are religious or irreligious.

A second observation is that no person is all of one type. We are sensitive to the traditions of our elders and at the same time we are open to the opinions of our peers, and guided by our inner experience. The inner person works over the data offered by the traditions of the past and the opinions of the present, never entirely free of them. Yet in choosing a future goal or setting a course of action from here, every person somehow decides within himself. Talat eventually departed to study abroad and pursue interests of his own choosing as an independent religious person. Dorothy turned away from the liberal church of her family and schoolmates, yet she chose to identify herself

156

with another religious tradition in faithful conformity to its teachings. Jeanne knew what she wanted and made up her own mind.

What then does it mean to struggle for freedom? To some it is a revolt against the established traditions whatever they may be. But freedom is not to be confused with rebellion against this or that. "Free love" may miss both love and freedom. It is a revolt against monogamous marriage, and like every negative protest it takes value by what it fights against rather than by its own positive achievement. Rebellion is an exciting struggle engaging one's energies violently and gaining a sense of victory in shouting down the enemy. But it is a reaction that gains its vitality and direction from its enemies, and remains a poor substitute for working out a system of values to affirm as one's own.

To others, freedom is seen as a kind of whimsical chaos in which everyone is to do whatever he wishes and nothing more. But freedom will not survive anarchy, which only invites the strong to rise up and take control of the weak. In such a state only the dictators are free to do as they please, and not for long; for the oppressed eventually rise up to overthrow the oppressor in a round of unstable contests for power. Out of such confusion men sell their freedom cheap, for it is false and not what it is claimed to be by its defenders.

Freedom, as Rollo May shows, is openness and readiness to grow. It means being flexible and willing to change for the sake of greater values. "To identify freedom with a given system is to deny freedom —it crystallizes freedom and turns it into dogma." [6] And yet freedom requires a structure to uphold life securely enough to realize values which have strength only as they cohere in a system of faithful meaning.

Freedom is man's capacity to take a hand in his own development. It is our capacity to mold ourselves. Freedom is the other side of consciousness of self: if we were not able to be aware of ourselves, we would be pushed along by instinct or the automatic march of history, like bees or mastodons. . . .

Consciousness of self gives us the power to stand outside the rigid chain of stimulus and response, to pause, and by this pause to throw some weight on either side, to cast some decision about what the response will be. . . . The less self-awareness a person has, the more he is unfree. That is to say, the more he is controlled by inhibitions, repressions, childhood condition-

[6] *Man's Search for Himself*, p. 159. Used by permission of W. W. Norton & Co., Inc.

ings which he has consciously "forgotten" but which still drive him unconsciously, the more he is pushed by forces over which he has no control.[7]

A person gains freedom, not by rebellion or planless *laissez faire*, but by "choosing one's self," as Kierkegaard would say.[8] The affirming of oneself means to accept responsibility to make the most of his potentialities in continuing development. To affirm oneself as created and loved by God is to gain a larger sense of freedom and responsibility to become one's best, even at the cost of struggle. To follow a religious vocation means to give one's best in the service of persons who are also potentially capable of growth in value. This power to shape our own development is what Nietzsche intends in defining freedom as the capacity "to become what we truly are." [9]

The prophets and founders of religions have exercised freedom in this way to open the potentialities of growth in personality. Jesus grew up in a family situation not very different from that of Talat's, in which each was dependent upon the other in affectionate regard for the values they shared religiously. When Joseph died, Jesus took his place as the elder son at the carpenter's bench to carry on the work and support of his family. But the time came when he laid down the tools in the carpenter's shop and strode forth from his home to enter upon a new vocation. This was not a hasty step or a sudden decision, for at the age of twelve when his parents returned to find him in the temple, he had said, "I must be about my Father's business" (Luke 2:49 K.J.V.). In following the call of God to heal the sick and teach the poor, he sifted the religious traditions of the past, and as one having authority spoke of a way of forgiving love that was to supersede the old law of an eye for an eye and a tooth for a tooth. When his family came to press their claim upon him he turned to the people around him and said, "Whoever does the will of God is my brother, and sister, and mother" (Mark 3:35).

This openness to challenge the past even while learning from it is the spirit of freedom. Not every religious person is so free to weave together the outer and inner sources of authority. But to fixate upon a rigid pattern of belief or behavior is to arrest the process of religious growth. The struggle for freedom is not won at the first victory over

[7] *Ibid.*, pp. 160-61.

[8] Robert Bretall, ed., *A Kierkegaard Anthology* (Princeton, N.J.: Princeton University Press, 1946).

[9] W. A. Kaufmann, *Nietzsche* (Princeton, N.J.: Princeton University Press, 1950).

inertia or tradition. Freedom is cumulative and requires one step after another, but not in dull repetition, for every step gives a new view of the possibilities ahead. There is weariness, to be sure, and no little anxiety as we shall see. But the exhilaration of such growth is that every step into freedom gives one strength to take another step and become more free to grow.

3. Anxiety and Distress

The struggle for freedom is not without anxiety and distress. Every step toward freedom is won at the cost of security. Otto Rank[10] has written of the trauma of birth as a tragic experience for the baby in being expelled from the security of the womb and having to endure the shock of separation as an independent being. It is his contention that the child never recovers entirely from the shock, and as he faces one deprivation or separation after another, he longs to return to the perfect environment of the womb, where every need was constantly met with no effort on his part.

Security is a basic need of the psychic life. And yet freedom to be oneself, to initiate separations and assert active strivings, is another need quite as urgent to growing life. This gives rise to the acute dilemma we have met before and will face again and again. For the security of dependent protection pulls in opposition to the free expression of independent assertion. The emerging of a self that is conscious of goals desired and ready to act upon independent choices, is a dangerous course fraught with the hazards of being hurt or disappointed, taking the risks of disapproval from parents or peers, in a costly venture of standing alone as a separate individual. The gains of freedom are always a struggle even when encouraged by parents and teachers. For the deeper struggle is within the person himself who wants both security and freedom in ways that are incompatible.

Because our anxieties arise most often in interpersonal relations, we try to cover up our inner distress by appearing as calm or happy as possible. The effort is often made to appear gay by joking and clowning to conceal the distress one hides within. Anne confesses in her diary that she tried to drive away the emptiness she felt with jokes and pranks. When she was confined in the "Secret Annex" with two families suffering their quarrels and reproaches, the only way she

[10] *The Trauma of Birth* (New York: Harcourt, Brace & Co., Inc., 1929).

could keep up some bearing was by being impertinent. Her loneliness, faults, and shortcomings were so distressing she would cry herself to sleep at night, but appear as nonchalant as possible during the day. She deliberately talked about anything that was farthest from her thoughts. Failing to draw her father to her, she resolved he was not to be her confidant any more. "Alone I had to face the difficult task of changing myself, to stop the everlasting reproaches which reduced me to such terrible despondency."

Another way in which we manage our distress is to accent the positive and to repress the negative aspect of the situation. This device is frequently used by religious people who have high ideals to live up to, and where positive attitudes of kindness and love, patience and hope, are cultivated. Negative attitudes and ugly moods are frowned upon as much as evil deeds, for the test of a religious person is in the spirit or inner attitudes by which one meets the difficulty. In telling the story of his family life, Talat so accents the positive that one must read between the lines to detect any negative emotions, which are almost completely repressed. The virtue and beauty of his father and mother eclipse any hint of the slightest fault. The happiness of their life together as a family is like the rhapsody of an unbroken melody, with no discordant note to mar the perfect harmony. If there was ever an unkind word or mood of resistance one to another, the loyal son and brother was not free to expose it in the narrative. It would be contrary to what is expected of a religious person.

There is a clue to hostility, however, at the time when the brothers were separated and sent to different schools. The brother Nasief then began to fail in his studies, as a result of "an emotional block." When a person is compelled to accept an unwelcome situation contrary to his desire, it is natural to feel resentment. But if the resentment is denied an outlet by a code of religious behavior which does not permit the expression of anger, it is stifled and repressed. This does not, however, relieve the anger which continues to smolder within the unhappy personality. The emotional resistance may then form a block which prevents learning and results in failure at school. This has been called educational suicide because one defeats himself by failing, and at the same time works revenge upon the parents or whatever authorities have invited his resentment. Nasief may have consciously wanted to succeed at school, yet he was failing by unconscious determination to reject the unwelcome situation and punish those who demanded it of him.

Another clue to anxious distress appears in Talat's courtship of Nargis. Knowing the family would not approve this adolescent romance, the couple were anxious enough to keep it secret. The very secrecy of the courtship would accentuate anxiety the more in stealing forbidden fruit, like Adam and Eve in the Garden. There would be the constant threat of discovery, with the disapproval and reproaches of parents who loved and trusted them to obey the moral code as defined by their religious and social tradition. The tragic conflict was not easily resolved, as they were caught in the ambivalence of contradictory desires—one to assert their independence as lovers and the other to hold the dependent security of family approval. As neither desire would yield, they continued to cherish each other in secret and appear to obey their family openly. The need for approval was too strong to consummate their love in marriage, while the need for mutual love was too strong to renounce each other. So their ambivalence prevented reaching a decision; they were "two nightingales just wavering the wings of happiness," yet unable to fly to a resting place at either horn of the dilemma. After years of indecision and wavering, the matter was finally settled by the intervention of the mother, who took Nargis away and married her to another man. The depth of his continuing distress at losing this struggle for freedom to love is penned in the lines:

> Where are you now? To overflow thee
> With my tears of kindness.
> Since you left me,
> I bade farewell to happiness.

In a similar dilemma Anne chose the bold course of open confession of the secret to her father in a declaration of independence. But she, too, was caught in the ambivalence of strong interlocking desires, yielding first to one and then to the other. She felt strong enough to stand alone when she declared her independence, but the response of the father overpowered her in remorse and blunted her self-assertion. "How could I do this to good Daddy?" It was not his scolding that overcame her resolve but his love that deserved more gratitude. It was the need for his approval, for the continuing security of his love to shelter her, that turned her back into the family nest. She had tried her wings and learned to fly alone for the moment, but she could not bear to leave the nest behind forever. Was it her love for her father that held stronger than her love for Peter, or was it her need to be loved by a father in the protecting security of childhood, not yet ready to endure the risks of asserting her own desires as an independent person? At any rate she wanted both loves at once.

Freud would view this struggle for freedom in the light of Oedipus in Greek legend and drama, who was driven by a fate he could not control to overthrow his father and marry his mother. This he considered the primordial struggle of primitive society as well as the recurring drama in every family, for a child to love the parent of the opposite sex, and to struggle against the dominant authority who stood in the way. But then followed the wave of remorse at having offended the established moral order in displacing the father, and the bitter repentance urging the son to seek reconciliation by renunciation of his self-assertive independence. This he considers the motive for religious behavior.

It is likely that Freud has overdrawn the violence of the struggle and overweighted the power of the dominant authority in the heavy-handed patriarchal family of his Austria in the nineteenth century. It is likely that religion has other motivations than the distress of sin and repentance. We do not well understand religious experience or any intricate and far-reaching system of values by reducing it to a simple formula like the Oedipus complex.

And yet who can doubt that religious experience is influenced by the basic relationships of family life? In the struggle for freedom the growing person gives up, one after another, the comforts of dependent security which he once enjoyed. To accomplish this he seeks elsewhere for new relationships to replace the values given up at each stage of his development. These new relationships cannot duplicate the earlier ones, lest he regress to infantile dependence again. Each new relationship, to be successful, will have to be appropriate to the enlarging outreach of his interests and capacities. As he learns a language he will need relationships with persons who can speak that language with him; as he learns new skills he will need playmates to enter into participation with him; as he learns new ideas he will want to share them with someone who understands. When he is ready for courtship and marriage he will need a mate, not to perform the functions of a parent for a dependent child, but one who will treat him as an equal and enter into a marriage partnership of mutual giving and receiving which is conjugal love.

Religious experience is first discovered in the glimpses of empathy and communication, of reverence and devotion, to be found in the basic relationships of the family. But growing through successive stages of widening relationships, what began in the local family moves out beyond the family to life as a whole. A religious person is searching for the whole meaning of his existence, and exploring his place in ever larger relationships. If God at first appeared as a member of the local family he comes through enlarging revelations in other relationships to mean the Father of all mankind. If my brother was at first the playmate who shared the meals at one table and laughed or cried with me within the four walls of one home, he comes through the universalizing of religious brotherhood to mean anyone on this planet who is hungry, or who claims my sympathy and concern as a fellow creature who laughs and weeps as one of us.

When Talat was nineteen his father died and the burden of grief was heavy upon him. He was then a student of medicine at the university, with a religious devotion to heal the sufferings of the poor. In that tragic moment he was plunged again into the struggle between separation and relationship. Should he continue his medical studies and carry out his independent desire for a vocation of his own choosing, or return to care for his family in their sorrow and loss? He may have preferred the independent role to continue his self-chosen career. But he gave it up to return home and care for his family. This came to him as his religious duty according to the tradition of his people and desire of his mother and brothers and sisters.

Was he drawn to his family, as Freud might say, by the oedipal desire to have his mother for his own and displace the father? Or did he feel guilt that he had longed for his mother, and so feel he must do penance to the memory of his father by this sacrifice? Could this feeling of guilt be entwined in his secret love for Nargis, which had violated the code of sex repression during adolescence, and in not trusting the parents to choose the proper mate in arranging the marriage? What of his decision not to marry? Was this a protest against the family that denied him the right to marry the one he loved, or penitence for the guilt he felt in loving contrary to the code of his people?

Whatever the unconscious conflicts may have been, he returned home for the conscious reason that he believed it was his duty. He was not the eldest son and might have left to the older brother Nasief the responsibility to look after the family. But the support of a family was no simple matter, and both sons were probably needed as breadwinners for the family. Or it might be that as Nasief was nearer to the completion of his university education, he was to continue in school to be able to earn more later. But these could hardly be economic decisions alone. As a religious person, Talat was motivated by spiritual values as well, and he felt it was a responsibility upon him to help rear two younger brothers and two sisters. The family loyalty was stronger than his own egoistic desires, and he saw his religious duty to sacrifice his own interests for the larger concerns of the family. His conscience was to be reckoned with, and he could not disregard such claims upon him.

4. A Religious Conscience

In this decision we see a religious conscience at work. Whatever the unconscious conflicts at this moment in the personality of Talat he pulls himself together to make a conscious choice that is his own. He might have left the burden to others, but he took it upon himself. His teachers may have advised him otherwise, and members of his family may not have wanted him to sacrifice his medical education in midstream. But whatever the opinions of others and the contradictory impulses within, he unified himself and cast the deciding vote. It was no easy decision. "All my hopes had collapsed." And yet in spite of the distress he made a responsible decision; he resigned from the university and secured a job in government service.

This is what we mean by conscience—the power to choose what to you seems best, all things considered. There are some who insist that conscience is but an echo of some external authority, such as tradition or the opinion of one's contemporaries. To Freud the super-ego was the authority of the parents or teachers, internalized, speaking within yet for the voices from without. If one is to continue under the rule of his parents, is the adult person still a victim of childhood training? Allport would say No; the growing person moves beyond the control of his earlier motives and sets up a new autonomy from which to guide his mature behavior. And Freud may agree, for when, after 1920, he speaks of the ego-ideal, he seems to say that the ego chooses its own ideals and governs its behavior accordingly.

A religious conscience, to be sure, may operate from different levels of autonomy along the progress of a person's growth. We have recognized variations among religious people and cultures, in that some are more dependent upon external authority than others. There are evidently degrees in which a religious conscience may be tradition-directed, and the culture in which Talat lived was highly traditional. He was not immune, nor can anyone be, to the traditions which entered the texture of his life and relationships. What others expected of him represented other-directed influences. He may have considered what his mother seemed to desire more than what she said at the time. But taking all these influences into account he was inner-directed in choosing what to him seemed best.

Another person quite as religious may have chosen otherwise, and that is the individuality of conscience that no other is to decide for you. Jesus faced a similar dilemma, as noted above, when wrestling with his vocation and his loyalty to his family. Traditions were no less powerful in his Nazareth, and there were obviously social pressures upon him to return to his family. Yet he decided not to return to the family who waited for him, but rather to follow his vocation as his conscientious duty. Speaking to others he was emphatic that the dead could better bury the dead than for a dedicated person to turn back from the ongoing imperative of his vocation. And in this struggle with the restraining ties of family loyalty, he said, "A man's foes will be those of his own household" (Matt. 10:36). In his religious teachings also he was more inner-directed than many of the religious teachers, not hesitating to set aside their traditions when his own clear vision saw reason to do so. He spoke as one having authority of his own.

And yet he was always consulting God as a higher authority, saying, "Not my will, but thine, be done" (Luke 22:42). His dependence upon God he was ready at all times to acknowledge, as the source of his courageous independence from the religious and civil authorities who challenged him, or brought him to trial and death. From him his disciples also took courage to speak boldly the truth as they consciously saw it and to obey God rather than men (Acts 4:19). In this way they followed the tradition of the Hebrew prophets who spoke out for God against the evils and injustices of their time. From early life Jesus was a faithful student of the Old Testament, drawing inspiration and guidance from the religious traditions of his people. He was other-directed in open and sensitive learning from these sources as a religious person in creative interdependence.

Anyone may be deceived by a private revelation, as Sullivan points out, mistaking his own fantasy or prejudice for divine truth. A religious person is frequently subjected to the temptation of a special revelation that gains for him the advantage in certainty or favor as nearer to God than his neighbors. The psychotic who suffers delusions of false identity may be in a mental hospital, or he may be leading a terrible crusade like Hitler's to ultimate destruction. These temptations Jesus met in the wilderness early in his career. He refused to have a private miracle for his own advantage by turning stones to bread, or by casting himself recklessly from the pinnacle, expecting the Lord to save him from danger and the angels to bear him up lest he strike his foot against a stone (Matt. 4:6). He declined the false promises of a special revelation to him alone as devilish, not divine.

Likewise the religious conscience is tempted to claim a private revelation which may seem higher and holier than the views of others. Every conscience needs to be educated and disciplined by tests of self-criticism and humble consultation as rigorous as the collaboration of scientists in the laboratory. What Sullivan called consensual validation is needed by the conscientious person to check private visions with the careful observations of others. It is possible of course that the majority may be wrong, and the honest thinker ought not to be subservient to popular opinion. And yet if one differs conscientiously with others, he will be conscientious enough to be as logical as he knows how in weighing the evidence and testing his hypothesis. For the feeling of certainty is often deceptive, and the intuition that claims to be true will need to be verified in the light of contrary evidence, all things considered.

Final certainty is not given to a finite mind. We must test and retest our conclusions to know what we think we know. Talat may well have been in a quandary when he gave up a medical career to take upon himself responsibility for his family. He made the best decision he could in the light of the evidence at hand. And he may have been besieged with doubts that he had chosen the wrong course, or that he had sacrificed so much he could never be happy again. He tried therefore to take a mature view of the situation and, confronted with disappointment, to control conflicting impulses by not giving in to

166

despair. He disciplined himself to become immune against sadness, and succeeded by virtue of an unfaltering religious faith.

Grim death, disease, or failure could not daunt me. Disaster would not touch my happiness, for I have found the unconquerable, unchangeable, ever new bliss of God. To be really happy, man must find what cannot be lost at all. I have found this in God, so I am happy forever. . . . I am free and happy. The truth made me free, and the love of God, people, and nature made me happy.

The victory over anguish and distress was not easy. It took him years to know himself and to understand his abilities, to control anger, hatred, and flesh desires. He disciplined his body by regular and strenuous exercise, believing that God lives in every cell of his body. As he came to know his limitations, he "welcomed reality as a sincere friend," and consequently was able to live cheerfully. Nor did he give up his dream of helping other people through healing. When he had discharged his responsibility to his family, he secured a four-year leave from government service to study abroad to be a clinical psychologist. In this way he hopes the better to understand emotional distresses and contribute something to the health and happiness of his people in the Middle East.

To "welcome reality as a sincere friend" is the true task of a religious conscience. We are reminded here of Freud's insistence upon the reality principle in the government of one's own behavior. Through education and sublimation "the pleasure principle is replaced by the *reality principle*." [11]

The reality principle does not abandon the intention of pleasure, but postpones the satisfaction and tolerates unpleasure as a step on the long road to a satisfactory goal. The pleasure principle demands the value of the moment, regardless of all else. The reality principle considers the value of the total situation, willing to sacrifice temporary satisfaction and undergo pain for the sake of the larger good. In the economy of personality the pleasure demands of the primitive id impulses are to yield to a higher wisdom to which we are responsible.

Freud identified the superego as conscience, but to our view conscience is more creative than merely to reflect the voice of parents and external authorities. We hold conscience to be the whole self in the

---

[11] *Beyond the Pleasure Principle,* in the Standard Edition of the Complete Psychological Works (London: Hogarth Press, 1955), XVIII, 10.

act of deciding what is best, all things considered. The inner needs of life as well as the outer demands of the social situation are to be considered by the person in taking responsibility for his own choices. The moral and religious traditions will be viewed as lessons from history adding valuable perspective, yet not holding the conscientious person in servile subjection. Such a conscience is more equivalent to Freud's view of "the coherent ego," [12] the executive function to weigh the claims of inner and outer demands, and then to decide what is best to do in the light of the total situation. To reinforce this obligation of a conscientious person, Freud finally, in his last book, [13] quotes from Goethe:

> What thou hast inherited from thy fathers,
> Acquire it to make it thine.

In his chapter "The Creative Conscience," Rollo May considers how a person can acquire the inheritance from his fathers in ethical and religious traditions. The past is to help us understand ourselves, but not to quench the vitality of our own creative insight. The more profoundly I confront and experience the meaning of historical tradition, the more adequately can I know and be myself. "Conscience" comes from the Latin, meaning "to know with," suggesting the cooperative enterprise of knowing with other seekers the true and the good. Yet the inner capacity to value and affirm is after all the heart of a creative conscience.

To the extent that an adult person has achieved some freedom and identity as a self, he has a base from which to acquire the wisdom in the past traditions of his society and to make it his. But if this freedom is missing, traditions block rather than enrich. They may become an internalized set of traffic rules, but they will have little or no fructifying influence on one's inward development as a person.[14]

A religious person from this inner center of identity and freedom will act conscientiously in the view of the total situation. He will be guided by the reality principle and subordinate the pleasure or pain of the moment to the value of the whole. In his devotion to the reality principle, Freud was moving toward religious affirmation. But in cir-

[12] *Ibid.*, p. 19.
[13] *An Outline of Psychoanalysis*, tr. J. Strachey (London: Hogarth Press, 1949), p. 79.
[14] May, *op. cit.*, p. 206.

cumscribing his theory by a narrow positivism which to him was equated with science, he stopped short of the larger religious meaning of reality. He declined to enter metaphysics and instead held his inquiry to what he termed "metapsychology." But to a religious theist, the total situation is more than the local environment of human society on this planet. It extends to cosmic dimensions and affirms God as the creator and sustainer of all existence. No view of the whole is complete without reference to the ultimate Being. If the whole creation is groaning and travailing together for some end, we need to consider it. If there is "one increasing purpose" that runs through all events and over all intentions, it is important for us to seek it out.

A religious person who wants to consider all things conscientiously will follow the reality principle as far as he is able toward ultimate values, not drawing arbitrary boundaries, but continuing to seek the whole meaning. If psychology is to follow the adventures of a religious person, every significant experience will be the field of investigation. The experience of conscience and religious decision seeks reality as its basic principle and asks, "What is the will of God—the larger destiny and purpose to which I am responsible?"

CHAPTER TEN

PERSONALITY
UNDER STRESS

~~~~~~

1. Threats to Security

Of the three whose biographies are before us, only Talat had basic security during his childhood. The others suffered serious threats to security, and each one consequently had disturbing anxieties. Anxiety, as Sullivan shows, is especially disturbing to a young child because he has "no capacity for action toward the relief of anxiety." [1] Other tensions, such as the need for oxygen, water, or sugar, are specific lacks and call for specific action to satisfy the hunger. But anxiety is that tension which has no specific remedy for its relief and is therefore not manageable. The need to be rid of anxiety consequently comes to special significance. It arises in relationships to the mother and father or other persons whose approval is important to the sense of well-being. To prevent these unmanageable distresses, the little person learns to respond with "security operations" to ward off the threat of anxiety. [2]

Dorothy began security operations by identifying with her mother and retreating into illness. Later when she was asked to perform on the piano, she was immobilized by anxiety which provided a tense security against making mistakes and suffering a reprimand. Still later she stayed up late at night to master her school lessons and win the approval of her father and teachers. Another reprieve from anxiety was granted her in visiting her grandparents, where she found security and learned to play more confidently with children her own age. Nature was also a refuge for her as she walked alone or gazed upon the stars and the peaceful landscape. Farm animals responded to her in friendly ways, and she found in them a security she had missed in human relations. Avoiding the boys in high school was another

---

[1] *Op. cit.*, p. 42.
[2] *Ibid.*, p. 191.

security operation, to cope with anxieties related to sex and the fearful warnings of her mother not to trust men. Eventually she left home at the suggestion of her father and, finding it possible to make her way elsewhere, declined to return to the nest of anxieties and tensions at home.

What part does religion play in coping with anxiety? Dorothy might well feel ambivalent toward religion. To begin with, it was associated respectfully with her ancestors, and assuringly with the farm family of the grandparents who hitched up the team on Sundays and rode to the old red brick Methodist church in town. But it was also entangled with the anxieties of her parents' quarrels, their divided religious interests in attending the Congregational church one Sunday and the Methodist church the next. Her father's changing religious beliefs, which he could not keep to himself, dragged the family through an unpredictable series of sectarian affiliations. When his ideas become too liberal for the townsfolk he was asked to leave the church, and his vituperations could only arouse further anxiety in Dorothy. Her father's violent reaction in forbidding her to enter the Episcopal church would further aggravate the religious insecurity. The esoteric symbols of the Rosicrucians, discovered with her brother in the forbidden room, and the seclusion of the parents in such ceremonies would, as she confessed, have a frightening effect upon her childhood.

And yet in spite of these uncertainties she did find security in religion. As a small child she was comforted to find a picture card bearing the caption "God is love." When she awakened crying in the night she told her parents she was afraid and wanted to pray. She recalls her first prayer as, "God I want to know you; I want to know more of your love. Teach me."

When she drew a New Testament from the library, she was disturbed by reading that "the wages of sin is death" (Rom. 6:23), and was stricken with guilt feelings because of hatred for her father, causing no little mental anguish. Religion seemed to increase her problems, and during the high-school years she tried to push it into the background. Church life was quite unsatisfying, and when the pastor upbraided the young people for singing "Rock of Ages" and referred to the blood of Jesus as old-fashioned and out of date, she gave up attending church since it was not satisfying her longings or resolving the problems with which she wrestled.

When her first "boy friend" was killed over Germany it was another shock to her. Before, death had seemed a release; now it was a robber and she did not know how to make terms with life or death. She was depressed when alone and knew that the round of ceaseless activities in which she had engaged was a futile effort to escape. She thought of suicide. She wanted to protest against injustices to Jewish and Negro friends. She vented her hostility in writing a cynical play, but she was in conflict because the play had ridiculed the very ideals she was beginning to formulate. She meditated upon the words of Jesus, "If you love me, keep my commandments," but was unwilling to do anything about it. Then at seventeen she was able to reach a decision which she tells as follows:

With such a mass of confused thoughts racing through my brain, I tried that night to pray, tried to find peace within; but there was no response. I felt a physical heaviness and the night seemed darker than any night had ever seemed before. I huddled close to the ground seeking warmth, and finally out of my misery came the words, "Jesus, show me thyself; have thine own way; I will keep thy commandments; I will observe thy Sabbath." Peace came; the weight was gone from my body, and the sky was dotted with stars. I do not know how long I remained there, but when I finally arose and went back to the house my decision was made. I had experienced God; I knew he existed regardless of what the higher critics or the psychologists or the ministers said. My life was dedicated to his service and I began attending the Seventh-day Adventist Church.

Not that her problems were all solved in one night, but this first step in finding a religious faith opened the way for others. When she changed to a Seventh-day Adventist school and studied with Christian teachers, she began to find more meaning in life and a desire to give her life in Christian service. This brought a separation from her family, but she found new friends and another congenial family to reinforce the security of life. She came to accept her unhappy childhood, to feel more kindly toward her father, and to be thankful for the problems that enabled her the better to understand other people. From college she entered into marriage with a man of the same faith and found new security in his strong and gentle love. Feelings of resentment and guilt have been the most difficult to overcome, and only in relationship with a loving and forgiving God does she find peace.

2. Security in Buddhism

It is evident that this is no isolated experience. The growing mastery of anxiety which Dorothy was able to find in religion has been the experience of numerous others as well. [3] There is reason to believe that the healing grace which she found is not limited to one denomination or to one religion. The history and literature of the religions of the world bear witness to the sources of security which are to be found in religious faith to cope with threats of anxiety and emotional instability.

Yoshi Nakama was born in the spring of 1924, the first son of a family which had hundreds of years of tradition in that district of Japan as upper middle-class landowners. In Japan the family system has been the basic unit of society and holds a place of importance prior to the individual. Security rested upon the ancient feudal system, in which the first son was destined to be the heir. At the age of twenty-four the father was married to a woman of equivalent social class who gave birth to a son.

In this well-established family Yoshi might expect to have a life of undisturbed peace and affluence. But three crucial events struck heavy blows to his security not unlike the shadows which fell across the lives of Dorothy, Jeanne, and Anne. First were the acute family tensions; second, the economic depression around 1930; and third, World War II. It will be instructive to see how Yoshi met these shocks and how he found resources to withstand their devastating effect. His earliest memory is regarding a dream:

My first memory is a dream about a rock which was in my garden. It was a grey, round rock about seven feet high. In my dream this rock gradually became bigger and bigger as a huge substance which was over against me. Sometimes I was wondering in vain what it meant. I do not understand why I remember so exactly as if it happened yesterday. I was alone in a vast space and felt loneliness. But I did not ask help. I was gazing at a monster-like rock.

He does not interpret the dream, but evidently the monster rock which grew bigger and bigger was a symbol of some threat greater than his own size and strength. He does not struggle against it or run away, but he feels lonely and anxious. Does it refer to his family, or

---

[3] See the classic work of William James, *Varieties of Religious Experience* (New York: Longmans Green & Co., 1902).

the external society, or some fate over which he has no control? Whatever the symbol means, it stands over against him and grows larger, while he feels smaller and weaker. But he does not ask for help; he accepts the monstrous threat and gazes at it helplessly yet resignedly.

The next memory was my deep feeling of wonder at Mr. Kim's poor life. Mr. Kim was a nameless Korean laborer who was working for us. He was a man of honesty and sympathy who was about forty years old. I was playing with my friends near Mr. Kim's house. By accident I saw him and his wife drinking near the fireplace in the dark room. When I saw his face, facing the fire and drinking, I suddenly perceived his sorrow and loneliness which is common among men who have passed middle age. He was a nice man but he did not do anything except carry heavy cargo. This made me sad. I wondered why we can live in a beautiful house and Mr. Kim cannot live in a comfortable house.

This was a remarkable insight for a little boy to have, so moving in its poignancy that it is highlighted in his memory across the years. By a sudden glimpse into the sorrow of this older man he discovered the tragic sense of life's emptiness and despair. From the gay excitement of a game he was playing with his little friends, he was unexpectedly given a revelation of the anguish and suffering of human life. He was first warmed with sympathy and then struck with the injustice of it all. Why should Mr. Kim's life be so empty with nothing to do but carry heavy burdens for others? And why should his own house, by contrast, be so large and well filled with beautiful things? He sensed at this early age the tragic insecurity of life, and discovered what in another land had so impressed Gautama that the young prince renounced his family and the kingdom of his fathers to seek enlightenment under the Bo tree. In the sadness of the little Yoshi was mingled the sympathy and renunciation of a Buddha.

Family tensions were an early threat to his security, as reflected in his dream. The family was the most intimate and powerful stability in his life, a strong rock to lean upon and to stand before in profound respect. It was for that reason the more disturbing to find tensions within the family, and he speaks of them guardedly. The mother had inclinations toward the modern, westernized culture, while the father and grandmother upheld the classical tradition. The mother wanted Yoshi to wear modern shoes and clothes, but the grandmother opposed it, saying there were many poor people who could not even

174

wear clean clothes. The relation between his mother and grandmother, he soon learned, was not harmonious.

The father was only eight years old when his father, Yoshi's grandfather, had died; and the grandmother ruled as head of the family until the father came of age at twenty. The grandmother was a daughter of the warrior class and firmly held the reigns of power as head of the family. On this account it may have been that the father developed interests away from home and was too busy elsewhere to give attention to little Yoshi. When he was four a baby brother was born who claimed the primary interest of the mother; and the older son was turned over to the grandmother. Eventually his parents were divorced and both of them moved away, leaving Yoshi entirely in the care of the grandmother, who became the most constant influence of his life.

She was the one strong rock of security in a changing and unstable world. In taking responsibility for his education she hoped to bring him up according to her ideal, which he describes as "composed of strict Confucianist ethics, Buddhist compassion, and feudal orderliness." But his anxiety and rebellion was to affect his work at school and for three years prevent his learning. In the face of every insistence that he should do better school work, he protested against the whole situation with hidden resentment and low grades.

In spite of people's expectation that I should be a brilliant student, I was a poor naughty boy who did not like school at all. I did not like the orderly regulation of the school system. I preferred to learn from my grandmother and did not study at home at all. However I might be scolded by parents or whatever incentives they might give, I did not study. I still remember my mother, with tears in her eyes, asking me to study. My father told me if I could get one A he would take me to Tokyo on a coming vacation.

I used to live with my grandmother in a separate house. My grandmother did not force me to study. Instead of that she used to tell me the history of Japan and China. I liked to hear from her various stories of heroes and religious teachers.

For three years the struggle continued between the generations, with Yoshi and his grandmother allied against the father and mother. It was a firm and unyielding world in the rigid structure of a feudal society overpowering the young heir. But within the external shell that appeared so calm was a hidden conflict seething under a strict code of classical virtue and repression. It is not surprising that Yoshi suffered anxiety as much from his own impulses rising in anger and protest as from the external tensions and insecurities.

Then came a blow to the entire structure of society in the form of an economic depression that depleted the family resources, undermined the established order of life, and caused everyone to give up the security of the past while seeking new ways to cope with the present distresses and deprivations. We have seen how the Schmidt family suffered from the same depression as economic values collapsed on the American continent. The Strongs were also distressed by economic losses requiring frantic efforts to care for family needs. The death of Talat's father brought economic crisis to his family also, leading to the sacrifice of his plans for a career and marriage. "All within the four seas are brothers," as Mencius said, and we all suffer from the same causes. What hurts one hurts another person also, and what destroys values on one continent undermines security on other continents too.

Let Yoshi tell what these losses meant to his family in 1931:

When I came to the third year of grammar school an unexpected thing happened which greatly influenced my later life. That was my family's economic disaster. Father went out somewhere. Mother and a brother and sister went out. Maids and servants disappeared. The main house was closed. My grandmother and I moved to a small house a mile away from home. I could not understand what had happened exactly, but I felt loneliness I could not share with anybody. People's attitude toward me became different. Now I was forced by my grandmother to help her in cultivating the field after I came back from school. . . . Until that time she had had no experience in field work but we had to eat.

There were gains as well as losses, however; for other values were found to replace the economic goods. Everything was changed and every value was reconsidered. Persons ascended in importance as economic goods declined. Though the family scattered never to be reunited, the life with grandmother became more meaningful; for Yoshi was given new worth and dignity as head of the family and representative of finite man in search of eternal verities. The child was promoted from an inferior position to that of the man of the house, and he began to feel a new sense of responsibility, against whatever odds, to uphold the human venture in the midst of adversity.

176

After this change of circumstance my grandmother's attitude toward me became different. She treated me as if I were the principal of my whole family. For example, she never took up the chopsticks before I did at dinner. She served me tea before she drank. My father's duties in religious matters were transferred to me. To set candle light and food in front of the Buddha's shrine and ancestor altar in the morning before we ate became my duty. To go to the festival of Shintoism in the village as the representative of my family was my duty. My grandmother made me a small classical Japanese suit to use at the formal occasions, and though I was a nine-year-old boy, I was treated as a gentleman.

It was the turning point in the life of a growing boy to be given this new value as a person in his own right and the representative of a great family. What he had formerly revolted against he was now allied with, and he saw with new appreciation the family tradition he had found so oppressive before. The cultural and religious heritage that had been his grandmother's now became his own, and he saw himself as a representative of his father and the ancestors before him.

> What thou hast inherited from thy fathers,
> Acquire it to make it thine,

as Freud says in the words of Goethe. In this new role as the head of the house, Yoshi moves suddenly toward maturity, with a new purpose to live for and a new sense of destiny that related him to other persons past and present. Here is security to cope with his anxieties.

This sudden change of my family life made me a different boy. My school grades came up close to the highest. When my grandmother received this information from school she did not praise me. I was disappointed. She did not care about my grades. But, in secret, she informed my father in Tokyo about my grades. Soon I got a big package from my father as a reward. I was happy, though father had never returned since he left home. It was a lonely life, but it was a pure, fulfilled life with my grandmother. She was respected by everybody. I willingly helped her, because she was already more than sixty years old. She taught me to respect life whatever it might be. She was a vegetarian. The first seed of religious mind was cultivated by the grandmother. She was not a sectarian but she was a lady of religious attitude. She taught me religion as a way of life.

When he completed grammar school, Yoshi was sent to the Koyasan Buddhist High School located some two hundred miles away. Koyasan is a religious town of over a thousand years of tradition in Esoteric Shingon or Mandala Buddhism. It is situated in a deep forest on the summit of the mountains. Surrounding the central cathedral are fifty Buddhist temples among the trees. It is one of the most historic sites in Japan, with courses of education from high school through university levels. The high school which Yoshi entered was a Buddhist mission school of four hundred students—boys from all over Japan, who lived together in dormitories with their teachers in the Eaton style. Yoshi had visited his father for a month and had met the stepmother. He thought it was probably because of his father's remarriage that he was sent away to school, but later it became clear that it was his grandmother's desire for him. He tells of a proverb that lions drop their babies from a cliff three days after birth so that they will be strong enough to be the chief of the animal kingdom. This principal was applied to his education, together with a provision for a religious atmosphere.

He was lonely at first but it put him on his own responsibility. His new mother sent him food regularly twice a month, and when he returned to visit his father and grandmother on vacations they were devoted to him. He felt it was for the best and was nothing but the outcome of their deep love for him. The teachers were all Buddhist and some of them were priests. Every morning and evening there were hours of meditation and religious services. At first he accepted the religious services, but gradually doubts arose from his reading of Western literature as well as from his own sexual awakening. He became antireligious. Several times he asked to be transferred to another school, but he continued and after five years entered the Koyasan Buddhist College.

Here the students were given considerable freedom to attend classes or be absent, so long as they could pass their examinations. They were treated like adults and often visited the teachers' homes and had discussions with them. A daily religious service was held at seven o'clock in the morning and a meditation hour at nine in the evening, and attendance was required. Yoshi decided to utilize these hours to think and to master the art of Buddhist Yoga. But these days, which he was finding so satisfying, did not continue long.

World War II was becoming more intense day by day, and in 1944 Yoshi was called upon to take the entrance examination for the officer course in the Navy. As a student in the Japanese navy he had serious thoughts about life and death, for in those days it was expected that every man in this service was meant to die sooner or later. Writing of this experience, he says:

I became conscious of my life and death, wondering about their meaning. I struggled with this insoluble problem of death until the war ended August 15, 1945. I saw the bottomless loneliness of those who faced death and who pretended as if they were transcending death and birth already. I saw a naked, powerless individual in myself and others. Not a few people died during training. Forced to establish my inner strength of self in these circumstances, I recalled all religious teachings and philosophy and found they were nothing; they were borrowed and not mine.

At last the day came when I had to be serious about religion. It was the end of spring in 1945, when suddenly in the middle of the night I was wakened by a captain who ordered me to go to the general's place which was about two miles away. I dressed carefully so that my friends did not wake up. I could not expect what would happen. When I arrived at the general's place, he opened the door for me and seated me in front of him. After asking several questions, finally he said, "I trust you and order you to be a secret member of the suicide group." I could only reply, "Yes Sir." That was the military life. Walking back to my camp I could not stop tears flowing endlessly. Through tear-filled eyes I saw Mt. Hiei, a black and towering mountain under the light of the stars, standing in front of me as though it scorned me. I suddenly recalled the life of numberless monks who dedicated their lives to find enlightenment on Mt. Hiei since it was established as a monastery for the meditation of Tendai Buddhism over a thousand years ago. I saw and heard the train speed away farther and farther, leaving its transitive fire behind. I heard the symphony of frogs crying mindlessly. It made me sad and lonely. From the bottom of my heart I realized that *I am an individual* and *I am responsible to myself.* I found myself as a stupid person who learned nothing. After I came back to my half warmed bed, I decided that if I could survive I would go back to the Koyasan Buddhist University.

Yoshi did not know that he would survive, and until the end of the war every day was agony as he struggled with uncertainties, not ready to die and yet not clear as to the meaning of life. When the war did come to an end he was almost dazed; however, he did begin to feel an inner thankfulness that he could live. When he returned home he found that his grandmother had died in 1944, and he stayed three months with his father. His father agreed that he should return again to the Koyasan Buddhist University. He went back with a searching mind, but no little confusion. Society itself was in chaos after the war, and he was determined to find the meaning of life in all the flux about him.

I had no ambition to be a president of Japan any more as it was my nickname in the grammar school. As for my future occupation I was thinking of being a farmer. I wanted to go back to my home country after I finished my university education and to live with people harmoniously and peacefully as a man who has an ambition only in personal integrity. I wanted to study as much as I could in order to make my intellectual soil rich. I mainly studied Buddhism, Western philosophy, Oriental philosophy, and the art of Buddhism. As a whole I tried to enlarge my horizon. Once I was an ardent admirer of Goethe and again I was a disciple of Buddha. Once I was a follower of social reformers and at other times I was a student of the Esoteric Mandala Buddhism.

His condition was not unlike that of many Americans returning from the same world war. They were nauseated with the slaughter of war and despairing of any solution to tangled human problems by violence or military intelligence. It was evident that no one can win a war, for the losses to the innocent are greater than the punishment of the guilty. With atomic weapons there is no longer a question of victory, but of survival for the human race on a planet turned into a death trap. There must be some better way out of human conflict than this; and, in the search for a better way, returning veterans tormented by these dilemmas may well turn to religion to change human nature from within and to open the heart to brotherhood. As American youth returned to the Christian or Jewish faith where they began the search, so Yoshi turned to the religion of his family and school years for the answer he sought. Finally his mind came to rest in Buddhism.

When I finished my graduate dissertation, I became a student of the Oriental religions and found them congenial with my temperament. Hinduism, Buddhism, and Taoism became more familiar to me than the Western thought and faith. I deeply regretted that I had not earlier discovered the deep meanings of Esoteric Mandala Buddhism as I had been in the midst of its living tradition more than ten years. I finally returned to the starting point were I began my high school education, yet with a wider and higher sphere of consciousness of religious meaning. As in the old days I participated in meditation and religious service with a simple mind, and realized how foolish I had been.

When I graduated from the University of Koyasan, the faculties recommended me to stay and continue my study so that I might someday be a teacher in that institution. I did not want to be a teacher because I could not have confidence in my capacity. I asked my father for permission and his support to continue my study and I was permitted to do that. I honestly wanted to understand and to experience Buddhism as the way of life.

I entered a temple and engaged in meditation as a disciple of Mandala Buddhism. During those days I gradually convinced myself that I could find my principle of life in Buddhism. If I could not attain to the world of cosmic consciousness, at least I could grasp the direction toward that goal. I used to visit my devoted teachers to ask questions and hear from them, face to face, their interpretations and experiences. It was a most blessed and fruitful era.

To enter upon a religious vocation had become the answer to Yoshi's ardent quest for the meaning of life. After the years of anti-religious revolt and the dark hours of despair and confusion, he decided that he could no longer postpone a decision. He would not run away from his problems but face them with all his might. He saw that intellectual answers are not enough and decided to commit himself in personal devotion to a religious way of life. Out of such dedication to a religious vocation he became a disciple rather than a spectator, to discipline himself in unwearied study and devotion to the way of peace and mercy.

I am a Buddhist. I want to dedicate my life in the understanding of Buddhism and in writing about Buddhism in modern languages. Concerning my grand principle of life, I want to establish it upon Esoteric Mandala Buddhism, which is almost unknown in Western countries.

It gives me fresh pleasure to recall my past, but at the same time I cannot avoid the feeling of what a young and stupid fellow I have been. Both bitter and warm experiences and thousands of trifles may compose what I am now. But they are like the earth on which I stand every day and have various experiences but of which I am seldom conscious. Though they are deeply sunk down into my vast world of unconsciousness, their influences still remain and are directing my unique way autonomously as the forces of my karma. I would like to be sensitive to my mission as an individual and at the same time fulfill the requirement of the larger destiny which affects all men.

In what direction is the peace and mercy he seeks? And how does he find that Buddhism contributes to this goal?

181

To Yoshi, as to Buddha who lived in the sixth century B.C., there are guiding clues to mark the way for man's religious quest. First there is karma, the sense of a moral purpose in the whole of existence, which shapes a destiny that is just to all, and that if followed opens the potentiality of enlarging good. Love of nature arises from this sense of goodness all around us that is trustworthy. Yoshi said of his boyhood feeling, "Nature was not my enemy. Nature is my friend, but we have to co-operate and keep harmony with it." To live in harmony with the trustworthy Reality is religious.

A second clue is compassion for suffering life. This Yoshi felt as empathy for Mr. Kim at an early age, and later for those who had to face the anguish of death in the cruel demands of war. Such compassion we have seen in Albert Schweitzer's ethical principle of "Reverence for Life"; in going to Africa he was seeking to fulfill his responsibility to share the sufferings of others and, insofar as possible, to heal them. There can be neither peace nor mercy without compassion, which cares enough to still the struggle for victory over others and to turn from ruthless aggression to love and kindness.

A third clue to a religious way of life is devotion and renunciation. If one finds a moral purpose that touches all men, and calls forth a sincere compassion for the needs and sufferings of others, the religious seeker will renounce selfish desires for the sake of other persons. Without this devotion man falls short of the religious meaning of life, and without renunciation he cannot fulfill the requirements of peace and mercy. Yoshi has come to that point in religious growth where he does not seek to be first among others, but where he would rather devote himself to integrity and co-operation with others. In renouncing selfish ambitions, he is on the way to more basic security, for he claims less to fight over and less that can be taken away from him. By devoting himself to spiritual values that are open to all who will seek them, he enters a way of life that invites peaceful co-operation rather than rivalry and contention. Whatever peace and security he hopes to find is to be in a larger destiny with all men.

3. The Problem of Hostility

In striving for goals, persons take risks of disappointment and suffer one loss after another. Threats to security result in anxiety difficult to relieve. Another stress arises in the denial of satisfaction and freedom, which we recognize as hostility. The feeling of hostility is a very disturbing emotion, and it may lead to destructive consequences in personal harm or in large-scale devastation of war. Because of this, psychology and religion are both concerned to understand and cope with hostility. What are its symptoms and what are its causes?

Hostility is a symptom of distress ranging from mild irritation to acute anguish. It may take different forms, as rage, anger, or resentment. When placed under physical restraint an infant will manifest rage behavior, similar to the tantrum which an older child will show when confronted with a denial of his wishes. Eventually, the growing child learns that rage is not a rewarding kind of behavior, for it is likely to bring further denial or punishment. It may then be modified to anger, which is controlled hostility directed toward a goal such as hurting another personality. The child may observe anger in the parent who punishes him, inflicting pain intentionally to teach him a lesson. Another use of anger is to relieve pent-up distress, and as the child learns this from the parent he may vent his anger upon a doll or toy as he plays the role of the parent.

But when the child shows anger toward the parent he may be punished the more, until he learns that anger is a dangerous attitude to show. In the pain that he suffers as punishment for showing anger, he fears to give open expression to his hostility, and learns to conceal it in the form of resentment. This does not relieve the hostility but preserves it in latent form and carries on the battle in covert ways as sullen rebellion or unyielding resistance. As the irritations of life accumulate, a civilized person may appear civil until some stimulus triggers an outburst of anger. Or he may carry a calm exterior but hide his hostility in preoccupations and evasions which block the wishes of another person, yet avoid an open clash.

So heavy are the consequences of hostility that the human race is sorely pressed to find a solution for it. To do this it is urgent to look into the causes of hostility. A theological view has contended that man is naturally evil, beset with unruly impulses known as original sin. We have met a psychological equivalent in the id of Freud, which knows no moral law or prudent reason but demands reckless gratification regardless of the consequences. In his later years Freud accented the drive toward destruction in his theory of the death instinct which works against the will to live. We need not wonder at these views of the evil in man, for every man offers evidence to support the theory that he is struggling with recalcitrant forces within his own nature.

And yet on closer observation we find in man good impulses that are fully as strong as the evil ones. It would be a hasty misjudgment to condemn man as essentially evil and ignore the impulses that strive for the good and the true with no less ardor. To "see life steadily and see it whole," other theologians view the infant as a bundle of potentialities, subject to the influences of his environment and capable of learning both good and evil, in situations where he has come to exercise choices of his own to seek after. Among psychologists today there is also less willingness to see human nature as predetermined by heredity packed in the genes or implanted in the instincts. There is more concern for the contemporary events and the interpersonal relations that invite responses of interest and learning as the child grows in the family and larger society. Increasing attention is directed to the conditions that encourage healthy and unhealthy emotions in the growing child.

Social psychologists have offered the hypothesis that hostility results from frustration.[4] The relationship is well established but many variables appear. Lewin, Barker, and Dembo conducted experiments, noted above, showing that with young children frustration leads to regression, with loss in range and organization of behavior. With adults, on the other hand, frustration sometimes stimulates more resourceful productivity. Hostility may be present in the regression of the child who resists activity, as well as in the increased productivity of an adult who "takes it out" in more vigorous work. It is evident that frustration is naturally irritating and therefore a cue for hostility. But more specific analysis is needed to show why some personalities have more frustration tolerance than others in the crisscrossing of human motivation.

From his studies Sullivan[5] reports that he is unable to find support for the theory that man is essentially a devil, or possessed of some wonderful thing called sadism. He finds anger to be a device to avoid anxiety. He is concerned that malevolence so often appears as a major pattern of interpersonal relations in childhood, and traces it to an unsatisfied need for tenderness. When children come to a certain age parents may cease giving them the tenderness which they earlier had enjoyed. Not only are they denied tenderness, but when they ask for

---

[4] John Dollard, *et al.*, *Frustration and Aggression* (New Haven, Conn.: Yale University Press, 1939).

[5] *Op. cit.*, p. 214.

it they are often treated in a fashion to provoke anxiety or pain. As the child learns that it is disadvantageous to show any need for tender affection, he comes to feel that he is living among enemies. And on that basis he may develop a malevolent attitude that makes it almost impossible for anyone to show him tenderness or treat him kindly. He has come to expect rejective attitudes in others, and so he beats them to it and gives back what others give to him. In thus denying tenderness, parents and other authority figures set in motion a vicious circle, which goes on multiplying ugly moods and juvenile delinquency, quarrels and hostile aggressions.

If the mother is hostile to the father, she may project blame upon a son by saying that he is just like his father. Or she may say to relatives and neighbors. "He has a bad temper just like me." When a child gets that view of himself and is punished for being just like his parents, he will have difficulty in understanding why if it is all right for mother it is not for him too. Sullivan considers such malevolence as the greatest disaster that happens in childhood, for it produces a serious handicap in the later development of personality as the person learns costly ways of avoiding anxiety by indulging in anger. He is thereby deprived of useful foresight in living and suffers from distortion of his fundamental interpersonal attitudes. Expecting the worst he gives the worst in a mood that implies: "Once upon a time everything was lovely, but that was before I had to deal with people." [6]

A significant study of hostility was made in 1955 by a group of student ministers at the Boston Psychopathic Hospital, with Robert W. Hyde, assistant superintendent of the hospital, and Joseph F. Woodson, chaplain of the hospital. [7] They were registered at Boston University for a course in group therapy, conducted as clinical training eight hours per day at the hospital. At the end of the course they submitted a joint report of their investigation. Hostility is defined as "a driving emotion against another person," and the general hypothesis is that it is one of various responses aroused by a threat to oneself. A threat is "real or imagined fear of damage, harm, humiliation, or deprivation to the self at some level."

A careful analysis of the causes of hostility points to specific threats, such as:

[6] *Ibid.*, p. 216.
[7] Presented here with permission of Dr. Hyde and Chaplain Woodson. The Boston Psychopathic Hospital became in 1956 the Massachusetts Mental Health Center.

PHYSICAL THREAT

1. To person or in-group

SOCIAL THREATS

1. Real or imagined rejection (in which hostility is a demand for love)
2. Threats to one's status or role
3. Inability to understand or communicate
4. Threats to one's in-group
5. Fear of being replaced in a relationship
6. Association with another person for whom hostility is unresolved

PSYCHOLOGICAL THREATS

1. To one's self-esteem (as one's sense of worth, independence as an individual, system of values, property, or education)
2. To one's front or defenses
3. To one's ego-image or estimate of himself
4. Rejection by others of one's best impulses
5. A threat to thwart one's growth and thus prevent one from achieving the selfhood he desires

These situations were then illustrated by incidents in the group experience or in the Bible, as well as other experiences cited by members of the group. Special attention was given to religious attitudes toward hostility in the concrete situations recorded in the Bible and met by the religious persons in the group. For hostility was recognized as one of the disturbing problems in human relations, which has been of focal concern in Judeo-Christian religion.

A checklist was constructed of the ways in which this group of twelve people expressed hostility. Upon a list of twenty-three items each member observed himself, and submitted to a frequency check by other observers, and finally to a group evaluation. Not a single person believed that he expressed hostility in as many ways as the group observed him to do so. In fact, the members were found to be using all or most of the ways of expressing hostility, yet each one had his favorite modes of expression. Hostilities were expressed as follows in descending order as observed in the group: tone of voice, 79; silent treatment, 78; intellectualization, 78; recognition and rigid control, 64; bodily expression, 62; unconvinced submission, 58; becoming more authoritative, 58; self-punishment, 55; projecting, 49; manipulation, 45; expressing a feeling of superiority, 44; direction of attention, 42; acts of discourtesy and selfishness, 40; humor, 38; oversolicitousness, 37; profanity, 33; aggravation, 25; continuous and comprehensive opposition, 25; embarrassing another person, 23; discrimination, 22; scapegoating, 21; subversion, 17; physical aggression, 3.

It would be of interest to have trained observers check the same list with other groups, e.g., patients in the hospital, medical doctors, social workers, unionized factory workers, or a high-school football team. The rank order of significance would surely vary from group to group, and from culture to culture. The present ranking as previously given indicates certain tendencies in a professional group in which educational advancement and religious dedication are significant determinants in behavior. A severe restraint has been placed upon the expression of hostility in this profession and also in the culture of college graduates. Consequently we note a tendency to avoid the crude and violent expressions of hostility, such as physical aggression, which had a score of only three votes. Subversion, or talking against a person behind his back, is the next lowest on the scale, along with scapegoating (picking on a weaker person), discrimination, embarrassing another person, aggravation, and continuous and comprehensive opposition. These are all flagrant violations of the code of the religious person who is serious about his ethical conduct.

Hostility is expressed rather in subtle and covert ways that are likely to escape the notice of the person himself. He has placed his hostility under heavy taboo, and, so repressed, it escapes around the seams and hatches rather than "blowing its top" in noisy blasts. And yet it is more visible to others than to the person himself, indicating that no matter how severe the repression may be, hostility leaks out and damages human relations. Everyone is, by long practice, skilled in detecting cues of hostility and responding in kind, usually with like signals and subtle manifestations. For the manner of concealing and expressing hostility is likely to conform anxiously to the cultural permissions and prohibitions. In this group of student ministers (except for one psychiatrist and one sociologist), hostility is revealed in tone of voice and silent treatment, both of which are habitual and often unconscious modes of expression, as are also bodily expression and intellectualization. By recognition and rigid control a conscious effort is made to hold back the hostility; from this position one may move either to unconvinced submission or authoritative assertion to cope with a situation that is getting out of hand. Self-punishment and projecting are ways of handling guilt which a religious person is likely to experience. Other devices, such as a feeling of superiority, direction of attention, and humor, are further conscious efforts to hold a position under stress. Acts of discourtesy and profanity are a way of blowing off steam more openly, while oversolicitousness is a resort to the opposite to accent the positive and perhaps shame the hostile person by overflowing kindness.

In conclusion, the group recognizes that hostility is either a two-way process or a mistake on the part of one person in the relationship. If you feel hostile toward another person it is likely that he also feels hostile, as each responds to the other's cues. It is further assumed that hostility, if it is felt by a person, will be expressed in some form. The pattern of our culture which prohibits expression of hostility is, therefore, based upon a fallacy. The question is not whether to express or repress, but whether to express hostility destructively or therapeutically. A destructive means of expressing hostility tends to destroy the rapport between the persons involved, while a therapeutic expression tends to give the persons a healing sense of wholeness in a more positive relationship.

What can a religious person do about these hostilities? A first step in a creative method of expressing hostility is to recognize the hostility as felt. This may be difficult under the rigid repressions of our culture, but honest acceptance of one's feelings is essential to wholeness.

A second step in dealing with hostility is to look inward and discover the contributing causes of one's hostile feelings. We may find actions and attitudes of our own that produce hostility in others. There may also be transference of attitudes from former hostile relationships, as toward authority figures from family and childhood. To see oneself more clearly is a step toward relieving the tensions and taking a more reasonable attitude that may be somewhat freer of hostility.

A third step is to try to build a better relationship with the person or persons toward whom one feels hostile. The method advocated in the New Testament is to go directly to a person who has anything against you and work together for reconciliation (Matt. 18:15). This has the advantage of expressing one's feelings openly, and then seeking a common understanding as to the reasons for the actions under dispute. In the sharing of honest feelings and the searching for understanding, one is already clearing the way to appreciate how the other person feels and what is meaningful to him. It is possible to communicate in nonverbal ways, but the use of words will open a channel for more effective communication. To feel that one is understood and accepted is therapeutic, and gives one a basis from which to extend that good feeling to the other person. As differences are acknowledged and accepted, there is common ground upon which to stand in seeking a reconciliation. The religious person will try again and again to offer the spirit of forgiving love to resolve enmities and achieve fellowship (Matt. 18:21-35).

4. Prejudice and Distorted Relationships

Whatever affects the individual person will affect his relationships. This is true because no man stands alone but lives his life from birth to death in a context of living relationships. A "threat oriented" [8] personality is rooted in underlying insecurity which governs his characteristic behavior. If he is fearful of himself and his own impulses and abilities, he will also be insecure in reference to other people and will take the defensive attitudes to protect his status among them. His perceptions are organized to distrust other people and suspect them of slighting him or working against him. To bolster up his feeble self-esteem, he will assume that he and his in-group are superior, while others whom he classifies as belonging to the out-group are inferior. The very traits which he admires among his fellows of the in-group, he resents and scorns among those of the alien out-group. He prefers to believe the worst about them, to treat them as all alike without awareness of individual differences, and to condemn and oppose them regardless of the truth or logic of the situation.

Such behavior is known as prejudice. It arises out of the stresses and insecurities of living, and cripples the personality who is caught in his own defense system. It also poisons the well of human kindness, distorts human relations, and carries hostility to cruel and destructive ends. It is defined as follows: "Prejudice is a pattern of hostility in interpersonal relations which is directed against an entire group, or against its individual members; it fulfills a specific irrational function for its bearer." [9]

Prejudice has two factors, as Allport[10] shows: an *attitude* of favor or

---

[8] T. M. Newcomb, *Social Psychology* (New York: Dryden Press, 1950), p. 588.

[9] N. W. Ackerman and Marie Jahoda, *Anti-Semitism and Emotional Disorder* (New York: Harper & Bros., 1950), p. 4.

[10] *The Nature of Prejudice* (Cambridge, Mass.: Addison-Wesley Publishing Co., 1954), p. 13 ff.

disfavor; and an overgeneralized, erroneous *belief*. In acting out the prejudice various degrees of hostility find expression in such negative action as talking against the objects of prejudice, avoidance as in the custom of segregation, discrimination as in denying equal opportunities to another group, physical attack upon the hated group as in gang warfare, and extermination as in Hitler's program of genocide. In all of these it is evident that prejudice is a distortion of perception that misconstrues interpersonal relationships, either to protect self-esteem or to conform to the opinion of other persons whose approval one desires.

As prejudice distorts human relations it emerges out of distortions within the personality as well. Recent psychological studies have shown it to be associated with a constellation of traits by which to cope with insecurity. The prejudiced person develops in a family setting where a relationship of power rather than love prevails. Obedience is demanded; otherwise he is threatened with punishment and rejection. He tends to operate from a rigid moralistic code in which he is quick to condemn minor faults, intolerant of his mistakes, and unable to live with his own impulses. He has learned to dichotomize in sharp contrasts as, "There are only two kinds of people: the weak and the strong," with no intermediate degrees between such extremes. He has a strong need for definiteness and does not tolerate ambiguity, but he insists that everything must be categorized either-or, and all or none. In the repression of tendencies he must deny in himself, he is likely to project upon others what he does not approve, and to externalize the problems of life as things that happen to me rather than for which I am responsible. A strong need for authority is also manifest to support his own inner uncertainty, and to find in heroic figures the decisive strength he lacks in himself.

When we inquire into the effect of religion upon prejudice, the signs are not altogether encouraging. The great ethical religions have all taught their followers the evils of hostility and violence and urged, instead, attitudes of appreciation and forgiving love. The Golden Rule, which appears in these religions, accents the need for empathy to put oneself in another's place and to do unto him what you would have him do unto you. Compassion is a cardinal virtue to suffer vicariously with others and to bear one another's burdens in openhanded generosity. Universal principles are also stressed to awaken a sense of responsibility to the stranger and recognize the unity of the entire human race as one family of God. And yet, in practice, religious communions have often shown hostility and prejudice against one another, with impassioned demands to separate and assert their own convictions against other sects who differ with them, until it would appear that religion in the record of history is one of the major causes of prejudice and conflict.

In reviewing recent psychological studies of religion and prejudice, Allport admits that the role of religion is paradoxical. [11] "People who adhere to different absolutes are not likely to find themselves in agreement." Piety may, however, be a mask for prejudices which have nothing to do with religion. Religion means different things to different people, and there are two kinds of religion highlighted by these studies. First there is the institutional religion which emphasizes loyalty to an external authority, wherein group association has a strong political and judgmental classification, by which to separate the sheep from the goats or the saved from the sinners. This kind of religion will manifest prejudice. The second kind of religion, which is more inward, upholds the cause of brotherhood with compassion and devotion to a God who loves all people and seeks the reclamation of all. This religion reduces prejudice. It is not likely that any religion can be reduced to a simple formula, for it is constituted of many complex and often conflicting tendencies. Furthermore, religious experience is dynamic, and open to change for better or worse in the process of growth, whether in a religious person or a religious community.

There is a striking similarity between prejudice and paranoia. The prejudiced person suffers from a rigid, cautious, segmentary approach, resorting to black-white solutions and arriving at premature closures. Once he makes an assumption he tends to repeat it again and again, to the neglect of contrary evidence which might otherwise correct a false theory. The paranoid patient is also rigid, cautious, and segmentary in his approach to unshared prejudices. He, too, insists on black-white solutions and arrives at a premature closure which disregards contrary evidence. [12] He is likewise threat-oriented and gives major attention to mobilizing his defenses against those whom he imagines are against him. Fear and hostility mingle in the projection

[11] *Ibid.,* pp. 444-57.

[12] Norman Cameron, "Perceptual Organization and Behavior Pathology," in *Perception: An Approach to Personality,* eds. R. R. Blake and G. V. Ramsey (New York: The Ronald Press, 1951), pp. 300-306.

191

that other people return hostility to him in reciprocal enmity. By his very actions he tends to arouse defensive attitudes of rejection and counteraggression in others, and this confirms his original hypothesis. The relationship is thus distorted by "reciprocal maximation" (as Norman Cameron terms it), by which the paranoid or the prejudiced person perceives himself at the center of mounting reciprocal hostility.

On a larger scale this same process operates between nations and ethnic groups who show prejudice toward each other. Take, for example, the cold war between Russia and the United States, with their respective allies, between 1945 and 1955. Fear and hostility mingled to make each national group suspicious of the other, with each making frantic efforts to defend itself against the other side. Neither could see the good in the other nation, but each perceived every official statement or policy in the light of a threat to its own security. Contrary evidence was ruled out and nothing could shake the rigid hypothesis by one nation that the other was working for its destruction. Black-white distinctions were constantly drawn between the evils in communism or capitalism, in mutual attacks and recriminations to convince neutral peoples that the other side was the devil seeking to destroy them, while our angels were coming to save them. The paranoid trend went so far that weapons were prepared for the total destruction of whole peoples, without distinction between the innocent and the guilty. Political leaders were heard to say that our nation should unleash an atomic war upon the enemies to destroy them first, without recognizing that instead of a preventive war it would be a suicide war for all combatants and millions of noncombatants, one that would reduce civilization to ruins and leave this planet virtually uninhabitable.

To such extremes have paranoid reactions carried us in recent international relations that waves of mass hysteria have swept over whole populations as they prepared for the destruction of "enemies." And by reciprocal maximation, threats called forth counterthreats, and the race in atomic weapons called forth counterpreparations to destroy the maximum number of people in a single trigger-happy explosion. Even at home patriots began to suspect one another, until congressional committees were frantically engaged in spying upon American citizens and, often upon flimsy evidence, publishing lists of respected members of our society who were accused as "Communist sympathizers," dismissed from positions where they had faithfully served, and hounded into public disgrace in order to satisfy the need for scapegoats and to support the paranoid delusions. The distortion of human relations can become a serious matter.

Is there not something to learn from recent world history that may apply to individuals as well as to nations? The way of hostility distorts interpersonal relations and accelerates the race to destruction, by reciprocal maximation and the increase of fear and suspicion which is preoccupied with defensive preparations. The paranoid is essentially a spectator, who nurses his prejudices and fears in isolation, refusing any activity or search for mutual understanding that might correct his delusions. But the way of good sense and mutual understanding may reduce distortions as people are willing to participate in open communication and to adjust their views to the evidence of good intentions in others.

There is more to learn from religion about reducing fearful suspicions by forgiving love that forgives again and again, "seventy times seven"; and goes forth from the altar to reconcile the brother who has anything against you. There is much to learn also in returning good for evil, and in loving enemies until love heals enmity. Nothing is more urgent in our time than to explore the possibilities of reducing prejudice and turning distorted human relations into healthy, open, and mutually growing appreciation for other people. Scientists are sensing the urgency of this need and giving attention to improving human relations. Social psychologists are showing a new understanding of group dynamics and opening the way for a more sane and constructive approach to group tensions and how to resolve them. The World Council of Churches and other representative church bodies are mobilizing public opinion, initiating research toward mutual understanding, taking steps toward unification, and developing resources to free mankind from the distortions that have crippled freedom to grow.

In Part II we have tried to see what it means to be religious. We find religious growth occurring in situations where basic relationships are close enough to provide empathy and identification. Such relationships permit communication of meaning and nourish reverence to deepen religious devotion.

From these basic relations a person emerges into selfhood, conscious of his unique individuality and capable of responding to the expectations of other persons. To be religious is a person-to-person experience of mutual appreciation that enhances the value of life. The ultimate devotion of a religious person responds to a Creator of Values by seeking to become creative himself. In his struggle for freedom the religious person will undergo anxiety and distress, but if he continues to grow his inner conscience will become a central integration of religious purpose to enlarge the worth of other persons.

He will suffer threats and frustrations that disturb his peaceful aspirations, and will need to cope with hostility and fear. A mature religious perspective, however, will correct distorted prejudice by mutual trust and love in an open community.

Part III will pursue the quest for wholeness in such a community of expanding dimensions. In the next chapter we shall journey with Anton Boisen through mental illness in search of wholeness.

PART III

To Be Whole

CHAPTER ELEVEN

ANTON BOISEN

~~~~~~

To be plunged as a patient into a hospital for the insane may be a tragedy or it may be an opportunity. [1] For me it has been an opportunity. It has introduced to me a new world of absorbing interest and profound significance; it has shown me that world throughout its entire range, from the bottommost depths of the nether regions to the heights of religious experience at its best; it has made me aware of certain relationships between two important fields of human experience which thus far have been held strictly apart; and it has given me a task in which I find the meaning and purpose of my life.

Sixteen years ago such possibilities were entirely undreamed of. Thus in the year 1920 I was riding on a train in the state of North Dakota when I noticed off to the south a large group of buildings standing in sharp relief against the horizon. I inquired of my neighbor in the seat what those buildings were. He informed me that I was looking at the State Insane Asylum. I thanked him and thought no more about it. It did not occur to me that I ought to be interested in those buildings or in the problem which they represented. And yet there were certain reasons why I ought to have been interested. During my course at the Union Theological Seminary nine years before I had centered my attention upon the study of the psychology of religion with particular reference to the problem of mysticism. And at that very time I was in charge of a sociological survey of the state under the direction of the Interchurch World Movement, and as a part of my task I was investigating the situation as regards church hospitals. Probably I should have remained uninterested for some time longer, if, less than a year later, I had not found myself plunged as a patient within the confines of just such an institution.

While it is not my purpose to tell how this happened, I shall give

---

[1] This biographical account of a mental illness and recovery is from Anton T. Boisen, *The Exploration of the Inner World* (New York: Harper & Bros., 1936), Introduction, pp. 1-11. Used by permission of the publisher and Mr. Boisen.

a few facts which will make clear the point of view from which this inquiry has been approached and also the biases which will influence my findings. The disturbance came on very suddenly and it was extremely severe. I had never been in better condition physically; the difficulty was rooted wholly in a severe inner struggle arising out of a precocious sexual sensitivity, dating from my fourth year. With the onset of adolescence the struggle became quite severe. It was cleared up on Easter morning in my twenty-second year through a spontaneous religious conversion experience which followed upon a period of black despair. An impulse, seemingly from without myself, bade me not to be afraid to tell. I was thus set free and given a new start in life. Two years later came a relapse into the land of bondage and then a desperate struggle to get free again. Following a decision to give up the teaching of languages, in which I was then engaged, and to enter upon the profession of forestry, there came a love affair which swept me off my feet and sent me forth on the adventure which has resulted in this book. This love affair was on my part a desperate cry for salvation. It led to my decision to enter the Christian ministry. The woman I loved was a religious worker of the finest type. On her part it was a source of great embarrassment, but she gave me a helping hand at the critical moment and stood ready to undertake what for her was a task of mercy. But I failed to make the grade. Then followed nine years of wandering. This included several years in rural survey work, five years in the rural pastorate and two with the Y.M.C.A. overseas. On my return I had charge of a state survey for the Interchurch World Movement. All this time I was hoping to be reinstated with her. It was as though my life depended upon it. In 1920 such a reinstatement did occur. The disturbance followed shortly after, coming just at the time when the hopes of so many years seemed about to be realized.

I had had, when the Interchurch World Movement disbanded, an enticing opportunity to go on with the survey work. This I had turned down, having decided definitely to go back into the pastorate. I wanted to work out what I felt to be my religious message. The call to a church was slow in coming and I went east. While waiting I decided to write out a statement of my religious experience, such as I had been required to do when I was a candidate for ordination. I became much absorbed in the task, so much so that I lay awake at night letting the ideas take shape of themselves, as I frequently do when I am writing. This time the ideas carried me away. First of all came the thought that I must give up the hope which meant everything to me. Following this there came surging in upon me with overpowering force a terrifying idea about a coming world catastrophe. Although I had never before given serious thought to such a subject, there came flashing into my mind, as though from a source without myself, the idea that this little planet of ours, which has existed for we know not how many millions of years, was about to undergo some sort of metamorphosis. It was like a seed or an egg. In it were stored up a quantity of food materials, represented by our natural resources. But now we were like a seed in the process of germinating or an egg that had just been fertilized. We were starting to grow. Just within the short space of a hundred years we had begun to draw upon our resources to such an extent that the timber and the gas and the oil were likely soon to be exhausted. In the wake of this idea followed others. I myself was more important than I had ever dreamed of being; I was also a zero quantity. Strange and mysterious forces of evil of which before I had not had the slightest suspicion were also revealed. I was terrified beyond measure and in my terror I talked. Of course my family was frightened and I soon found myself in a psychopathic hospital. There followed three weeks of violent delirium which remain indelibly burned into my memory. There is probably no three-weeks period in all my life that I can recall more clearly. It seemed as if I were living thousands of years within that time. Then I came out of it much as one awakens out of a bad dream.

I remember distinctly one incident which helped me to find my way out. The idea which had first bowled me over was, as I have said, that of a coming world catastrophe. This same idea was dominant throughout as the premise on which my reasoning was based. I was therefore much impressed one night, as I lay awake out on the sleeping-porch, by the observation that the moon was centered in a cross of light. I took this as confirmation of my worst fears. Did not the cross stand for suffering? What else could it mean than this, that the moon —which, as so often happens in acute disturbances, I had personified —is in mourning over the coming doom? In order to be sure I called an attendant and inquired if he also saw the cross. He said that he did. I was greatly impressed and agitated. But some days later in the early watches of the morning as I lay awake looking at the moon, speculating about the terrible danger which that cross betokened, I made a discovery. Whenever I looked at the moon from a certain spot the cross did not appear. I immediately investigated and found that from that particular spot I was looking at the moon through a hole in the wire screening! With this discovery the edifice I had reared upon the basis of the original premise began to fall. And only a few days later I was well again.

Concerning the severity of the disturbance I may say that the diagnosis was "catatonic dementia praecox" and that my people were told there was no hope of recovery. In consequence, when I did recover I had difficulty in convincing them that I was well enough to leave, and my stay in the hospital was for this reason longer than it would otherwise have been. I may also say that during those three weeks I lost thirty pounds in weight, but three weeks after I had made the discovery in regard to the moon I had nearly gained it back and felt physically as fit as ever. And I was also fit mentally except for certain lurking fears which I stowed away in the back of my mind with a question mark after them.

Very naturally I became interested during the days that followed in the attempt to find out just what had happened to me. I began by observing my fellow patients. I soon learned that there was a group of them that once each week took certain treatments. It seemed that they had a disease called "general paresis." There was one young man who had something the nurse called "post-encephalitis." She explained that this also had an organic basis. Then there were several old men on the ward, some of whom had hardening of the arteries in the brain. But aside from these my fellow patients seemed well enough physically. And some I met who had been inmates of the hospital twenty-five, thirty, and even forty years, all the time apparently in good physical health. But they were on the whole a rather discouraged lot of men. I arrived at the conclusion that what had happened to me had happened also to them. Their inner world had come crashing down. They had perhaps been thinking intently on something until they had put themselves into an abnormal condition. I came also to the conclusion that the particular thing most of them had been concerned about was of the same general nature as that which caused some people to "hit the sawdust trail" at the meetings of evangelists like Billy Sunday. It came over me like a flash that if inner conflicts like that which Paul describes in the famous passage in the seventh chapter of Romans can have happy solutions, as the church has always believed, there must also be unhappy solutions which thus far the church has ignored. It came to me that what I was being faced with in the hospital were the unhappy solutions. Most of the patients whom I saw around me would then be in the hospital because of spiritual or religious difficulties.

Of course I spent much time puzzling about my own case. I tried to get a chance to talk with the doctor about it. In this I met with little success. That particular hospital took the organicist point of view. The doctors did not believe in talking with patients about their symptoms, which they assumed to be rooted in some as yet undiscovered organic difficulty. The longest time I ever got was fifteen minutes during which the very charming young doctor pointed out that one must not hold the reins too tight in dealing with the sex instinct. Nature, he said, must have its way. It was very clear that he had neither understanding nor interest in the religious aspects of my problem.

I was very happy to find that there were religious services on Sunday afternoons. But I soon discovered that the ministers from the neighboring village who conducted those services might know something about religion, but they certainly knew nothing about our problems. They did no visiting on the wards—which may not have been entirely their fault, as they probably received little encouragement to do so. All they did was to conduct a formal service on Sunday afternoons, and for lack of anything better they usually gave us the same sermons they had given their own congregations in the morning. There was one kindly old minister who gave us a series of sermons on missions—missions in China, missions in Africa, missions in Japan. Another preached on the text, "If thine eye offend thee, pluck it out." I was afraid that one or two of my fellow patients might be inclined to take that injunction literally.

For four and a half months I gave most of my attention to the attempt to understand my experience and also to convince my friends that I was as well as I had ever been. But the harder I tried the less they believed it. The result was to increase my own fears and my own sense of helplessness. There followed then another period of disturbance quite as severe as the first and ten weeks in duration instead of three. This also began suddenly and ended abruptly. On coming out of it, I changed my tactics and said nothing about release. Instead I looked around for something to do. I was struck by the number of patients in my ward who spent most of the day sitting still, looking off into the distance and thinking apparently very gloomy thoughts. I suggested some games in which it might be possible to interest them. I ventured to suggest and write out a program for a play festival on the "Glorious Fourth" which was then about three weeks in the offing. I also looked around for a regular job and suggested several things I should enjoy doing, among them wood-working and photography. It so happened that they wanted someone to do photographic work, so they gave me the job. It will be seen that the doctors were really kind and responsive and that I did find something to do that I could enjoy. And I had an opportunity to study the hospital inside and out.

The question of what to do with myself after I left the hospital was of course a knotty problem. I myself had a very definite idea of what I wanted to do. I had not been three weeks out of the psychopathic ward before I was clear on that. The new-formed purpose was expressed as follows in a letter of February 14, 1921:

This catastrophe has of course destroyed my hopes and my plans. I came back east in July with the intention of taking a pastorate. From that, I take it, I am now turned aside. My present purpose is to take as my problem the one with which I am now confronted, the service of these unfortunates with whom I am surrounded. I feel that many forms of insanity are religious rather than medical problems and that they cannot be successfully treated until they are so recognized. The problem seems to me one of great importance not only because of the large number who are now suffering from mental ailments but also because of its religious and psychological and philosophical aspects. I am very sure that if I can make to it any contribution whatsoever it will be worth the cost.

There were of course many difficulties to be overcome. The doctors did not favor it. My friends had to be convinced, and that was no easy task. Some even thought it was my duty to remain in the hospital as a patient for the rest of my life. Others assumed that something in the nature of simple manual work was all that would now be open to me. The following letter, written on August 14, 1921, will give an idea of the situation with which I was confronted at that time:

I am quite cheered by the fact that my cherished plan for the coming year meets with your approval. . . .
I had a most welcome visit the other day from my old friend P. who

has now an important church in M——. P. brought with him some good advice which he hatched out coming down on the train. He thought that some work which would keep me right down to concrete things would be the best way to regain or retain my sanity! I said to him: "Hang the sanity! You can't ever make life worth living if all you're doing is to try to keep from going insane. The object of life is to accomplish things worth while, to solve problems and to make contributions of some sort to this world in which we live. As I see it, a man ought to be willing to go through Hell if thereby he has even a chance of doing something which is really worth doing."

This reminds me of a little incident from my forestry days. One day during my sojourn in Washington in 1907, I walked into one of the rooms in the Forest Service Building and found there quite a little gathering. One of our old classmates at Yale had just returned from two years up in the north woods and was busily engaged in dishing out yarns about his experience in the wilds. One of the questions and its answer I'll never forget. "Say, Bill," asked one of the group, "have you ever been lost?" Bill straightened up, glared at him and replied with some heat: "Lost? Of course I've been. It's only the dubs who never go five miles from camp, who don't get lost sometimes." Now I do not mean to imply that those who do keep their poise and their sanity are able to do so only because they never venture off the beaten path. I only mean that for me to stick right to camp and wash dishes all the rest of my life for fear of getting lost again would take out of life all that makes it worth living for me. I am not afraid. I have always managed to find my way through; and I do think that in a very real sense I have been exploring some little-known territory which I should like now to have a chance to map out.

In the end my plan went through. My mother gave her consent, conditioned upon the approval of Dr. Elwood Worcester. With him I had a series of helpful conferences which have left me with a high opinion of his insight and wisdom. In February, 1922, I enrolled for special work in the Andover Theological Seminary and in the graduate school of Harvard University. I was fortunate enough to be included in Dr. Macfie Campbell's seminar at the Boston Psychopathic Hospital. I found much help also in some work I took with Dr. Richard C. Cabot. The following year I continued my work with these men together also with Professor William McDougall. At the end of the second year I looked around for an opening. I wanted a chaplaincy in a hospital. I soon discovered that there were no such jobs. What is more, the hospital superintendents were not enthusiastic over the idea. I even tried to get a job as attendant with the stipulation that I might have access to the case records. But that stipulation barred me out.

The year 1923-24 was therefore spent at the Boston Psychopathic Hospital. I worked during the summer in the psychological department under Dr. F. L. Wells. In the fall I transferred to the social service department under Miss Susie Lyons. Here I found just the opportunity I was looking for to study cases from all angles. From the standpoint of one who had spent three years in the making of sociological surveys, I made an interesting discovery. Before, as a mere inquirer, I had had to stop at the very points in which as a student of religion I was most interested. I did not dare in my survey work to inquire into the moral conditions or the inner experiences of the people. I would not have got anywhere if I had. But now I was beginning with precisely those problems embodied in the cases of individuals in difficulty. And because my purpose was that of helping those individuals rather than that of mere inquiry the friends were ready to talk, and I received insights into the social situation otherwise impossible. In the course of this work at the Psychopathic Hospital I became interested in certain of the missions in the Negro section in Roxbury and most of the last four months was spent in making a special study of their activities and influence.

The next year there came an opening at the Worcester State Hospital. In Dr. William A. Bryan I found a superintendent who rejoices in making it possible for men with very different points of view to work together at the same problem. He did indeed have to put up with a good bit of chaffing from his fellow superintendents for such an unheard-of innovation as that of bringing a full-time chaplain into a mental hospital. This he met with the reply that he would be perfectly willing to bring in a horse doctor if he thought there was any chance of his being able to help the patients.

In the spring of 1925 through my friend, Professor Arthur E. Holt, who has done more than anyone else to help me in getting the new start, there came an opening as research associate in the Chicago Theological Seminary. I spent the fall quarter there. My first task was an experiment in a small mining community near La Salle. I sought to approach from my point of view the problems of some ordinary group of people such as the minister has to deal with. The time was too short to accomplish much in the way of results beyond the new insights into pastoral work and its possibilities which it gave me. The following fall quarter I had my first course at the seminary and until the fall of 1930 I continued to spend three months of each year in Chicago.

In the summer of 1925 I was given the opportunity to try the experiment of bringing some theological students to the hospital. These students worked on the wards as ordinary attendants. My own experience had convinced me that there is no one upon whom the patient's welfare is more dependent than the nurse or attendant who is with him hour after hour during the day. I felt also that such work provided an unequaled opportunity to observe and understand the patient, and I was much concerned that theological students should have the opportunity to go to first-hand sources for their knowledge of human nature. I wanted them to learn to read human documents as well as books, particularly those revealing documents which are opened up at the inner day of judgment. These students were allowed to have information in regard to the cases. They were permitted to attend the medical staff meetings and for their benefit we held special conferences. There were four students the first summer. The plan was sufficiently successful to warrant another trial. Since then the number has increased rapidly and whatever success my undertaking has had at Worcester and at Elgin as well has been due to the fine work of these students and the favorable impression they have left upon the hospital community.

During the last week in November, 1920, three weeks after I had made my little discovery in regard to the moon, I had written a long letter setting forth my explanation of what had happened to me. I had at this time done no reading whatever in psychiatric literature and I did not even know that such a man as Freud existed. The conclusions were drawn entirely from my own experience and observations in the light of the work I had previously done in the psychology of religion. In the years that have followed the original hypothesis has been considerably modified and elaborated, but in its essence it remains unchanged as the working hypothesis which has determined all my subsequent work. The following paragraph from that letter may be taken as the thesis of this book:

As I look around me here and then try to analyze my own case, I see two main classes of insanity. In the one case there is some organic trouble, a defect in the brain tissue, some disorder in the nervous system, some disease of the blood. In the other there is no organic difficulty. The body is strong and the brain in good working order. The difficulty is rather in the *disorganization of the patient's world*. Something has happened which has upset the foundations upon which his ordinary reasoning is based. Death or disappointment or sense of failure may have compelled a reconstruction of the patient's world view from the bottom up, and the mind becomes dominated by the one idea which he has been trying to put in its proper place. That, I think, has been my trouble and I think it is the trouble with many others also.

In the pages that follow I propose to examine, in the light of my own experience, the experiences of other persons who have been forced off the beaten path of common sense and have traveled through the little-known wilderness of the inner life. I shall seek, so far as possible, to arrive at some comprehensive view of this inner world throughout its entire range. I shall examine not only the unhappy solutions of inner conflicts but also the happy ones. This I shall do with the ever deepening conviction that only as we study the one in the light of the other shall we be able to understand either one or to gain any insight into the laws of the spiritual life with which theology and psychiatry are equally concerned.

Any value that this study may have will lie primarily in the fact that it is a report of one who has himself explored the country which he describes, one who has passed through an experience which was at once mental disorder of the most profound and unmistakable variety and also, for himself at least, of unquestionable religious value.

CHAPTER TWELVE

PSYCHOTHERAPY
AND RELIGION

1. A New Approach

We are deeply indebted to Anton Boisen as a pioneer explorer in this frontier territory of religious experience. He has entered into the crisis of mental illness and suffered the burden of its anguish as have many others. But instead of hiding his sorrows or giving up in despair, he has wrestled like Jacob with the unknown angel until he could discover the religious meaning of it. Since his recovery he has devoted his life in tireless research and faithful service to others who suffer.

In seeking to understand the nature of mental illness, he was in a fortunate position to take an inside view of what it means to the patient. While others looked on and shook their heads or formulated remote hypotheses, he was able to know what it meant as a participant observer. Yet not content with one man's personal experience he studied with the best minds in the field and joined a research team headed by Dr. Roy Hoskins[1] to explore the meaning of such illness to 173 schizophrenic patients. This study was followed by continuing research to the present time bearing fruit in a series of publications in the psychology of religion and mental illness. He concludes that the mental patient is seeking to find his role in relation to other persons, and while he may be at times confused yet he has valid insight into a creative process at work. Like a religious conversion it may center in a desperate struggle to find what is supreme in his system of loyalties.

From this understanding is coming a new approach to mental illness. Instead of looking at the mental patient as a curious specimen of unchanging and permanent deviation from the norm of human behavior, we are seeing him as a striving and growing personality like

[1] Roy G. Hoskins, *The Biology of Schizophrenia* (New York: W. W. Norton & Co., Inc., 1946).

one of us, who has come into a temporary distress he cannot manage in the customary way. Custodial care has not proved a satisfactory goal for mental patients; [2] the costs are too high to society as well as to the patient who is not led to recovery of health. Leaders in the field of mental health are now recognizing that the only proper and feasible goal is to treat the mental patient as a potentially healthy person, and to give him every opportunity to learn from his experience how to cope more effectively with his distresses.

Every person seeks to be whole. The crisis of illness, whatever its nature may be, is a breakdown of wholeness. The goal of recovery is therefore health, to restore the ability to function as a whole personality. Organic illness may disturb the unified functioning of cells and interactive processes within the body. Mental illness may disturb the effective functioning of a person in his social relations with other persons. The recent work of psychosomatic medicine has discovered emotional factors in every form of illness. If a personality is to enjoy health, he will need to be whole emotionally and socially. For the mind and body function together as a living unity in a network of social relations, and we contribute to the health or illness of other persons by our emotional attitudes toward them.

This chapter will consider resources whereby persons may come through mental illness to health and wholeness.

The mental hospital is becoming a therapeutic community, in which each patient is treated as a citizen worthy to participate in activities for the welfare of all who share the goal of recovery. Massachusetts Mental Health Center (formerly the Boston Psychopathic Hospital) is following this approach with a record of 82 per cent of regularly committed patients recovered and returning to the community after an average stay of ninety days.[3]

In seeking to understand the causes of illness psychiatrists (accord-

[2] There are 750,000 patients in mental hospitals in this country, cared for by 2,156 doctors, 12,000 psychiatric nurses, and 84,750 psychiatric attendants as well as other professional and maintenance service. See Robert W. Hyde, *Experiencing the Patient's Day* (New York: G. P. Putnam's Sons, 1955).

[3] J. S. Bockoven, Milton Greenblatt, and Harry C. Solomon, "Treatment Results in Major Psychoses," *New England Journal of Medicine*, 244 (May, 1951); Robert W. Hyde and Harry C. Solomon, "Patient Government: A New Form of Group Therapy," *Digest of Neurology and Psychiatry*, 28 (April, 1950); Joseph F. Woodson, *The Meaning and Development of Empathy* (Ph.D. dissertation, Boston University, 1954).

ing to one of them[4]) have been dominated either by superstition or by physiological and mechanistic thinking. Various fashion trends have had their day, such as viewing mental disease as the result of witchcraft or of bacterial invasion. In the last hundred years the search has been for immediate causes of a disease or malfunction, and psychiatrists have followed the class-theoretical approach of Aristotle to classify symptoms into categories or disease entities.[5] To answer the question "Why?" the aim was to point to a class of diseases in which the symptoms might come to rest. In contrast to this is the field-theoretical approach which is concerned with how the personality functions in relation to its environment. Instead of searching for a "Factor X" which is responsible for schizophrenia, and assuming that one cause can be classified and localized, a broader view is taken of the whole situation in which many factors interchange with many others.

Freud was among the first to treat the personality as a whole process in dynamic relatedness. But he did not sufficiently explore the relationships of the individual personality to the entire social situation. He did give significance to the primary relationships in the immediate family and the traumatic effects of experiences in infancy and childhood. But it was left to Lewin, Sullivan, and others to extend the horizon to assess the social scene as a whole in its many intricate relationships. In our time psychiatrists are increasingly viewing mental illness as disturbances of interpersonal relations, and particularly of communication.

Psychopathology is defined in terms of disturbances of communication. This statement may come as a surprise, but if the reader cares to open a textbook on psychiatry and to read about the manic-depressive or the schizophrenic psychosis, for example, he is likely to find terms such as "illusions," "delusions," "hallucinations," "flight of ideas," "dissociation," "mental retardation," "elation," "withdrawal," and many others, which refer specifically to disturbances of communication; they imply either that perception is distorted or that expression—that is, transmission—is unintelligible.

Psychiatrists who devote their time to psychotherapy believe that the rehabilitation of patients suffering from psychopathology can only be car-

[4] Jurgen Ruesch and Gregory Bateson, *Communication: The Social Matrix of Psychiatry* (New York: W. W. Norton & Co., Inc., 1951), p. 74.

[5] For such a classification see Emil Kraepelin, *Clinical Psychiatry*, tr. A. R. Diefendorf (New York: The Macmillan Co., 1907).

ried out within the context of a social situation; they think that contact with human beings is a therapeutic necessity. If one attempts to analyze the events which take place in a social situation, the interaction between patient and doctor, and the efforts directed at influencing the patient by means of psychotherapy, one must arrive at the conclusion that these events fall into the realm of communication. Therefore one can state with certainty that the therapeutically effective agents contained in psychotherapy are to be found in communication.[6]

It may be true, as Ruesch says, that communication is implied in most of the psychiatric literature, but it has not generally been acknowledged as the chief consideration. Traditionally, the mental patient has been approached as an isolated individual, who is taken as a self-contained unit. He may send forth and receive signals to and from other isolated persons but they are viewed as incidental and subsidiary to the real causes contained within the individual himself. This view of self-containment is most evident in the physiological etiology, but it is also apparent in the diagnostic labels of disease classification implying a fatalistic view that this is it and always will be. Every typology is subject to the fallacy of hasty generalization by crowding many variables into a simplified and rigid type. And with this there is the illicit assumption that to label a condition is to explain it.

Even psychoanalysis, with its dynamic view of personality, has explained behavior largely as resulting from instinctual drives and unconscious mechanisms which operate for the most part in a closed psychic system within the separate personality. Interpersonal relations are in the background and may prove decisive at critical periods of early childhood, but the determinants of character are held to be urges and reactions of inner forces. The concept of "transference" is specifically relational, and does indicate a significant process going on between the patient and the therapist; but the emphasis has been upon two separate persons who stand apart and parry the sallies of the other with cunning resistance or manipulation. Neo-Freudians, however, have played an important part in developing the new approach to mental illness as a problem in communication.

In this new approach the dynamics of interpersonal relations come into central focus. The individual personality has never lived apart

[6] Ruesch and Bateson, *op. cit.*, pp. 79-80. Used by permission of W. W. Norton & Co., Inc.

from his context of social relations, and from these he has learned the goals for which he strives and the anxieties that beset his efforts to attain them. The goals of striving as well as the conditions that advance or frustrate his progress are social in nature, for persons are crucial in the life of every person. To isolate a mental patient may give him temporary respite from conflictual relationships that have aggravated his distress, but he will need to work through the anxieties which distort his interpersonal relations if he is to recover his poise or feel at home in his world. The isolation is not a cure, but a temporary phase in a reconstruction that must be worked out in relation to other persons.

The aim is to find for the mental patient a therapeutic community to replace the pathogenic relationships that have so disturbed him. If the hospital is to become such a therapeutic community, the patient must be respected as a person in his own right, who, though momentarily afflicted and confused, is potentially able to reach sound decisions and manage his own life in relation to the persons with whom he will live. He will need to have some freedom within limits to express his inner feelings in verbal communication with friendly persons, who have empathy for his predicament and some understanding of his needs at each step of recovery. The therapeutic team of the hospital will include a number of related professions such as the psychiatrist, the psychiatric nurse, the psychiatric aide, the social worker, the chaplain, the clinical psychologist, and occupational and recreational therapists. Other patients must also be counted on the therapy team, for they, too, have frequent communication with the patient and may do a good deal for his recovery. This is possible especially when the patients are given genuine respect with democratic privileges to act as citizens of a self-governing community in which open communication is invited and appreciated by the hospital authorities.

One of the principal reasons patients are in the hospital rather than at home is because they are unwilling or unable to communicate satisfactorily with their families and friends. One of the attendant's primary contributions may be that of understanding patients' communications which cannot be understood by others. He may also develop the capacity to communicate with the patient in a way the patient can understand. This may mean learning how the patient's actions and expressions replace words, and how words may be used in unique ways. The patient likewise is trying to understand the attendant's communication; but the entire burden cannot be placed on either the patient or the attendant. In every difficult situation with patients, the attendant may ask himself: "What is he (the patient) trying to tell me with his behavior?" [7]

It is evident that communication is more than speaking words just to hear oneself talk; the important thing is a sharing of meaning with another person. Confusion and misunderstanding are the natural result in using a language or any symbols not understood by the other person. What Dr. Hyde, of the Massachusetts Mental Health Center, is saying to the psychiatric attendants is that while communication is very important it may also be very difficult. To understand another person, whether a patient or a psychiatrist, one must begin by listening with careful attention and empathic imagination to see what is the meaning he is experiencing, and what he is trying to tell us. Then it is our part to try to respond in language or symbols that he can understand, so there will be a mutual exchange of meaning. Only in this way are we able to accept a person with his meanings; for without comprehending what life means to him, we have only a remote and detached view of external features which may miss the essential focus of experience that is most important to him. And to feel that one is not accepted or understood is so distressing that it causes him to distort further the relationship, which accentuates the isolation the lonely person suffers and prevents the correction of misapprehensions and delusions.

In the training of psychiatric attendants, Dr. Hyde began with didactic lectures on the basic principles of psychiatry but found that such lectures had little meaning or inspiration to the attendants or to himself. He found that he was "peddling an old vocabulary, very poorly defined from the standpoint of the actual experiences in which the attendants were immersed." But whenever digressions occurred into their actual experiences with patients, he began to learn a good deal about an aspect of psychiatry that has scant mention in the conventional textbooks. A new approach was immediately successful when group discussions were focused upon the patient's life within the hospital, and the feelings which the attendants have in working with

[7] Hyde, *Experiencing the Patient's Day*, pp. 2-3. Used by permission of G. P. Putnam's Sons. See also Alfred H. Stanton and Morris S. Schwartz, *The Mental Hospital* (New York: Basic Books, Inc., 1954) ; Maxwell S. Jones, *et al.*, *The Therapeutic Community* (New York: Basic Books, Inc., 1953) .

the patients. In thus considering "what the patients mean to us psychologically and what we mean to the patients," there was marked increase in both interest and understanding, with a consequent beneficial effect upon the recovery of the patients. Subjects for discussion arose spontaneously out of the ward situations which concerned the attendants, and how they were involved as participant observers. Instead of standing off and looking at the patients with unconcern, the attendants now became active participants in the therapy program as they sought to understand and communicate with the experiences of the patients. This procedure has also been followed with patients in the practice of group therapy at the Boston State Hospital. Small groups of five to ten patients are invited to meet regularly with a therapist, who listens to whatever they desire to say and who participates in their interaction with each other. In this way the isolation of mental illness yields to open communication with those who are interested in how one another feels and what life means to each. The progress of therapy is essentially related to the experience of the patient, and his ability to communicate his experience so as to be understood and accepted by other persons. There is also gain in exchanging meanings with persons who differ in their perceptions and valuations, for this is how we learn to modify rigid prejudices and alleviate unfounded fears and anxieties. There is further progress in the confidence that one can express himself so others will understand, and the realization that his meanings are meaningful to other persons also.

Little therapy can result from conversations in which two people such as patient and therapist talk a different language about meanings that are not shared but held apart in different frames of reference. For true understanding a person must become a participant in a social situation in which events are experienced in common. Then, as Ruesch[8] says, they can be used as a basis for further discussion of principles, and the consideration of differing viewpoints will have concrete meaning. It should be clear that every such relationship is a two-way process in which each person learns from the other when both participate in observing common events and sharing experiences. The therapist is affected by the feelings of the patient even as the patient is affected by the attitudes of the therapist. No one is secure in his

---

[8] Ruesch and Bateson, *op. cit.*, p. 84.

self-contained infallibility, and each one will need to learn from the other, if the relationship is to progress toward understanding in seeing life together. Otherwise the therapist responds erroneously to the meaning of the patient and this in turn frustrates the patient so he is more likely to distort and less likely to correct his false perceptions. But as the therapist accurately responds to the meaning of the patient he prepares the way for progressive understanding which will enable the patient to communicate with other persons; and this is the road to mental health.

The psychiatric interview, according to Sullivan,[9] is a situation of vocal communication in a two-group to elucidate characteristic patterns of living. As a group of two, the client and the expert form a relationship of mutual participation in which each listens to the other and seeks to understand what life means as he sees it. Apart from such participation the expert is of no value in the treatment or the diagnosis, for detached observation of external behavior is not sufficient to understand the inner distress. The focus is upon the client, and the profound respect in which he is approached by the helping person is essential to the recovery. He is accepted as a person of unique worth and potential growth, whose characteristic patterns of life have real significance not only for the patient but also for other persons. The role of the expert is not to seek satisfaction for himself but to devote himself faithfully to helping the client to understand himself and learn to communicate with other persons.

2. Resources for Recovery

Psychotherapy may be difficult with psychotic patients, especially in the acute stages where their fears, suspicions, and self-blame manifest obsessive and irrational attitudes. Schizophrenic patients may be withdrawn and noncommunicative, or disoriented and out of contact with reality. Radical measures may then be employed under such conditions as insulin or electric shock therapy on the one hand, or relaxation by means of medication which relieves emotional distress and permits the patient to talk more freely with the therapist. Acute disturbances, however, are like the opening of an abscess, and those of a sudden and dramatic character are more likely to recover than the indecisive form. The acuteness of the crisis is in itself a means of re-

[9] Harry S. Sullivan, *The Psychiatric Interview* (New York: W. W. Norton & Co., Inc., 1954).

covery, like a fever which mobilizes the energies of the organism to combat the danger. There is a self-corrective process in the human organism, noted by Cannon and other biologists as "homeostasis," and by psychiatrists like Adler and Jung as "compensation." [10] Within every person there are resources for mental health and growth which may be relied upon to work through difficulties as obstructions are removed. This is a basic assumption of all counseling and psychotherapy, emphasized by Rogers[11] as "self-actualization," and by Karen Horney[12] as "self-realization."

This struggle to work through difficulties and find a viable solution is what Allport calls propriate striving toward integrative goals. Where this will to live and grow is strong there is good reason to expect recovery in either mental or physical illness.[13] A more ominous condition appears in the tendency to give up the struggle and drift hopelessly in apathetic despair. Unwilling to deal with the realities of the situation, such patients yield to fantasy, daydreaming, and hallucination. If they refuse to acknowledge defeat and resort to denial by projection, delusion, and face-saving devices, their prospect of recovery is less hopeful. And yet delusional systems may be necessary for a time to protect a sensitive person from intolerable depreciation, and give him a kind of partial integration by which to maintain some poise and dignity under stress. Everyone has his defenses by which he denies his defects and keeps up a sense of value and self-respect, but those who are content to remain indefinitely within contradictions and delusions may give up the struggle for reality and health.

In the growing child we have noted how the stimulation to learn and arrive at selfhood arises in interpersonal relations. So now in the lonely crisis of mental illness such relationships are essential to recovery. In his desperate feeling of estrangement he needs to be accepted by another person who is willing to enter into his suffering with him. If someone is willing to stand by him in his distress and reach out a hand of friendly concern he may feel less estranged and begin to respond in faltering ways to a living relatedness. The isola-

[10] Walter B. Cannon, *The Way of an Investigator* (New York: W. W. Norton & Co., Inc., 1945); Alfred Adler, *Understanding Human Nature* (New York: Garden City Publishing Co., 1932); Carl G. Jung, *Psychological Types* (New York: Harcourt Brace & Co., Inc., 1923).

[11] *Op. cit.*

[12] *Neurosis and Human Growth* (New York: W. W. Norton & Co., Inc., 1950).

[13] Arnold A. Hutschnecker, *The Will to Live* (New York: Thos. Y. Crowell Co., 1951).

tion in which he suffers is self-imposed because he believes other persons have given him up, and this needs to be corrected by gestures of friendly interest from persons who bridge the chasm by keeping in contact with him.

If mental illness is a breakdown in communications, then it is essential to recovery that communication be restored on a more satisfactory basis. Interpersonal communication gives opportunity for catharsis and the unburdening of pent-up feelings to an understanding listener. Isolation and confusion are reduced when one can talk openly about these concerns with another person. Fears and anxieties are thus clarified to be less foreboding, more intelligible, and therefore manageable. As the patient feels less threatened by these dangers, he is more open in his communication and better able to establish good relationships with other persons.

The inner meaning of a functional psychosis is the sense of personal failure and loss of self-respect. In his study of 173 patients, Boisen finds three typical reactions in a psychosis. The first is *drifting* without a struggle or much show of resistance. These patients do not try to do very much about it; they withdraw into a world of fantasy, aided perhaps by drugs or alcohol. The drive for self-realization is short-circuited, and instead of striving for goals, they become listless and unable to take care of themselves, eventually reaching a point where the dream world is preferred to the real world. He found thirty-five cases of drifters.

A second reaction is *self-deception,* shown by those who refuse to admit defeat and error but concern themselves with efforts to save face. They turn to delusion by which to evade the sense of failure and to keep up appearances. They may shift responsibility to other people or situations by projection and are likely to be surly, fault-finding, and suspicious. Their efforts at concealment of the difficulty postpone the search for a solution, and instead rest in a deceptive stalemate. He found thirty-nine cases of self-deceivers. Neither of these first two reactions led to a satisfactory recovery. Only three were classed improved.

A third reaction is *panic* in the face of recognized danger which is neither accepted or evaded. These patients are acutely disturbed and may show their emotional distress in excited hyperactivity or a stupor of profound despair and hopelessness, in which interest is withdrawn from the external world. Often the sense of peril is magnified by feeling that it threatens the entire world and human destiny as a whole. Ideas of death and cosmic catastrophe predominate, as in the experience of Boisen himself. He found ninety-nine patients who had such profound disturbance, and their panic reaction was effective in producing a marked change for better or worse. Acute emotional disturbances seem to be attempts at cure by rallying the whole organism to emergency action. There is in this a reorganization of personality similar to the crisis experience in religious conversion. Even when the reactions are mixed, a panic may serve to break the delusional shell and set the victim free with better prospects for recovery. It is from this group of patients who reacted with panic that the largest number of improvements and social recoveries were recorded.[14]

Morale is essential to recover from any illness or disaster. Moral responsibility is a dynamic sense of urgency to recover values in opposition to either drifting or deception. It is because one cares for his values and is loyal to a sane way of life that he meets the danger of psychosis with panic and struggles so to find a solution. A psychosis may serve the purpose of problem solving.

The struggle for mental health is fought on the battleground of character. It is no trivial mistake that brings one to a sense of personal failure, but a deep and inclusive disharmony which radically diminishes the worth of life as a whole. The conscience represents the moral standards which are actually the core of his self-esteem. The guilt which a person feels when he believes that he has failed has therefore a social as well as a personal condemnation. In the crisis of moral failure he suffers acutely from social isolation, as much as from self-rejection that goes with it, in not measuring up to the ideal goal to which he is committed.

Some Freudians view conscience as a punitive superego which causes the disturbing conflict.[15] Their counsel would be to soften the voice of the censor and reduce the demands of the conscience. They would seek a compromise of some kind to relieve the anxiety and unleash the instinctual drive for pleasure. But Mowrer[16] has found a "conscience pleasure" needing to be fulfilled even more than "id

---

[14] *Op. cit.*, pp. 15-57.

[15] Edmund Bergler, *The Battle of the Conscience* (Washington, D.C.: Washington Institute of Medicine, 1948).

[16] O. H. Mowrer, *Learning Theory and Personality Dynamics* (New York: Ronald Press Co., 1950).

pleasure" as personality moves toward maturity. The problem of neurotic anxiety, as he sees it, is not one of overlearning but of underlearning, in which the solution is to increase the investment in conscience rather than regress to the demands of the infantile id. With this view Boisen would agree, as he sees the patient deeply concerned with his interpersonal relations and usually sensitive to the need of moral approval. He finds that the moral struggle to move toward ideal goals is essential to recovery.

He is no defender of a rigid moral code based upon the *status quo,* unwilling to acknowledge new values. A thoroughgoing honesty is needed to accommodate new experiences in a growing reorganization of personality.[17] There must be no refuge in disguise or subterfuge, but rather a definite reaching out to ever higher values and larger loyalties. A dynamic morality rather than a static defense of the *status quo* is the basis of continuing growth and self-respect. It is not the outward correctness of behavior that counts most, but a kinship of purpose with other persons in a responsible society. Of his own moral struggle Boisen says:

My conscious self was indeed down in the lower regions at the mercy of all the strange and terrifying phantasms which were to me reality. It was a terrific life and death struggle in which all accepted beliefs and values were overturned, and I did not know what to believe. I was sure of just one thing, that things were not what they seemed, sure also that my loved ones were in danger and that their welfare meant everything to me. Many of the ideas that came to me were shocking, horrifying in the extreme, but even so I can say that there was no giving way to the lower tendencies. If I am today not still behind locked doors, I find in that fact the explanation. Throughout those entire periods it was my best self that was dominant, something strong and deep and tender and intense, which was, I still believe, more than just myself.[18]

Religious concern is another resource for recovery. Acute psychotic disturbances may represent a kind of religious experience. They are attempts to deal with the crucial issues of life as one wrestles with what means most to him and his fellows on this planet. In the 173 patients studied, 74 did not show religious concern in the prepsychotic life, while 89 showed moderate concern and ten were very religious. But

---

[17] See Gordon W. Allport's chapter "Conscience and Mental Health" in *The Individual and His Religion,* pp. 75-98.

[18] *The Exploration of the Inner World,* p. 116. Used by permission of Harper & Bros.

at the onset of the illness many of the patients became intensely interested in religion, spending much time in Bible reading and prayer or attending religious services. This increase of religious interest is especially evident in those who had panic reactions, while it declined with those who had reactions of drifting and concealment. Religious concern appears wherever persons are trying to face their difficulties and deal with them in reference to the whole life situation.[19]

The conclusion from this evidence seems to be that religious seeking is not an escape from reality, but rather a serious attempt to find a reality by which to cope with threats to ultimate values and loyalties. Where it does figure in delusions it tends to interpret life in socially acceptable terms rather than the bitter antisocial attitudes of paranoid reactions. Religion in this context seeks a relationship to affirm the best in the largest sense.

The religious quest is a determined effort to counteract isolation by relating oneself to a loving community. Isolation is ultimately death, and to save life from destruction the religious attempt is to become related to God as the creator and sustainer of the life we share together. The sense of cosmic catastrophe is a projection of inner danger not as a lonely individual, but in reference to those we love and even mankind as a whole. This perception of the psychotic is no delusion for it recognizes that together we are bearing our life for better or for worse.

If the patient is preoccupied with ideas of death he may also have premonitions of new birth. Rebirth is not an accidental idea but an actual goal to get rid of impulses that are alien to the ideal self and to reconstruct life around a new center of meaning and value. Punitive tendencies may relieve a sense of guilt, and also seek to gain new control of the impulses by self-discipline. These tendencies are frequently to be found in the experience of religious mystics and may indicate a determination to put off the old man at whatever cost, to attain a new life that will better fulfill the ideal needs of personality. In these efforts the aim is to restore a right relationship based upon mutual respect and regard, whereas before there had been tragic estrangement. The religious meaning of this quest for relatedness Boisen sees as follows:

[19] See Wayne E. Oates, *Religious Factors in Mental Illness* (New York: Association Press, 1955) ; and Carroll A. Wise, *Religion in Illness and Health* (New York: Harper & Bros., 1942).

The real evil in mental disorder is not to be found in the conflict but in the sense of isolation or estrangement. It is the fear and guilt which result from the presence in one's life of that which one is afraid to tell. For this reason I do not consider it necessary to lower the conscience threshold in order to get rid of the conflict. What is needed is forgiveness and restoration to the fellowship of that social something which we call God.[20]

So closely is life related to life that whatever separates me from another person causes an alienation within myself.[21] In the effort to heal this breach, psychotherapy meets morality and religion. To accomplish the inner unification so desperately needed if a personality is to be whole, a new experience of creative relationship is required. It is the unassimilated impulse of which one is ashamed or afraid that breaks personality apart. And because one is afraid or ashamed of what other persons will think, there is social estrangement as well. With the help of another person who will accept and try to understand my unacceptable distress, I may be able to work through the barrier of fearful defenses into a new integration of personality.

Sex impulses are likely to emerge in unacceptable ways. To express them in their primitive urgency is disastrous to values we cherish in family and society, and yet to repudiate them causes a division in personality. Segmental cravings need to be integrated with whole processes in a larger perspective of ethical love. Sex desire is short-circuited when expended merely upon a convenient object of gratification. In its largest meaning sex love is seeking the infinite; it is seeking union with the idealized other. "Sex love thus seeks not just the finite love object but the infinite, and when it ceases to do so it is no longer love." [22]

Religious seeking is a social experience and its direction is outward bound to the ultimate relationship with God. There is good to be found in local relations as they enrich the meaning of life in the sharing of whatever value is mutually appreciated. Some morality and some religions are tribal in character, strictly limited to the in-group against the out-group. But these limitations are essentially divisive in personality as well as in society, and the quest of persons growing toward maturity is for larger dimensions of social experience beyond the

[20] *Op. cit.,* p. 268.

[21] See Sullivan, *Conceptions of Modern Psychiatry* (New York: W. W. Norton & Co. Inc., 1953).

[22] Boisen, *op. cit.,* p. 278.

narrow boundaries of ethnic pride and fancied superiority. Whether for the strong or the weak, the sick or well, there is no satisfactory solution short of progressive socialization that moves toward the universal. It is not enough to be free from inner conflict, if that were possible; there is the greater need for fellowship with other persons.

Such fellowship in universal dimensions is the aim of the religious quest, wherever it is to have maximum healing power for the human spirit torn amid conflict and despair. Mental health is not an individual affair, but a growing into effective relationship with those whom we count worthy of love and honor.[23] The Christian religion was founded by Jesus, who himself passed through deep distress in his concern for the whole human race, which he saw even as today in the travail of desperate conflicts. To him came a revelation of the love of God as the saving force in the chaos of this conflict. In the redemptive power of this love he invited others to join in the new society which he called he kingdom of God. To belong to that new and spiritual society of God was a treasure of such value that no one need hesitate to give up all for it, even life itself. Upon the cross he demonstrated the relationship of vine and branches, giving his life to God and his fellow men in the spirit of forgiving love.

3. The Function of Faith

Psychotherapy, which means literally "mind healing," is the concern of many professions which approach mental health from different viewpoints. Psychiatrists advance from the medical sciences, whose tireless research has brought amazing resources to the problems of health. Clinical psychologists are coming with their knowledge of human behavior and diagnostic testing and methods of research. Social workers and cultural anthropologists are bringing their knowledge of human relations and community life. The professions of nursing and occupational therapy, psychodrama, art, and music therapy, and vocational and educational counseling, are devoting their services to emotional health.

Since 1925 when Anton Boisen was appointed chaplain of the Worcester State Hospital in Massachsetts, the religious ministry to hospital patients has come to new significance. At that time hospitals were

---

[23] *Ibid.*, p. 289. In psychotherapy the relationship is of primary importance (*ibid.*, pp. 240, 245). This is also stressed by Otto Rank in *Will Therapy*, tr. J. Taft (New York: Alfred A. Knopf, Inc., 1936).

providing only a brief hour of formal worship for those who volunteered to attend once a week. Realizing how urgent are the religious concerns of mental patients and how unprepared were the clergy who came to minister to them, Boisen offered himself to pioneer a new vocation. As the first full-time chaplain of a mental hospital, he invited theological students to work and study with him as summer residents in the hospital. This led to the clinical training of theological students, a movement which he founded in collaboration with Richard C. Cabot, of Harvard University, and Austin Philip Guiles, of Andover Newton Theological School. Today some ten thousand Christian and Jewish pastors have had clinical training, learning better to understand personality and minister to the human spirit in the toils of mortal life. Theological schools now require clinical training[24] as essential preparation for the pastoral ministry, while increasing numbers of chaplains and pastoral counselors are devoting themselves to the cure of souls.

The cure of souls has a long history, and the spiritual counselor is well known in religious circles from ancient times.[25] Most of us suffer emotionally in one way or another, and we turn to counselors to find a new perspective in which to cope with life situations. In the tensions of modern life in a mobile and insecure society it is evident that anxieties are mounting and the search for peace of mind has become one of our urgent quests.[26]

Religion and psychotherapy meet in recognizing faith as essential to mental health. Whatever the orientation of the counselor or therapist, no one who understands the predicament of man in our time will deny that faith is a basic requirement for healthy living. Faith may not mean the same thing to everyone, and yet whatever you believe will make a difference in how you behave. Faith is more than belief, for it involves the whole attitude of a person toward his world, his emotional response and purpose to deal with the total situation which he confronts. As such it permeates all of life, affecting a person's concept of himself and his relationship to other persons. The quality of personal faith is a determinant second to none in human behavior.

---

[24] In co-operation with the Council for Clinical Training, 2 East 103rd Street, New York, N.Y.; and the Institute of Pastoral Care, Massachusetts General Hospital, Boston.

[25] John T. McNeill, *A History of the Cure of Souls* (New York: Harper & Bros., 1951); and Charles F. Kemp, *Physicians of the Soul* (New York: The Macmilan Co., 1947).

[26] Joshua L. Liebman (*Peace of Mind* [New York: Simon & Schuster, Inc. 1946]) has led a procession of popular writings to meet this hunger.

Faith is important for mental health because it is the antidote to anxiety. As we come to understand how anxiety pervades human experience from birth to death we become aware of the magnitude of the problem it presents. Anxiety, as we have seen, disturbs emotional security, blocks learning, distorts perceptions, and upsets interpersonal relations. To cope with anxiety a person may entrench himself behind rigid barriers and with the best of intentions deceive himself as to the real situation. Plagued by anxiety he may misconstrue the meaning of other persons' behavior or fail to communicate his own meanings effectively. In seeking to counteract the devastating effects of anxiety, psychotherapy aims to provide a relationship of trust essential to mental health.

Such faith arises in a secure and permissive interpersonal relationship wherein one may explore his anxieties more openly and develop more trusting emotional responses which can be generalized to other relationships.[27] What is needed is an "emotionally corrective experience" [28] to counteract habitually disturbing and crippling anxieties. It will need to be a learning experience, in which insight is gained through making the unconscious conscious,[29] and communication may find channels for open expression. As a person learns to communicate his true feelings and perceived values to another person, he gains confidence to accept his feelings and courage to act in view of his inmost desires when all things are considered.

To the psychologist the function and purpose of faith is to integrate character, for genuine faith should move a person toward more unified living. Psychology also recognizes that a person does not save himself but is saved within a relationship undergirded by trust. Within a trusting relationship the person becomes integrated as he affirms himself with both his capacities and limitations.[30] From this realistic appraisal he will then be better able to discover his inner aim and co-operate with others for mutual goals.

Psychotherapy may also learn lessons from religion. What are the religious dimensions of faith? Religious faith is the deepening and

[27] Edward J. Shoben, "Some Observations on Psychotherapy and the Learning Process," in *Psychotherapy: Theory and Research*, ed. O. H. Mowrer *et al.* (New York: Ronald Press Co., 1953), pp. 120-39.

[28] Franz Alexander, *et al.*, *Psychoanalytic Therapy* (New York: Ronald Press Co., 1946).

[29] Freud, *The Ego and the Id*.

[30] See Charles W. Stewart, *The Function of Faith in the Light of Psychotherapy* (Ph.D. dissertation, Boston University, 1955).

enlarging of a trustworthy relationship between persons. A religious person trusts his life to the creative relationship with God as the ultimate source of values. In the security of this relationship he may better have the courage to realize his inner aim and exercise his creative potentialities in the face of anxiety, the threat of meaninglessness, and the tragic separation of death. In this relatedness a religious person can accept the forgiveness of God and his fellow men despite the guilt and condemnation he feels in view of his failures. As he discovers that his self-affirmation is upheld by a sustaining relationship that affirms his value, he can communicate his feelings and seek more productively to fulfill his personal and community life.

In terms of religious experience, faith is a relationship of I and Thou, revealing larger possibilities of truth and deeper possibilities of love through reverent appreciation to enhance all values and meanings.

4. The Work of Love

Faith is the hallmark of religion and its importance can scarcely be overestimated. The followers of a religion are known as believers, or "the faithful." Faith is essential, as we have seen, to mental health and psychotherapy. It is the meeting ground and battleground of science and religion. And yet it is not the ultimate need or the ultimate cure. Jesus gave first place to love (Matt. 22:35-40) and Paul held that faith without love is nothing (I Cor. 13).

The fact is that faith is not self-originating or self-perpetuating. It is a derivative of love and arises in trustworthy relationships. Until a person is loved he is unable to love, for without loving relationships who can believe that life is good enough to put one's trust in it? We have reason to believe, therefore, that love is the ultimate need of human life and the ultimate cure of emotional ills. If this is true it will be the central meeting ground of psychotherapy and religion. And there are signs among the workers in these psychological and religious disciplines of converging upon love as the crucial issue.[31]

Freud was the pioneer psychotherapist to discover the significance of the affectional life to mental health. Within the primary social unit

[31] See Albert C. Outler, *Psychotherapy and the Christian Message* (New York: Harper & Bros., 1954); Izette De Forest, *The Leaven of Love* (New York: Harper & Bros., 1954); Smiley Blanton, *Love or Perish* (New York: Simon & Schuster, 1956); Erich Fromm, *The Art of Loving* (New York: Harper & Bros., 1956).

of the family, as we have seen, the infant's first love object is the mother upon whom he depends in the oral stage for nourishment and emotional support. During weaning and toilet training the little person is threatened with the loss of love which arouses sadistic impulses to hurt the one he loved. As he comes to the phallic stage he wants to possess the mother for himself and rival his father in the struggle for a favored position. This causes reprisals and guilt feelings through which he must learn to inhibit his sex aim and sublimate his primitive impulses to form a character that is socially acceptable to other persons. To Freud the struggles and neurotic patterns of later life are repetitions and devious efforts to resolve these earlier conflicts.

In psychoanalytic therapy the focus has come upon what is called the transference neurosis. As the patient enters upon a course of daily interviews he projects his emotional conflicts upon the physician as the prototype of his earlier struggles to gain a love object. From the acute distress of his hunger for love which was unfulfilled asccording to his desires in childhood, he has ambivalent feelings where love mingles with hostility toward the person who does not gratify his demand. As he has been hurt by these frustrations he tends either to hurt another or to defend himself against more hurt by a repertoire of ego-defenses such as repression, rationalization and deception, or substitution and displacement of these feelings upon another person who stands for the parent. This is what happens in transference, as the patient transfers his ambivalent feelings upon the therapist and shows hostility or love toward him that is inappropriate to the real situation. The value of this step in the process of therapy is that it brings the distortions of the past into the arena of the present and demonstrates the deceptions and defenses that are preventing healthy relationships with contemporaries. The task of psychoanalysis is to work through distortions of the transference by careful interpretation in a supportive relationship, until the patient can gain the insight to free himself from the distorted perceptions that afflict him and come into a mature capacity to love in productive ways.[32]

Another psychiatrist who gives attention to the origins of love and hate is Ian Suttie, and he takes issue with Freud in his theory of motivation. His research leads him to reject Freud's view of love as essentially sexual and to find it social in nature. In the basic relationship

---

[32] Freud, *Collected Papers*, tr. J. Riviere (London: Hogarth Press, 1924), II, 312-22. The paper entitled "The Dynamics of the Transference" first appeared in the German in 1912.

of the infant with the mother the need for companionship is essential to his self-preservation. This need for companionship is independent of genital appetite and takes the place of the Freudian libido. Social longing is rooted in the biological need for nurture but in human life it is more than a physiological necessity; it is pleasure in responsive companionship to overcome the loneliness of isolation. The love of the mother is primal for it is the first emotional relationship, a love-bond which has from the beginning the quality of tenderness. It is not sexual desire degenitalized or "goal inhibited," but a desire for response and sympathy.

Freud conceives all motive (a) as a "letting off steam," an evacuation or detensioning, and (b) as a quest for sensory gratification. Anxiety, he consequently thought, arose when an *outlet* was denied and tension consequently rose. . . . Against this I regard expression not as an outpouring for its own sake, but as *an overture demanding response from others*. It is the absence of this response, I think, that is the source of all anxiety and rage whose expression is thus *wholly purposive*. Even the sexual act aims to elicit response; and surely the aims and satisfactions of maternity transcend the evacuation of the mammary glands! [33]

While Freud viewed the individual as a separate entity who learns to love first by loving himself (narcissism), Suttie would hold that the infant is first aware of his relationship to a responsive person and is motivated to participate in social responsiveness. While Freud explained hatred as the product of a destructive or death instinct, Suttie finds it to be a protest arising from the denial of love and an effort to gain love by claiming a better response from the other person. In this way the child tries to attract attention and induce the mother to accomplish his wish for responses of tenderness. In our culture a taboo on tenderness has arisen from these disappointments, manifest in repression of feelings by separation of parent from child and competitor against his rival. Mental illness is a failure or distortion of social development, following a vicious circle in which every hostility or social lapse invites antipathy from society, which in turn disturbs the person further.

Psychotherapy aims to correct this social distortion by providing a relationship in which social love can be rediscovered. Common to

[33] Ian D. Suttie, *The Origins of Love and Hate* (New York: Julian Press, Inc., 1952), p. 35. Used by permission.

PSYCHOTHERAPY AND RELIGION

all psychotherapeutic processes is the quest for a basis of companionship that will overcome fear and anger with trustworthy love. Suttie finds Freudian practice better than Freudian theory. In psychoanalytic therapy the patient's need for love is met by such means as unfailing interest and inexhaustible patience. Tolerance for the distresses and distortions of the patient leads to understanding and co-operation in dealing with his grievances and facilitating his progress. Looking together at the meaning of the patient's difficulties develops a mutual appreciation for what life means to the other person, and a sustaining relationship in which there is security to take steps of needed growth. As Ferenczi says, "The physician's love heals the patient." In these ways a fellowship of suffering is created where the isolation is overcome and the loneliness yields to a sense of being understood and accepted. Recovery is therefore a social reconciliation.

From other viewpoints in psychotherapy there is also a converging upon "the full experiencing of an affectional relationship." [34] As Carl Rogers presents it from the approach of client-centered therapy, this is a learning to accept fully and without fear the positive feelings of another person. In our defensive moods we may find it easier to accept the hostility of another, for we are schooled to expect it and prepared to meet it. Lest we should be hurt by expecting love and meeting disappointment, we are not open to accept it, for it seems to involve a risk we might better not undertake. This comes out in a series of interviews with Mrs. C., who in the thirtieth interview had this to say:

C.: Well, I made a very remarkable discovery. I know it's—[laughs] I found out that you actually *care* how this thing goes. [Both laugh.] It gives me the feeling, it's sort of well—"Maybe I'll let you get in the act" sort of thing. . . . I mean—but it suddenly dawned on me that in the—client-counselor kind of thing, you *actually care* what happens. . . . And it was a revelation, a—not that. That doesn't describe it. It was a—well, the closest I can come to it is a kind of relaxation, a—not a letting down, but a—[pause] more of a straightening out without tension if that means anything. I don't know.

T.: Sounds as though it isn't as though this was a new idea, but it was a new *experience* of really *feeling* that I did care and if I get the rest of that, sort of a willingness on your part to let me care.

C.: Yes.

[34] Carl R. Rogers, "Some Directions and End Points in Therapy," in *Psychotherapy: Theory and Research,* edited by O. Hobart Mowrer. Copyright 1953 The Ronald Press Company. Used by permission.

Rogers comments that this letting the counselor into her life with his warm interest was a turning point in therapy. In the following interview she mentioned this as being the outstanding experience. This is not transference, which is understood to be one-way and inappropriate, for this was a mutual and appropriate interest in the meaning of the life they were considering together. And from this common interest in exploring the meaning of this life, they came to appreciate each other in a new perspective.

As therapy goes on, the therapist's feeling of acceptance and respect for the client tends to change to something approaching awe as he sees the valiant and deep struggle of the person to be himself. There is, I think, within the therapist, a profound experience of the underlying commonality —should we say brotherhood—of man. As a result he feels toward the client a warm, positive, affectional reaction. This poses a problem for the client, who often, as in this case, finds it difficult to accept the positive feeling of another. Yet, once accepted, the inevitable reaction on the part of the client is to relax, to let the warmth of liking by another person reduce the tension and fear involved in facing life.[35]

Mrs. C. then meditates on the phrase "love of humanity," saying that she does not love humanity but that she does *care* terribly what happens to her fellow men. She is not ready to give herself on the auction block with the finality she identifies with love, but she does care in a given situation what they suffer and is willing to enter into their feelings with them. What she is trying to say is that the counseling relationship may have this simple outgoing human feeling of one person for another which is more basic than sexual or parental feeling. It is caring enough about the person that you do not want to turn him to your own advantage or interfere with his development, but stand by him in his effort to claim his own destiny in life. Mrs. C. continues:

C.: I have a feeling . . . that you have to do it pretty much yourself, but that somehow you ought to be able to do that with other people. [She mentions that there have been "countless" times when she might have accepted personal warmth and kindliness from others.] I get the feeling that I just was afraid I would be devastated. [She returns to talking about the counseling itself and her feeling toward it.] I mean there's been this tearing through the thing myself. Almost to—I mean, I felt it—I mean I

[35] *Ibid.,* p. 50.

tried to verbalize it on occasion—a kind of—at times almost not wanting you to restate, not wanting you to reflect, the thing is *mine*. . . . I've got to cut it down myself. See? . . . I'm still in the thing alone, but I'm *not* . . .

. . . .

T.: In all of this, there is a feeling, it's still—every aspect of my experience is mine and that's kind of inevitable and necessary and so on. And yet that isn't the whole picture either. Somehow it can be shared or another's interest can come in and in some ways it is new.

Here we see a groping for socialization in which she discovers that it is not devastating to accept the positive feeling of another, that it need not come to hurt, but may actually feel good to have another person with you in the struggle to cope with the difficulties of life and find a way through them to clearer and truer caring. Such learning, as Rogers shows, is more than verbal; it is totally organismic or existential in the deeper sense of emotional understanding and interpersonal appreciation. As this learning occurs in a creative relationship, a person is better able to experience the whole self with his yet unrealized potentialities, and to like himself with a new sense of his worth as he finds that the core of his personality is positive in spite of his mistakes and disappointments. By working through these growing experiences he finds himself in relation to other persons who with him may be able to enhance the values of living.

How does the therapy of love occur in religious experience? To Christian experience the healing therapy or saving grace so urgently needed in human life is a new kind of relationship. As portrayed in the New Testament the tragic evil of life is to be lost, that is, separated and estranged. In the parables of the lost sheep and the prodigal son, as well as in the Sermon on the Mount and the teachings of the Gospels and Epistles, the aim is to reconcile the lost in a new relatedness of forgiving love. The one who is lost by his own waywardness and estranged by his own enmities is to be saved by an outgoing love that forgives and seeks to save him in spite of his offenses. What the law could not do in its stern insistence upon unswerving obedience and self-righteousness, can be wrought only by a love that overflows all rigid boundaries of strict justice and takes the offender back into a creative relationship of accepting and renewing grace.

There are two kinds of love which theologians, returning to the Greek, denote as *eros* and *agape*. Eros love is a self-seeking to enhance the status or gratify the desires of oneself. Agape love is a self-giving to enhance the worth and fulfill the needs of another person. Sherrill [36] points out that the first love one experiences as an infant is eros love, seeking nourishment and affiliation with the mother to satisfy his own needs. To keep himself alive he must seek to satisfy his own needs, and this striving is to him good. But as he meets disappointment he responds to thwarting with hostility. Suffering the thwarting and the punitive responses to his own hostility, he becomes anxious and feels guilty in disturbing ways. The growing person is trapped in a prison of hostility, which induces anxiety and guilt in himself, and at the same time invites hostility from the persons who mean the most to him as givers of love.

Into this prison of hostility and guilt we are led by eros love, and the more eagerly we seek to gain love by self-seeking the more we are caught in a vicious circle of malignant relationships. Eros love only intensifies the contest; it does not provide the way of deliverance from our distress. Another kind of love is needed, agape love that seeks to enhance the worth of the other person in spite of his anxiety and hostility, without seeking reward but only to give love in the overflow of generous and forgiving affection. Wherever therapy is affective this kind of agape love is present, to enhance the worth and growth of the other person. This is the healing power of love that desires to enhance the other one, and such agape love is able to dispose of the guilt and hostility which arose in a malignant relationship by a new and therapeutic relationship.

The drama of human life has ultimate significance to religious experience in relation to God the creator of life. In our self-seeking demands we are disappointed that God does not give us whatever we desire, and reactions of hostility and guilt are then felt toward God. Impulses to rebel against God set up feelings of enmity and reprisal in which a person may seek to escape or deny God to avoid the penalty of divine judgment. Jesus reveals the character of God as agape love, a heavenly Father who forgives the sinner and seeks to restore him to a new relationship of faithful love.

Basic anxiety is the threat of nonbeing, the experience of our lost condition when estranged from ultimate Being.[37] Every other separa-

[36] Lewis J. Sherrill, *Guilt and Redemption* (Richmond: John Knox Press, 1956). See also Anders Nygren, *Agape and Eros*, 2 vols. (New York: The Macmillan Co., 1932-39).

[37] Tillich, *The Courage to Be; Love, Power, and Justice* (New York: Oxford University Press, 1954).

tion is a token of the ultimate loss, and every temporary gain is empty unless it comes to terms with the eternal meaning of existence. There is a limit to what man can do for himself; there is also a limit to what one man as therapist can do for another. As we resist one another so we can resist God, the ultimate source of value, in our hostile reactions desperately seeking love, yet caught in a bitter anguish of anxiety and guilt. Somehow if we are to be healed or saved, we must be reached by a new kind of love that breaks into the circle of malignant relationships and offers a way of deliverance. It is the experience of God's overflowing agape love, seeking us when yet unworthy in spite of our faults and failures, that opens the door of our prison and sets us free in a new community of love.

To find our way into this community, we shall in the next chapter explore the dimensions of personality.

CHAPTER THIRTEEN

DIMENSIONS OF PERSONALITY

1. An Integrated Theory

If we have learned anything in our journey together it is to discover the complexity of personality. *E pluribus unum* may characterize personality as well as a nation of many states, cultures, and individual interests, yet bound together in one organic and indivisible life. The fallacy in most theories of personality is oversimplification. Whatever we say is fragmentary, and however we describe or analyze we do not go far enough, for the whole is more than we think. The intricacy of the subject does not entitle us to give up in despair, but it does require us to be inexhaustibly persistent in our searching and invariably humble in not claiming that we know it all.

In the four theories of personality viewed in Chapters III and IV we have found needed wisdom. No one account is the whole story, and none is irrelevant. Each has corrected and complemented the others until we come to a better understanding through each approach when they are seen together in perspective. Looking back over the road we have traveled, we could not do without any one of these guides. It may be that the heyday of rival schools was due to the immaturity of psychology, which is about to yield now to a more co-operative enterprise. As the evidence accumulates, there is a converging of theory from rival extremes toward a common meeting ground.[1]

What remains to be done at this stage of investigation is to relate the many facts and theories, so far as possible, into a system which will serve as a network for communication and collaboration. To make an effort toward integration we will undertake to draw together the theories into a dimensional view of personality. To outline these dimensions in their relation to the person at the center we construct a design that will intersect as four highways coming together within a circle. This design is shown in Fig. III, p. 233.

[1] Kurt Lewin, *Field Theory in Social Science* (New York: Harper & Bros., 1951), pp. 1-4.

Personality is an intricate system of relationships whose focal center is a conscious *I*, the subject of experience. This unique self we have recognized as the "person" who is aware of his relationships through many

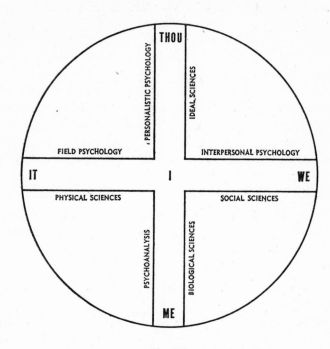

Fig. III

INTEGRATED THEORY OF PERSONALITY

dimensions that radiate from his self-experience. Of these intersecting dimensions we have charted four principal highways to explore in this chapter. A theory of personality integrated in this way we shall call "dynamic interpersonalism." At the center is the *I* who is actively participating in these dimensions of dynamic relations simultaneously. He is interacting with biological, physical, social, and ideal relationships at the same time in complex and often conflicting needs and interests.

A theory which holds the person central is personalistic. There are two historical traditions here: the personalisms of Bowne and Stern. Bowne[2] clearly saw the failure of any mechanistic attempt to piece to-

[2] Borden P. Bowne, *Introduction to Psychological Theory* (New York: Harper & Bros., 1886).

gether elements or sensations into a whole person. The very thinking employed in constructing such a theory is impossible except through a unitary, abiding, and active self. The self can only be denied verbally; for the nature of thought and language makes it impossible to maintain the denial without contradiction. To Bowne and his successor Brightman,[3] personality is equivalent to conscious experience. To Stern and Allport personality includes bodily functions with mental in one psychophysical system.[4] Our theory might be called "neo-personalism," in holding the person central, yet going beyond classical personalists to emphasize the dynamic motivations of the unconscious, the body, the environing culture, and interpersonal relations.

Writing in 1886 Bowne perceived this boundless openness of the person in his relationships.

No complete knowledge of the human mind can be gained by a study of the individual consciousness alone. This consciousness itself is evoked only under social conditions; and the individual is never a complete or perfect specimen of the human race. To escape the narrowness and one-sidedness of individualism we need to go out into the open field of the world.[5]

Stern[6] defines the person as a living whole that is at once self-contained and open to the world around him. In his theory of personalistics, he finds inward and outward dimensions. As the physical world has dimensions of space and time, so the personal world has its polarities between inner depth and outer relations, the here and there, before and after, rhythms and patterns which indicate multidimensions. Brightman[7] in his final lecture also proposed a theory of personal dimensions: "A person is a process in many dimensions."

Our dimensional view of personality seeks to integrate the outgoing interests of the person with the interactive richness of these relationships. It would be folly to hold defensively to a rigid theory of personality that refuses to incorporate the growing knowledge of recent scientific research. No theory can claim to be final or complete, unless

[3] Edgar S. Brightman, *Personality and Religion* (New York: The Abingdon Press, 1934).

[4] William Stern, *General Psychology from the Personalistic Standpoint,* tr. H. D. Spoerl (New York: The Macmillan Co., 1938).

[5] *Op. cit.,* p. 6.

[6] *Op. cit.,* pp. 70, 88-100.

[7] Edgar S. Brightman, *Persons and Values* (Boston University Press, 1952), p. 20. This university lecture was delivered April 16, 1951.

abstractions spun in remote corners are preferred to the give and take of open conversation where each is willing to listen and learn from the others.

The interpersonal theory we offer is open-ended rather than final, seeking not to complete the system with a last word, but to be completed by ongoing participation with other minds. It is not identical with the view of Sullivan, who neglects the inner content of the person for the events which take place between persons. The person is essentially focal in one's experience, yet his experience is actually of relationships that enrich and complicate his goal seeking.

Each of the psychologists whom we have studied is concerned with one of these dimensions. Freud and the psychoanalysts explore the I-Me relation of body and mind. Lewin and the field theorists explore the I-It relation to the environing field of interacting forces. Sullivan and the interpersonalists explore the I-We relation of group membership. Allport and the personalists explore the I-Thou relation of man and his values in their ultimate meanings.

These are not arbitrary schemes superimposed upon the unsuspecting person. Psychological dimensions arise from the basic relationships of personal life. No personality stands alone in complete isolation; for we have seen that isolation is death, and only inert matter can be cut off, dissembled, or taken apart. To live is to participate continually in the outgoing and inflowing stream of interaction by which to supply essential needs and extend the range of relatedness. A person is inseparable from these relationships because they are the dimensions of life in which and through which he finds the meanings and values of his existence.

2. The I-Me Relation of Mind and Body

At the center of personality stands the person. This center of conscious experience has been known by theology as the soul, by philosophy as the self, and by psychology as the ego. Other forms of life are conscious; animals are aware of pleasure and pain, learning from such experiences to guide their behavior to avoid pain and satisfy hunger. But a person is uniquely self-conscious, with capacity to draw together a multitude of experiences into focal unity as one's own. This self-awareness is periodically lost in sleep (though recurring in dreams far more than we are likely to recall). But in the morning a person awakes to remember what he was doing and thinking the day before,

235

with continuity of interest and purpose to take up again the unfinished tasks and plan the next steps in his career as the unifier who holds together many fragments of living in one ongoing life. The person has been called a time-binder in holding past and future together in one perspective; he is a space-binder in weaving steps and journeys of many directions into a unified pattern that has meaning to himself. He has been called "a fighter for ends," [8] which he chooses to strive toward as worth the effort in fulfilling desires and purposes he pursues as his own.

When you look at human beings from a distance in detached curiosity, as they dash madly to and fro, or start and stop in hesitating indecision, you may say to yourself, "They are crazy," or remark confidentially to a friend, "Aren't they absurd!" Yet when we act that way the behavior is not so crazy, for we know the inner meaning of it with some idea of what we are trying to do. So long as we approach each other externally as objects to push and pull around mechanically, we shall persist in stubborn misunderstandings. Mechanists have taken this approach in seeking to explain human behavior as determined by push-pull causes which reduce man to absurdity. In conscientious effort to work strictly within the limitations of natural science, we may be confined to barren conclusions in spite of ingenious and elaborate research procedures. But a deeper understanding is possible in viewing personality from within the center of unifying experience. Then the inner meaning of behavior is revealed, what appeared mechanical is seen to be purposive, and hidden relationships are clarified. Behavior which appeared to be causally determined from the past is now seen to be orientated to the future, in the dynamic process of means and ends as a person moves toward goals of his own choice.

To explore the dimensions of personality, let us take the internal point of view, starting at the center of conscious experience and moving outward to see what these relationships mean to the person himself. The subject of all relationships is the self we call *I*. As I perceive myself there is more than the subject perceiving; there is *Me*. The Me is what others observe, as well as what I think and expect of myself. What others observe is my body (classified by them as tall or short, fat or lean), and their comments help to shape the image I have of me. Such physical characteristics as posture, gait, and expressive movements rep-

[8] William James (1842-1910).

resent Me—as well as the clothing selected for the day or the evening, the haircut, the jewelry and personal equipment which add up to a style that is uniquely my own. This style is in part consciously chosen to fulfill the image of the personality I am or want to become, and in part unconscious as through trial and habit I will settle into a pattern of life that becomes my character. The unconscious aspects of Me are far greater and more influential in my behavior than I know, or than others know.

There can be no shadow of a doubt that I am related to Me. We live together, in one existence (the dwelling poetically named the "tenement of clay"), so intimately and continuously in the span of this earthly life that we evidently belong together. I cannot jump out of my skin, but I may forget while in meditation or sleep that my body is here too. Yet more often than not I am conscious of my body through hunger pangs, sensory stimuli, muscular movements, temperature changes, and restless urges that come to attention. Through the brain and nervous systems mind is informed of bodily conditions as continuously as body is stimulated by mental activities. Materialistic concepts as well as mentalism have equally failed to account for the complexity of human life in simplified abstractions of either body or mind. Medical efforts to cure bodily ills in a closed system of physical causations have proved as incomplete as religious efforts to rule out the flesh as having no significance for the spirit.

Psychosomatic medicine is now demonstrating the intricate inter-relationships of body and mind. A study of two thousand consecutive cases in the medical clinic of the Boston Dispensary showed 35 per cent to have no discoverable organic cause for painful symptoms. The emotional attitudes are increasingly seen to affect organic processes such as glandular secretions, heart and circulation, respiration, digestion and elimination, and sex and reproduction. No organ or condition of the body is impervious to psychic influences; neither can mental attitudes function apart from the biological processes. Personality so evidently functions as a unity of body-mind that these dual processes may be separated only by artificial dichotomies, which are obviously abstractions for logical analysis, not independent entities detachable one from another.

Granting the relation of body and mind as one functioning system in living behavior, what are we to understand as to the nature of the relationship? How am I related to Me? If a cue may be taken from grammar, the subject I refers to Me as the object of an active verb. In the once popular song "I love Me," the active relationship of affection is initiated by the subject for himself as the object. In the sentence "I know me better than you do," the subject again initiates a relationship (of knowing) in which he claims superiority due to his unique opportunity to observe the object. This grammatical usage is clearly equivalent to what we find in the psychological relationship, where I as perceiving subject initiate an active relationship to Me as the object of my perception. What is significant about Me as the perceived object arises from the experience I have in perceiving my whole being as one system of relatedness. The unity of personality which we recognized first as a biologic necessity is now seen to be a psychologic discovery. The Me which is biologically necessary to the mortal survival of the I is psychologically projected as the concept which I select or construct as an act of choice.

It is therefore evident that the psychologic Me is not exactly equivalent to the biologic Me; for my perceptions are variable and notably subject to error in misrepresenting objects. It would be an easy solution to this dilemma if we could set up a simple classification of duality by which the biologic process (body) would operate by causal necessity, while the psychologic process (mind) would operate by choice. But this would be an obvious oversimplification of the complex interacting processes of personality. Not only am I aware of Me now as body and then as mind, but there are aspects of both I am not aware of. Biologic processes like circulation, respiration, glandular secretion, digestion, and cell chemistry go on without my conscious awareness. Psychic processes are also at work unconsciously, and motivations affect behavior in purposive goal-seeking beneath the threshold of awareness.

We need, therefore, to give a larger place than is often realized to the unconscious dynamics of personality. Here is a third estate in the economy of personal life in which biotic and the psychic processes meet and commingle. Hungers arising from biotic needs interplay with wishes arising from psychic tendencies that are goal-seeking. Choice factors operating in the wishes (more or less conscious) intercharge with necessity factors operating in the organic processes (more or less unconscious). Together they carry on elaborate plots to fulfill hidden designs that are not ready for exposure to conscious examination. Browning's line has new relevance when applied to these designs—"A man's reach should exceed his grasp." What we reach for unconsciously exceeds our conscious grasp.

Freud has considerable evidence for his hypothesis that conscious experience is fragmentary, while the basic motivations and continuities of life are unconscious. Not that consciousness is less significant or consequential, nor can we ignore its achievements in relating ends and means, constructing systems of thought into elaborate meanings, and making acts of choice all things considered; but life has ongoing needs and purposes that emerge only partially and intermittently to conscious awareness.

Stern agrees with Freud that life is more primary and basic to personality than experience. His thesis is that "experience develops out of and into life." [9] As a living whole, personality is a life, individual and unique, that is capable of having experience. Only that which lives can have experience, and such experience is more or less conscious according to the particular situation which tends to dim or sharpen focal awareness. In human beings life appears in three modalities: (1) *Vitality* seeks to fulfill its functions in the biosphere; (2) *experience* is differentiated under cleavage and tension to be aware of the world of objects; while (3) *introception* seeks to affirm a world of values by incorporating or realizing them, that is, making them real in oneself. The more acute the tensions the sharper is the conscious awareness of this goal-seeking life.

The relation of mind and body is organically united in this ongoing personal life that is both physical and psychical. The individual is not partly body and partly mind but a personality with the capacity for experience. This goes beyond the traditional positions of parallelism and interactionism, resting in the fallacy of separate entities, to a whole organism emerging into experience. The connections are meaningful as they serve the total life purpose of personality. Every relation has instrumental and intrinsic significance for the person, in the goal-seeking by which he integrates his energies and relationships.

The body has more than physical usefulness; it has symbolic meanings as well. The social significance of the body with its component members has value far beyond instrumental use. The body build, facial expressions, posture, and gestures have values or disvalues that add or subtract from what the personality means to others, and by their re-

[9] *Op. cit.,* pp. 70-82.

flected appraisals to himself. The body is very expressive of attitudes, dispositions, and character traits which are communicated to others. In these ways the human personality is probably the most intricate of all systems of communication for the receiving and sending of meanings. It is not the most efficient, however, because of ambivalent desires and intentions that conflict, block, and confuse the expressions and impressions of personality.

Freud observed this first in the study of hysteria, as with Breuer he discovered the conversion of emotional conflicts and repressed motives into bodily symptoms.[10] In his case study of an English governess in Vienna, Miss Lucy, he showed how the active process of repressing an incompatible idea (a forbidden attachment to her employer) resulted in the substitution of a bodily symptom, hysteria. This discovery opened the way for psychosomatic concepts in medicine, as Freud continued to demonstrate how painful ideas may be repressed and diverted into somatic channels. The myth of a closed physical system apart from the psychic life is now dispelled by the weight of accumulating evidence that mind and body are functioning as one organismic whole. His analysis of psychosexuality further demonstrated how somatic drives are sublimated and modified into new and enlarging meanings where love has spiritual meaning.

The I-Me relation expands in these activities far beyond the original connections of mind and body. In its dynamic associations with mind, the body is more than body even as the mind in associating with body is more than mind. In fact they are constantly growing through the accretions of successive experiences in multiple relationships until the infantile mind-body system has been transformed a thousand times. The unfolding of these developments has been traced in the interpretations above of growing personality. To achieve maturity is the goal of every potentiality, and such a goal is not reached at a single bound, but "we mount to its summit round by round." We may find it convenient to speak of the educational ladder, but actually there are many ladders reaching out in all directions like spokes extending from the hub of a wheel. Not only does the wheel of life revolve, it also expands as personality reaches out in many directions at once through all of one's relationships. (See Fig. III, p. 233.)

The Me which I experience is therefore changing from day to day

[10] *Studies on Hysteria* (1895).

through every experience and modifying relationship. There are biopsychosocial spheres of activity constantly intersecting until I find my concept of Me always out of date. For Me is an expanding network of communications between the person and the intricate ramifications of his world. There is an openness about Me that will not stay within former boundaries, but ever and again moves across frontiers to occupy, or at least view, new territory. For I am that restless person who must grow or perish.

3. The I-It Relation to Environment

There can be no doubt that a person is related to his environment. From birth to death he is dependent upon it for air and nourishment, as well as the materials and energies he operates with to fulfill his life purposes. The environment is well defined by Webster as "the external conditions and influences affecting the life and development of an organism." The person and his surrounding environment taken together constitute what Lewin calls "life space." Into this field a person extends his interests and pursuits with room to move about and occupy himself in a variety of activities.

This environment is not empty space but a dynamic field of interacting forces in which the person seeks goals, meets barriers, and explores detours to overcome them. No object or region stands alone; each item is in a dynamic system of associated meanings and interests, anxieties and uses for the person. He selects items from his environment for attention, as a spotlight illuminates a sector of a dark landscape, and brings into focus what concerns him at the moment as related to his ongoing purposes.

He is evidently not a thing among other things added to a collection of discrete articles or related by external contiguity. The person is selector and organizer of the material world about him. Two people living on the same farm or dwelling in the same home on a city street do not have the same identical environment. Rather, each person has his own particular environment consisting of the features of his world to which he gives attention and which have special meaning to him.

Every person deals with impersonal objects which he gathers around him and with which he carries on a career of purposive living. Some objects he may create or purchase, as the tools of his workshop or the furnishings of his home. Other things such as mountains and streams,

241

fields and roads, are already there and he accommodates his behavior in reference to the given. The institutions of his society and the cultural patterns of his world are also given to him and stand around him as the structure of his life space. They resist his desires for they have a structure of their own. He may violate their demands upon him, as in the case of traffic laws; and one time he may get by, but another time he may be caught and penalized for his reckless defiance of their claim upon him.

The impersonal environment is something every person has to come to terms with. In some ways it assists him to realize his desires, while in other ways it limits and obstructs his freedom to gratify his wishes. One who ignores the realities of his situation indulges in fantasy. He may escape for a while in the make-believe of play, but he must return to realities or remain in deceptive hallucination and live by error rather than truth. This may have disastrous consequences, such as mistaking poison for food or refusing food for fear it may be poisoned. Freud insisted that a life which follows the pleasure principle without regard to the reality principle will destroy itself.

And yet conformity to the environment is not the whole answer to human need. To feel helpless and submit to the *status quo* may keep one out of trouble but timid and unproductive. To fulfill potentialities a person will have to initiate steps of his own and venture forth at some risk. To be creative he will shape these raw materials and energies to his purposes. He will clear the ground, plant and cultivate, to bring in the harvest. He will dream and design what is not yet, then go to work and build according to specifications agreed upon. Lewin urged us not to beat down the creative imagination of growing children to literal conformity, but to encourage them to work at the irreality level of fantasy. We are to orient our behavior to realities, not as slaves but as inventors who make history as well as read it, changing the world even as we depend upon it.

In this way we personalize our world. Every person restructures and remakes his environment to fit his own needs and serve his purposes. The space of Euclidian geometry and Newtonian mass attraction is not centered, but the personal world is. Each person is the center of his own world, as Stern says.[11] As perceiver I look out upon my world from a center of experience which is my own, radiating like a compass

[11] *Op. cit.,* p. 88.

in all directions from where I stand. To orient my position I reckon that this house is north of me, and then I proceed in that direction. When I arrive at the house which was my destination, I find myself at the center of that life space; and to take my bearings again, I must view the world from where I am now. Wherever I may be, as Lewin shows, I am a particular person at a particular time.[12] Before and after, here and there, are always linked to a person who has the experience and operates in his field.

There is a dynamic and progressive character to this incessant intercourse of a person with his world. Not only the person but also the environment is developed in this perpetual commerce between the person and his world. The milieu of a person is more than that part of the environment which happens to be in his vicinity; it is the portion of the world that the person brings near to him as he is sensitive to it. His environment is that part of the world which he recognizes as the context of his living, and to which he seeks to give form appropriate to his interests and concerns. This commerce, as Stern indicates, is so intimate and continuous that there is no separating cause from effect. The person is no more determined by his world than he determines the character of his world and its meaning for him. He is not merely a product, he is also a producer of his world; he initiates as well as responds, and his relations with the world are multiplied and extended by his spontaneous activities.

Lewin shows that the physical environment has psychological meaning to the person.[13] In a person's field he is influenced by psychical more than physical forces. The physical sciences have contributed useful concepts to the understanding of man, but psychical events are not reducible to physical energies, for man whatever he is cannot be treated as a robot moved by mechanical forces. Rather he is motivated by his own perceptions, insofar as he gives meaning to events and guides his behavior toward the goals he seeks. The stimulus to perception (e.g., the disfigured face of a wounded soldier) is to be assessed not by its physical contours, but according to its psychological meaning to the person. Such perceptual experience may create needs and initiate purposes which were not present before. Consequently there may be a release of energy in weeping, or first aid to help the wounded soldier, yet

[12] *Field Theory in Social Science*, p. 238.
[13] *A Dynamic Theory of Personality* (New York: McGraw-Hill Book Co., Inc., 1935), pp. 46-48.

more than energy is at work in this situation. Perception of meaning is nonphysical, and there is "a *steering* of the process by the perceptual field."

Yet we differ with Lewin when he seems to reduce the person to a fractional part of an impersonal process, as one item in a field of tensions. To him the field of coexisting forces is final and continuing, while the person is incidental and temporary. The unity of the ego, or self, is not central to Lewin, but is "merely one system or complex of systems, a functional part region within this psychical totality." [14] What then provides the unity to hold the entire psychic field together? Departing from perception, which is unmistakably person-centered, he arrives at a unity of tension systems by analogy to the equilibrium of physical forces. Actually, the equilibration of forces is a construct, or mental image, by which the theorist comes to rest in a formula. That this falls short of empirical unity is admitted by Lewin in concluding that there are "a great number of relatively separate tense systems." [15] By reducing personal experience to impersonal forces, the unique integration of psychic experience is given up and the essential character of the person is lost to energy systems modeled upon physics.

It should be noted, however, that this view comes from an early period, and in his later writings Lewin gives more weight to the inner-personal motivation. Needs have the power to "organize" behavior. Intention to attain a goal is a decisive factor giving direction to behavior. Intentions aim "to secure a certain behavior" in the future which is expected to fulfill needs.[16] The work of intention is to centralize the field and give to it a new structure and dynamic in reference to the goal sought to attain personal needs. In this way we can see how the person is constantly recentralizing all of his dimensions as he interacts with his world.

In so recreating his world a person is the one who attributes value to objects as they become desirable to him. He reaches out through perception to discover the meaning of these objects in his own experience. And their value is a measure of what they mean to him as a valuing person. There is conflict and tension in such experience, to be sure, with gains and losses, anxieties and doubts. But even so and because

[14] *Ibid.,* p. 56.
[15] *Ibid.,* p. 60.
[16] *Field Theory in Social Science,* p. 284.

of these contrasting experiences, the continuing person in his dynamic goal-seeking is able to actualize the potential value of his existence. He may also find satisfaction in enhancing the values of life for other persons.

The basis of ethical living, as Kant shows, is to treat all persons as ends not means. For a person is the experiencer to whom values have perceptible meaning. Persons are in the environment yet stand out above the impersonal environment. The relation of person to person will therefore become an important dimension of personality.

4. The I-We Relation of Group Life

Life begins in a relationship of social integration which Kunkel calls "the Primal-We." [17] In this early experience the child has not yet discovered the dividing line between I and You. The mother does not stand as an object to the child as subject, but together they form a common subject. The unity of this primal we-experience is difficult for an adult to understand, for he is so well established as a separate individual. Yet in suckling as the mother feeds the child, she wants him to drink and the child wants to drink. They have a unified goal, and while their actions are different, they together complete the act of nourishment.

To have a unified goal is different from having the same goal. If two hungry children find an apple that each wants to eat, they have the same goal, yet as both cannot eat the whole apple they stand in competitive opposition to each other. But as the mother nurses the infant it is not a case of one acting for another, or each acting for himself. If the mother had not given to the child she would be uncomfortable from the excess of milk, while the child would be in hunger distress from lack of milk. Not only was the value of nursing common to both, but also the personal well-being of each. "Injury to one would mean injury to the whole, hence an injury to the other as well."

The mother is of course not living wholly in the Primal-We. She participates in it with some of her functions, but she has other interests and relationships with which she is also occupied. For the young child, however, the unity of his first relationship to the mother is the original and undifferentiated experience of group life. Something of

[17] Fritz Kunkel, *Character, Growth, Education,* trs. Keppel-Compton and B. Druitt (Philadelphia: J. B. Lippincott Co., 1938), p. 15.

this unity may be experienced by primitive folk, described by Levy-Bruhl as "mystical sympathy" and by Max Scheler as a "feeling of oneness," or the racial affinity which Jung calls the "collective unconscious." [18] Longing for this earlier unity may come upon the adult person with overpowering emotion as nostalgia for a lost paradise.

The affiliative need for companionship may well be the basic need of human life, as Suttie[19] perceives it to be. Yet there must be a ripening of the we-experience for the Primal-We when shattered is gone forever, and it is regressive folly to seek to restore what has been outgrown. The timid child will withdraw and the aggressive child will show anger and resistance; both tactics are working against the learning most urgently needed, to achieve a mature we-experience.

New relationships will be attempted and old ones approached from a new perspective if the We is to be reconstructed. This will call for courage to venture forth in spite of anxiety to explore the possibilities of new affiliations. The indulgent parent who binds the growing child to him thwarts these new adventures by defining security possessively as the *status quo,* and instilling fear of change. To move beyond the original We, the growing person must participate in other groups and exercise a variety of roles in different contexts.

Mature persons are free to assimilate new affiliations and extend mutual regard through a repertory of interpersonal relations.[20] These are not a series of one-to-one relations, but a network of groups in which the individual comes to belong and participate with meaningful roles and status. Kunkel believes that the dialectic of the corporate life does not occur as I and You, but as I and We, the individual and the group. The group which moves visibly in the outer world has its counterpart in the experience of the We in the developing character of the individual.[21] If the behavior of the group is doubtful (as a family at odds with itself), the development of the We in the child will be weak, as he waits in vain for something that does not exist.

The family is the primary social group in our culture. As the growing personality introjects these affiliations into himself he will employ

---

[18] *Psychological Reflections: An Anthology,* ed. Jolande Jacobi (New York: Pantheon Books, Inc., 1951).

[19] *Op. cit.*

[20] Sullivan traces these successive relationships in *The Interpersonal Theory of Psychiatry.*

[21] See also the object-relations theory of W. R. D. Fairbairn, *Psychoanalytic Studies of the Personality* (London: Routledge & Kegan Paul, Ltd., 1952).

this "internalized family" as a model for other relationships that he comes to experience. Other face-to-face groups will tend to symbolize a family as he perceives them, and he is likely to transfer former attitudes to new affiliations. The leader of a group may represent the parental figure, and the members may be unconsciously cast in the role of siblings. Freudians have noted that the kind of sharing and co-operating of which a person is capable emerges largely from his earlier experiences in his own family. A psychological group is formed of two or more people who have set up similar models or ideals in the super-ego and are able to identify with each other. Affective forces of attraction (libido) draw individuals together by interstimulation according to personal needs and group circumstances, forming dynamic valences or linkages of unity. Hostility and divisive tendencies may be released by group experience as well as affectional and cohesive forces.

A psychoanalyst has noted the following potentially constructive ways in which groups can further personality growth:

1. the feeling of belonging and status;
2. protection from real or fantasied threat;
3. the enhancement of self-esteem;
4. the loosening of the façade of defensive mechanisms and the opportunity for testing these against the reality;
5. proper conditions for sublimating of basic drives;
6. the curbing of infantile desires and behavior, and internalization of group standards in exchange for the love and protection received;
7. the diverting of undue aggressiveness onto real evils and its use for purposes of self-control and defense.[22]

Religious groups have often functioned in these ways to meet the basic needs of individual members. It is significant that every religion has grown when its group associations have been satisfying, and declined when group associations became inactive. To be a follower of Jesus has, from the first disciples, required membership in a group, which was an essential means of grace and growth. The Christian fellowship Paul declared was the body of Christ, wherein each one is organically related to and interdependent with every other member (I Cor. 12). Religious leaders who wonder why church groups are not more vital and dynamic may well investigate how the actual needs of

[22] Saul Scheidlinger, *Psychoanalysis and Group Behavior* (New York: W. W. Norton & Co., Inc., 1952), pp. 139-40.

the members are being met by such groups. Are they occupied merely with keeping up formal traditions? Are they concerned altogether with external goals and tasks such as raising money? Or do they care for each other as persons and contribute to deeper personal needs, which, though unconscious or dimly recognized, are central to self-esteem, protection from anxiety, reality testing, sublimating of infantile desires, diverting of aggressiveness into constructive channels, and love and mutual enhancement of values through sharing and identification with ideal figures?

Religious groups are not merely to meet the ego-centered needs of their members, urgent and rightful as these may be, but also to meet the altruistic, other-centered needs which are equally significant to the person if he is to fulfill his potentialities. It would be a false and misleading view of a human personality to assume that he has only hedonistic and egocentric desires. The desire to serve other persons, to be a responsible member of a community, to share his values with other persons, to sacrifice the local and temporary for the larger and enduring interest—these are essential to a growing person and characteristic of his maturity. But unless personal needs are also met in vital satisfactions, group experiences have shown that the worthiness of external aims is not alone sufficient to make a group cohesive.[23] The kingdom of God is both within and beyond; the deepest personal needs are met in serving the needs of other persons.

Individuals are attracted into group membership by the character of the group, by response to its goals and programs, type of organization, and position in the community. The objective characteristics of the group may interest a person and appeal to him as good and worthy of support. But when we ask why the group appeals to him we come to the nature of the person himself and his needs for affiliation, recognition, and participation which the group may be able to meet. Church groups which are abstractly intending to meet human needs may decline, unless there is accurate hitting of the target of actual member needs in the concrete situations of everyday living. Rather than take this for granted, each group, to be effective, will need to explore the immediate needs of its members, and guide the group experience into productive channels of need fulfillment. To love and serve one another in genuine concern for the interests that are most vital to each person will

[23] Dorwin Cartwright and Alvin Zander, eds., *Group Dynamics: Research and Theory* (Evanston, Ill.: Row, Peterson & Co., 1953), pp. 73-91.

deepen the sense of fellowship and heighten the value of the group experience.

Group membership may be peripheral, as when a person keeps his name on the roll of a church but neglects to attend or contribute to the activities. If the group does not have central meaning for him, it is ego-distant and does not involve his loyalty to the point of active participation. He may drift away from the group or be disgruntled by any demands made upon him to take on more responsibility. Not recognizing how the church is meeting his needs, he turns his attention elsewhere and resists efforts to enlist him in its program. The church fails to reach him by not touching him where he lives, and he declines to participate as he feels alienated and out of touch with the church.

How does it come about that a person once interested drifts away, or one whose family participates will not himself come into the fellowship of the church? Each case is unique but we can recognize a complex of inner and outer conditions which combine unpleasant memories with emotional tensions in association with the group, assertions of independence from authoritarian figures, symbols and behavior that seem threatening or meaningless, as well as the inertia of drifting toward careless habits that make fewer demands upon leisure, and a stifling of spontaneous expression by rigid formalities which diminish the we-feeling.

Such indifference toward a religious group may continue until some crisis occurs which brings a sense of personal need to focal awareness. Then the easygoing complacency is shattered and he is confronted with urgent needs he can not ignore. If the crisis is a private affair he may take the lonely road of battling his way apart from group life, especially when the group appears to him as unsympathetic or antagonistic. Such a lonely road may lead to the psychotic distress of mental illness which we have seen as a desperate attempt to solve a problem single-handed when communication breaks down and one feels terribly isolated from the understanding love of other persons.

Boisen[24] has investigated the effect of social crisis upon religious groups. He finds that a social crisis breaks through the customary defenses when the values of life are challenged and persons are forced to think about fundamental problems. Out of distress comes a depth of experience unknown before with a new sense of urgency. In seek-

[24] *Religion in Crisis and Custom* (New York: Harper & Bros., 1955).

ing to cope with the unmanageable crisis, one is thrown back upon basic considerations of what life is for and how to gain the strength and courage to live through the time of stress. Larger resources are needed than had been required before, and a sympathetic group is a welcome asset. It is natural then to turn to religion which deals with the meaning of life and to search for God, the creator and sustainer of life.

It is notable that Pentecostal religious groups had a tremendous growth during the economic crisis of 1928-36. While other churches were declining statistically, they doubled and trebled in membership. From his field studies Boisen found that people who came into the Pentecostal sects felt that they were not welcomed in the older churches, and that their needs were not met by the formality of traditional churches. They sought a message and a revitalizing power for the sick and distressed soul that would make a decisive difference in their lives. They did not undertake to change the world, but they did intend to change themselves through confession of sins to release the burden of guilt and disappointment in material values. To satisfy their deeper needs they sought an emotional revival of religious devotion, a conversion from external goods to inner and spiritual resources, a new birth in eternal life.

In other periods of history, social crises have broken through the superficial veneer of man's complacency and revealed new resources for personal growth. Insights won in time of crisis have led to the formation of new groups or have been assimilated by the established ones. Religious groups have both a creative and a conservative function to quicken new discoveries and to conserve them in the ongoing stream of custom and culture. For the I does not stand alone in self-sufficient independence, but emerges out of the living relatedness of the We, and will need again and again to return to the group for creative awakening as well as for emotional and moral sustenance.

5. The I-Thou Relation to God

The quest for wholeness begins with every personality by integration of mind and body. "No man is an island," complete and sufficient in himself, however; he has other dimensions to explore and other relationships to develop in outreaching and incorporating growth. He will relate himself to the world of things in myriad ways as he responds to the environmental stimuli and seeks to organize his world around himself. He will relate himself to the world of persons and find new meanings through interpersonal experiences in groups to which he belongs.

Another dimension opens before the human explorer in his search for something greater than himself. He searches for the ultimate of all being and wonders if he can comprehend how he is related thereto. He takes up the fragments of local and little interests, and tries to find what they mean altogether in larger perspective. He remains unsatisfied with every partial good and will not give up his restless search for that larger goodness he confronts in God.

In his own restless search for the meaning of life Freud gave enlarging significance to the superego. From childhood every person is aware of someone greater than himself to whom he is responsible. The parents are the first authority figures for the child in his dawning sense of responsibility to control his impulses in deference to their demands upon him. Eventually he takes into himself their ideal code, and censors the id impulses by self-control, acting for the parents in regulating his own behavior. The superego becomes an inner guide or sense of obligation to submit primitive wishes to a higher authority. This continues into maturity long after the parents have departed, in seeking to fulfill one's responsibility to a greater order of Being.

Morality and religion, no less than all the achievements of civilization, arise from this struggle to remake human nature. Not content to let his impulses run wild or to remain in native unconcern, man ever seeks to improve himself. He aspires to be better than he is, to sublimate his impulses and attain to the ideal person that is higher than the present ego. To do this he projects his desire upon someone greater as a model with whom he identifies his ego-ideal. Then he introjects that ideal and internalizes the relationship until the greater superego is incarnate in his own personality acting from within as his guiding authority.

This upward dimension of personality we will call the *I-Thou* relation. *I* stands for the ego seeking to regulate his impulses to become a better personality. *Thou* is the ultimate authority to whom I am responsible. To the infant the parent is the ultimate authority to whom he is responsible. But as the child grows upward and outward he moves from the home into a larger world where other authorities hold sway and claim his allegiance. There is the teacher, the policeman, the mayor of his city, the governor of his state, and the heads of national

251

and international units. There are church authorities and saints as well as the founder of his religion. There are scientific and medical authorities whom he consults and whose wisdom he respects or rejects.

Eventually, he might be confused by so many conflicting authorities, unless he is able to hold them in a hierarchy of lesser and greater significance in his life. Not that he decides all at once to make a formal list in rank order, but rather this hierarchy grows upon him gradually and somewhat unconsciously as he observes who defers to whom, and senses the currents of authority as they flow among all of his relationships. The aspiration level is ever moving upward as we begin with local persons and objects of interest, from whence we turn to more universal values and ultimate authorities.

Thou may at first refer to the child's mother or father in the home. Brothers and sisters defer to them too as the authority figures to whom we are responsible. When the parents lead family worship and pray to God as "Our Father who art in heaven," there is reference to a more ultimate authority. When the growing person approaches religious maturity in the direction of a monotheistic religion, informed by a comprehensive theology and intensified by personal devotion to responsible living, his Thou will have greatly enlarged. That ultimate Being may to one person be an abstract norm in his detached speculation, that which philosophers talk about. To another person who is moved by deep religious devotion, Thou will represent the Supreme Person to whom he is committed in worship and whole-hearted dedication.

The Thou whom I approach in religious devotion is more than superego. Freud viewed the superego as a segment of the psychic apparatus, a part of Me caught in neurotic conflicts and submerged in the internecine contests of the unconscious. Standing for the reality principle in opposition to the pleasure principle, it was only an image, not the reality. But Thou is the objective Reality, and no mere image or fetish. The religious seeker is convinced that he confronts a Being beyond himself, that he is not alone but meeting an Other. This is the basic premise of religious experience, the essential meaning and excitement of every religious quest and symbol, that I am meeting Thou.

Psychology as a natural science is not equipped to deal with questions of ultimate reality. Freud was a devoted scientist who did not expect to find what science could not give. And yet he was concerned about the larger questions of religion and sought to deal with them by speculative reasoning he called "metapsychology." In this way he undertook to circumvent religion with concepts developed in his psychology. Finding the Oedipus complex in mythology of ancient cultures as well as in the contemporary family of his time, he saw the religious quest as a serious attempt to be reconciled with the Father. It is natural for the young man to revolt against the authority of the father, and then suffering guilty remorse for having offended him, to seek earnestly a reconciliation to restore the filial relationship.

This is a remarkable insight into the basic motivation of religion. It is a theme central in the teaching of Jesus (the Prodigal Son) and Paul ("while we were yet sinners, Christ died for us"), as well as the broken covenant and the forgiving God of the Old Testament, the Oedipus story of Hellenism, the Osiris myth of other civilizations, and the *Bhagavad-Gita* epic of Hinduism. Theologians of many persuasions agree that alienation from God the ultimate Being is the great evil of human life, to be restored in one way or another by religious devotion. By separation one is cut off from the Creative Source of life and love, mistaken as to the truth, and wandering as a lost soul in the maya of illusion and empty defeat.

Our difference with Freud is that he does not acknowledge the Reality to which the epic points, that to him it is only a myth. To him there is no such Being to forgive our offenses, nothing but a projection of the father-image. He reduces theology to psychology. Instead of someone greater who is approached as Thou, he turns to the image which reflects a super-ego. Instead of a dynamic meeting in the living present where I confront Thou, he sees the link as a fixation, chained to the past in repetition of a childish anxiety. If this were all religion can mean, it would be no more than a haunting illusion, "the universal obsessional neurosis of mankind." Such a religion is fantasy because it ends with the lonely person isolated in a deathly solipsism.

The superego is a poor substitute for the religious concept of Thou. Like a puppet in a shadow play it seems to have no voice or will of its own, but to move by the pulling strings of the psychic apparatus. Its function is largely negative to censor and restrain the id impulses according to a code of prohibition. Its demands are harsh and punitive, a "tyranny of shoulds" [25] enforced by guilt feelings and accusative anxieties. Like the Furies in Greek legend the superego relentlessly

---

[25] Horney, *Neurosis and Human Growth.*

pursues the unfortunate culprit, giving him no rest or peace, but always avenging his hapless mistakes.

Freud might be the first to admit that this is a neurotic view of religion. It would seem to emerge from the obsessions and anxieties that he found in neurotic patients. It is not surprising that neuroses distort religion, as well as other human ventures and perceptions, which he analyzed so clearly in his epochal writings. From his work we may be able to distinguish between neurotic and healthy religion. But for some reason he does not make that distinction himself; rather he leaves the reader with the impression that *this* is religion. If we can avoid the fallacy of hasty generalization, we may see that one religion is regressive and neurotic while another religion is mature and growing. What empirical analysis he gives will aid us in detecting neurotic tendencies in some religious experience. At the same time his speculative generalizations may help us to recognize the danger of bias in the presuppositions even of great thinkers.

For if we do not recognize the danger of biases in our own thinking we may go as far afield in some other direction, even to assume that all religious experiences are true and healthy. Jesus warned against this procedure in his comment on removing a speck from another's eye without noting the log distorting the vision of one's own eye. Granting that a finite mind can neither prove nor disprove the being of God, we seek a view of God that is coherent with our empirical evidence, that makes sense in such experiences as we are able to communicate to each other. What do we mean by Thou?

When I meet Thou in this living moment something creative happens between us. No description of this creative encounter can be more than halting analogy. It is as if a creative spark leaped and charged the event with dynamic energy. It is a waking experience, as if something inert and slumbering had suddenly come to life and consciousness. The moment of meeting Thou is radically serious and awe-inspiring, as if to shatter complacent self-satisfaction with a new urgency to rise to the occasion. There may be a sense of mystery and fascination that is overpowering (as Otto[26] finds), or a calm security that undergirds life with deeper trust and energizing repose, with overflowing light and warmth. I feel as if I am meeting a personal Being who responds to my quest instantly in the deepest kind of intimate under-

---

[26] *The Idea of the Holy.*

standing, who knows the worst yet believes the best, who clearly sees the fault yet with forgiving love that affirms the true intent and hidden potentiality.

Though imperceptible to the external senses, there is a definitive inner perception that I meet Thou through interpersonal relationship. The response is mutual and there is a feeling of confrontation by person to person that I cannot set aside even for logical considerations. I can agree with theologians who insist that God cannot be one of a class; he is unique in his transcendent creativity beyond all finite creatures who are his creation. And yet what can be more unique or transcendent or creative than personhood? To be less than person is to be less than we are. To be more than person is to be even more unique, transcendent, and creative. For of all beings we know, it is the person who best represents these attributes. And if we speak of God as responding with forgiving love to the penitent man or woman who prays for reconciliation, do we not assume a person-to-person relationship?

If Thou is ultimate to the religious seeker, we do not mean in any quantitive measure of space or time, but in a qualitative sense of heightened meaning and spiritual values. We address Thou by the personal pronoun because He has personal meaning for us that cannot be less, and therefore must be more of what we know as personhood. Whatever we know of science or religion is anthropomorphic, arising from human experience, in the categories and structure of our finite viewpoint. In this sense we do project our concept of God from our own dynamic needs to fulfill our ultimate expectation that Reality out there meets what is most real in us. To see this as a finite quest for infinite response is also to recognize a mutuality in which there is infinite quest for finite response. If every living relation is dynamic, the relation of I and Thou is intensified by the energizing of ultimate Creativity. For I seek the Thou who initiates creativity.

To enter such a dynamic relationship means a new dimension for personality. "The ego needs a Thou to build up an assertive self with and against this Thou." [27] For no finite person is self-sufficient, however he may try to be so. Without his living relationships he cannot be a person. Augustine acknowledges this for God also in his social theory of the Trinity, which the Godhead requires in order to be complete in mutual relationships. However this may be, we can affirm for man his depend-

[27] Otto Rank, *Beyond Psychology* (1711 Fitzwater St., Philadelphia: E. Hauser, 1941), p. 290.

ence upon these sustaining relationships. We have seen how the person enters into relation with his body, his environment, and his social group. More ultimately he is dependent upon God as the creator and sustainer of life. No man creates himself nor does he sustain himself by his own efforts alone. Life is given to him from a more ultimate Source beyond human knowledge, and he is sustained from breath to breath by a destiny he does not invent. He may be quite unconscious of the ultimate Giver.

But as he does become conscious of Thou, life takes on a dimension of new significance. Then, as Rank notes, he asserts himself in a new direction, with and against this Thou. Acknowledging dependence, yet he will no longer be merely dependent. He rises up to assert his own creativity. Only the self-conscious can assert freedom of choice. In reference to Thou, I become conscious of myself as a person, responsible to exercise my freedom in view of all the relationships of life.

To assert the id impulses recklessly is destructive even of the pleasure so lustily sought. To defy the punitive superego is like offending a petty official who is too mean to forgive, and too intolerant to discharge the penalty. Consequently, the culprit is always guilty and there is no escape from the guilt. Life is eternal hell here and now when a person suffers the damnation of unyielding condemnation. So a person becomes his own worst enemy caught in the cross fire of interminable conflict between id and superego.

Confronting Thou is quite a different situation. The entire climate changes, for Thou is someone greater than my petty legalism and conflict. Thou communicates this greatness to me, so that I take on new stature and dignity. My freedom to choose is upheld by his purpose and continued with his permission. He sustains even my right to revolt against him, and in view of his unfailing love my revolt is no petty misdemeanor, but a tragic denial of the best I know, a betrayal of my ultimate potentiality turning into self-defeat. Yet the way of return to Thou is always open for he does not cast me off or lock me out. Before I call he is answering, and while I hesitate with faltering indecision he is waiting to receive me with patient and forgiving love. What was a means of guilt becomes a means of grace!

Such love is too wonderful for me in my fickle deceits; it is high beyond what I can attain, and yet this love overflows from Thou to me insofar as I am willing to accept. To enter this dimension is a new birth in freedom and ability to love, which changes the other dimensions of personality and transforms all other relationships.

Martin Buber [28] gives an eloquent portrayal of the meeting of I and Thou. In the world of things we command whatever we find to our own use and take exploitative attitudes even toward our fellow men. In the I-It relation nothing is sacred in its own right, but instrumental always to our desires. With the discovery of Thou a new relationship is open to reverence, as I come to respect the intrinsic worth of a person in his own right. The reverence I feel toward Thou changes all the relations of life, and profound respect displaces my former attitude of exploitation. Every person emerges to new dignity when I feel reverence for Thou. A radical change has taken place in me, and consequently the world is different to me because I perceive everything in a new light of intrinsic worth.

This new awareness the Hindu mystic calls the superconscious. When the religious seeker comes to union with God he breaks through the maya of illusion that clouds his earthly life. Then as if the bright sun had dispelled the clouds, he is in a radiant atmosphere where everything appears in a clearer light. In the ecstasy of his union with God he rises to a higher dimension above the ordinary way of looking at life. He finds the superconscious a new and transforming center from which to view all of his relationships. Returning to his fellow men, he finds that they take on added significance, that he is related to them more closely through God, and that he desires to serve them more joyously as he finds God in them.

No person can long be content to live in one dimension, or plod along a step at a time without looking before and after. For man is that being who ever seeks to transcend himself. He is finite, yet knowing that he is finite he views his predicament in transcendent ways. He seeks to put the fragments of experience into whole meanings, to sense the direction of his trending and the overarching purpose that shapes his destiny. Every dimension and living relationship links him to a larger wholeness.

In this quest all roads lead to Thou, when pursued to their ultimate meaning. For it is the ultimate goal that brings all intermediate steps into a course of ongoing destiny. Yet until I meet Thou, they are only a heap or collection of fragments in the aggregate. The inner sense of

[28] *I and Thou.*

unity is lacking until meeting Thou consummates the meaning that was lost. The body was once exploited for work or pleasure; now it has intrinsic worth and dignity before the Creator who breathed into it the breath of life. The world of physical things was then instrumental to my self-seeking ambition; now it is the garment of the Spirit who moves upon the deep to bring chaos into order and pronounce it good. Other persons who once counted as rivals or tools to my egocentric schemes have come to hold the matchless beauty of individuality, each in his own way and right, a bearer of intrinsic and unique value.

Is it reverence that makes the difference? Recalling the central place that reverence holds in every religion and the motivation it gives to ethics, we could well magnify the attitude of reverence. To Schweitzer the integrating principle for all human striving is reverence for life. Psychology is inclined to find the meaning of religion in the inner motive that stirs a person to respond to greatness with profound appreciation. But to enthrone any attitude is a ghostly abstraction that mistakes the part for the whole. Nothing less than a whole person can be religious. And even a person cannot be religious in isolation. To be religious is to achieve community where spirit with spirit can meet in relationships of reverence. In the meeting of I and Thou we come to the creative event that transmutes life into reverent wholeness.

CHAPTER FOURTEEN

FOREVER SEARCHING

~~~~~~~~~~~~~~~~~~~~~~~

1. Becoming

Man is no static, inert thing. He is on the way to becoming more than he is at the present moment. As we observe the growth of a child from birth as a helpless infant to the ripe development of later maturity, the changes are quite astonishing in behavior and external appearance. And if you should write a full-length autobiography fitting together all the details of memory and record, wherein external events take on the significance of inner meaning as experienced by the person who lived through them, the changes would be even more astonishing. Who can unravel the myriad threads of causation and comprehend what shapes the destiny of each personality in his unique development? The biographical chapters of this book are too brief and fragmentary for such causal analysis. Too many significant events and hidden motives are overlooked to give the whole story, and yet these accounts do have the merit of portraying the drama of life as the person himself sees it at the time of writing.

How is personality dynamic? Biologists have studied the *genetive dynamic* of growth toward maturity. There is much to learn from the genetic approach of heredity as transmitted in the genes and the unfolding of life from stage to stage of its development. What makes life grow according to the pattern which replicates the species and resembles the parents, yet arrives in each case at such unique individuality? To some investigators this maturation appears gene-determined, and there is little to do but wait for the preordained developments to occur. Darwin's theory of evolution held that chance variations are sifted by natural selection with survival of the fittest. Plant and animal species are improved by selective breeding in which the purpose of the eugenist may guide the evolution.

The power of growth can hardly be overestimated. It is the basic dynamic of life so long as the organism continues to live. Even in maturity after the full stature has been attained, cell growth continues to repair losses and replace deficiencies. Psychic growth is most character-istic of human life in learning and the pursuit of enlarging interests. Psychotherapists as well as educators rely upon the growing capacity of persons for self-actualization in which potentialities may be increasingly developed through persistent striving.

Here we come upon another dynamic to which psychologists have given major attention, the *goal dynamic* of individual striving. To study this goal tension in its elementary simplicity, they have experimented with animal behavior motivated by hunger as a basic physiological need. But hunger may not be typical of human motivation, which is far from simple and operates from a hierarchy of motives. It is true that physiological motives are prepotent when the organism suffers a deficit. Maslow[1] shows, however, that when the physiological needs are satisfied then a person may be motivated from higher needs that gain ascendancy. A well-fed person who is satiated with food is consequently free to follow other interests.

There is little use in making lists of needs by which personality is motivated, for most drives or goal tensions are not isolable, nor localized upon a specific somatic base. The typical desires are evidently needs of the whole personality. They are means to ends rather than ends in themselves, and many purposes may find expression through the same channel (as when food is taken as a substitute for love). Drives are not equal in potency nor are they mutually exclusive. But it may be useful to note the hierarchy of motives in which physiological needs are first in urgency, then the safety needs which organize behavior in defenses against threat. When the physiological and safety needs are met, the love needs and belongingness emerge. Upon this foundation there will appear the needs for esteem and self-actualization, the desire to know, the aesthetic and religious aspirations. This does not mean that the exact order is rigid, but that human needs are related in series, so that as one need is satisfied others will emerge.

This evidence will contradict the theory of Freud and others who assume that tension reduction is the goal of life, seeking only to reach a state of quiescent equilibrium. Actually, in human life we find no such tendency to lie down and rest at every goal line, but rather a desire to start out in quest of other goals. A satisfied need is not a motivator. What was a value in deprivation is no longer sought when that

---

[1] A. H. Maslow, *Motivation and Personality* (New York: Harper & Bros., 1954).

need is satisfied, and the person is ready to move on to other goals which now have higher motivating power. To be thwarted in any of the basic needs is to be sick and preoccupied with deficits. The healthy person is one whose basic needs are so gratified that he is free to act in reference to long-range goals of his own choosing. No longer dominated by the emergency of deprivation he can live at a higher need level with greater efficiency, more serenity and richness of the inner life. In so doing he is able to participate with other persons in a wider range of values with desirable social consequences for civic and community life. He enjoys a larger circle of love identification and yet with truer individuality. Maslow finds that the higher the need level, the more effective is psychotherapy and self-actualization.[2]

This persistent striving for many goals may lead to distraction and conflict among desired values that pull in opposing directions. Neurotic indecision and "nervous breakdown" appear in laboratory animals subjected to experiment in conflict situations. It is evident that some higher executive capacity is needed to manage a complicated array of diverse interests and choose among alternative goals. Otherwise the goal progress bogs down like a traffic snarl at a crowded intersection, and acute frustration extinguishes desire. Goal striving is not a self-regulating mechanism sufficient to cope with deep-seated dilemmas.

What is needed to resolve conflict is an *integral dynamic* to unify diverse impulses into effective teamwork. This, according to Freud, is the chief function of the ego, which is most in contact with the reality of the total situation and able to adjudicate the conflicting demands of id and superego. The integrating work of the ego is increasingly acknowledged by contemporary psychologists, and Allport has proposed that we call this "propriate striving." The ego function is more than defensive operations, it is open and outgoing participation in a whole spectrum of colorful interests that may fulfill one's potentialities and round out the meaning of life. No one wants to be a fraction unless he is so crippled by anxieties and wounded by defeats that he has given up the struggle. The growing personality, with zest for living, wants to exercise his powers and actualize his enlarging capacities.

To this extent every person is the integrator of his diverse impulses and the organizer of fractional interests into dynamic unity. He does this by selecting a centralizing principle to orient his course and guide

[2] *Ibid.*, pp. 146-50.

him in deciding what is more or less important to his long-range goals. To decide upon a medical vocation is to form such a centralizing principle. It will guide the person in the years of preparation, and in the exercise of countless decisions in the day-by-day work of a practicing physician. In view of this major purpose he will set aside certain values as less essential and give himself unstintingly to other activities (daily house calls, hospital rounds, office appointments, laboratory or surgical procedures, reading professional journals, and attending professional meetings). When these centralizing principles become regnant, they are constantly employed to unify the whole meaning of life and to bring diverse interests into working harmony. As junctures arise requiring a decision, the choice is made in view of the larger purpose, and the issues at stake find their place in a scale of ascending values.

Not that every person works out a complete design like a blueprint with every step detailed in perfect order. In less formal ways, however, we are constantly systematizing the impressions we receive and the intentions we project into every situation we meet. The life of illiterate people is regulated by proverbs by which general principles are recalled as occasion may arise to solve specific questions of how to proceed. Every perception is an act of selection where attention comes to focus upon a figure in a background. Every recognition is a judgment noting how this resembles that, and thus relating percepts and concepts into a perspective. From moment to moment, unconscious as well as conscious purposes are regulating the ongoing life as each item presented is taken into integral patterns of meaning. There is structure, therefore, in all experience by which order emerges from chaos, and yet the whole process is forever dynamic in a continuous reshaping of means and ends to make sense and follow purposive striving.

Allport shows that becoming is motivated by a dynamic of futurity, even more than reaction to past and present stimuli. To be sure, we are beset by conflicting impulses and environmental demands that distract and disorient us from the main purpose. Mature persons will be "aware of, and in some way partner to, all the discordant conditions of our own existence." [3] To the social scientist who views man from a detached point of view, there may be no room for freedom among the many determinants and causal sequences he plots for the human scene. Yet the acting person has to assert choices at each step of his life course,

[3] *Becoming,* p. 79.

which he may do from a central orienting principle of intentionality. Intentions are the characteristic ways in which we address ourselves to the future. By these intentions we select stimuli and make the choices of our becoming.

Paul Weiss notes this dynamic of intention in saying that "we know our fellows because we know the kind of future they are bringing about." [4] Personality is not what one has, it is the "projected outcome of his growth." [5] It is this unfinished business that has dynamic interest for a growing personality. Whatever may push me from behind or pull me from before is a mechanical operation in which I am likely to be either passive or resistant. But whatever interests me as a value to seek in relation to the whole meaning of life is an integral dynamic of personal choice. And the larger perspective offers more alternatives among which to choose in the light of a regulating principle by which I can make a clear choice. Freedom advances with the ability to perceive whole meanings.

Integral becoming is more than linear progress toward a goal. It is more like a spiral that ever widens as it ascends. There is an outgoingness about this kind of growth that moves into widening areas of experience to appreciate their meaning. The one who perceives them may enter through empathy into the feelings of other persons, to discover what life means to them. He may participate actively in group life and co-operate in the pursuit of mutual goals where values are shared. He may incorporate these relations into his own personality and incarnate the ideals and principles which have become his cause to uphold with other persons.

And yet he is not just flying off in one tangent after another which can result only in distraction and disintegration. Rather he lives from the center of his being and guides his behavior from a core of ongoing purpose as a centralizing principle. Secure in this inner core of vitality he need not be ego-defensive, but open and outreaching to meet other persons on their ground and acknowledge the merit of their viewpoints. He is not carried away by claims of others, for he knows the value of his own intentions and has no need to surrender, though willing at any time to modify them in view of new perspectives. This behavior is neither one-sided self-seeking or self-denying, but a continuing balance

[4] *Man's Freedom* (New Haven, Conn.: Yale University Press, 1950), p. 170.
[5] Allport, *Becoming*, p. 90.

of outgoing and incoming action. A circle is repetitive in returning only to the starting point, while the spiral of true growth ascends by coming to higher integration.

This is what we find in religious growth, not merely the repetition of childhood experiences or regression to the comfort of infantile dependence, as in neurotic manifestations. Full-grown religion is far more than its early beginnings; it is not reducible to an anxious cry in the night. "Hence the developed personality will not fabricate his religion out of some emotional fragment but will seek a theory of Being in which all fragments are meaningfully ordered." [6] In this way religion contributes wholeness to man's becoming.

Growth may of course be arrested in one way or another. Freud found the root of neuroses to be a fixation upon some object in the childhood of the patient. The object of this fixation comes to have an absolute value which he can neither escape nor reduce to moderation. This may be viewed in a religious context, as Daim[7] does, by seeing the fixation as "idolization" (Verabsolutierung). This is the act of treating a relative object as if it were absolute. When a person is fixated to an object in his past as a false absolute, he has a mistaken view both of reality and of his own needs. He therefore continues to act from a distorted view of life in devoting his energies to some childish attachment which is irrelevant to the contemporary situation. Instead of addressing himself to a well-oriented futuristic goal, he is preoccupied intensely with an outdated demand of childhood.

The religious meaning of idolatry is equivalent to the absolute fixation upon some object of relative value. It is a tragic example of arrested growth, in which the longing for salvation is diverted upon some lesser object unworthy of such devotion and incapable of effecting the needed salvation. Psychoanalysis seeks to remove the fixation by transference into a contemporary relationship where a new and better solution may be found. The disorienting and debasing character of the fixation is the inability of the neurotic to live up to his real self, or fulfill his true mission as a mature human being because his temporal development is so arrested. By making the patient conscious of his fixation the longing for salvation is intensified into a new crisis. The feeling of being imprisoned, disoriented, and debased reaches a climax

[6] *Ibid.,* p. 94.

[7] Wilfried Daim, "On Depth-Pyschology and Salvation," *Journal of Psychotherapy as a Religious Process,* II (January, 1955) , 24-37.

in which the patient experiences a kind of hell. He struggles more violently to break the fixation in the supportive relationship with the therapist, to gain more freedom to live in the present.

Yet he concludes that even the best psychoanalysis can only be a partial salvation. It finds its larger meaning in the metaphysical process of total salvation by a divine Savior. For man longs for a true absolute and has an undeniable need for orientation to the ultimate Being. When he idolizes a finite object he represses this need and denies himself the larger fulfillment which he actually seeks. Instead of God, the idol—the false absolute—now dominates his distorted values and leads to inadequate reaction to reality as a whole. Salvation in the ultimate sense beyond any partial adjustment calls for a reorientation and re-dedication of the person to the infinite God, which opens to him a healing and recovery of perspective that is a resurrection, or new birth, into a larger life.

Every person is limited by his relationships. They may close in upon him like a prison house in a bondage of fixation, with stifling and constraining finality. When the past overreaches the present he is not free to assert his potentialities toward real and contemporary goals. But when his relations are open, they invite growth and confident exploration. They have a releasing quality that permits the person to exercise real choices and transcend earlier limitations. The first steps to a new life may require the faith and understanding of a resourceful counselor who offers to go a part of the journey with him. The total salvation so earnestly desired, however, will require an ultimate confrontation with the Creator, whose infinite love and unfailing redemptive purpose are devoted to this becoming.

2. Belonging

Man is cruciate. Standing erect among all the creatures of earth, with arms outstretched, the light may fall upon him so as to make the shadow of a cross. He will appear in other postures according to his mood and the intention of his striving in each particular situation. For he is a versatile creature of many interests and varied activities. We may look at the man from many different points of view, but from the light of this study of personality and religion he is cruciform. This is to say that he bears in himself the dimensions of a cross, which are essential to his very nature.

This is more than body form: it is the structure of his nature as personality. Within himself is a meeting of opposites: first in the mating of genes; then in the subdivision of cells and their development into organic structures with diverse functions, yet interdependent upon each other to maintain life. The psychic nature of man is even more complex in the meeting of opposing tendencies seeking unity without loss of diversity. Every attempt to portray the nature of personality falls short of the intricate character of his actual being. There is an insoluble mystery here, an irreversible complexity of human nature that is not reducible to a simple formula.

In the preceding chapter we have taken a dimensional view of personality, the better to comprehend this complexity. Four dimensions have been noted, which you will quickly agree is a crude oversimplification. We know from our own fleeting experience that our living complexity is too great to be encompassed in any series of descriptions we may offer. Why then have we come to rest with four dimensions? Because a quarternity is a convenient symbol to represent the meeting of opposites. No symbol can be adequate to the subject in all its complexity, but this symbol of cross in circle (known in the East as *mandala*) has a universal character whatever may be the local meanings invested in it. Like the compass which guides the traveler anywhere on this planet whatever language he may speak, it can indicate directions in which a person may go.

We have recognized that man is a creature of relationships. The person he is at the center of his being we have designated "I" to denote the subject of these relationships. As he knows himself in his inner experience he is a lonely person unique in his own individuality. This may give one a sense of isolation as set apart from all others who have their separate centers of experience. And this feeling of separation we have seen to be one of the tragic dilemmas of his existence. He may want to be independent and do all in his power to be self-sufficient, yet he is not, and eventually to his sorrow he learns that he has only deceived himself and hastened his own downfall by contending that he is self-contained. For his life hangs upon his relationships and in the final outcome to be isolated is to die.

This truth may not dawn upon him immediately. Man does have inner resources to a greater extent than any other creature, and he can choose in one way or another what to do with his life. He can assert his independence in useful and creative ways so long as he works through his relationships. But whenever he scorns them defiantly and begins to drop this one or break that relationship or cut himself off from his connections without replacing them, he reduces himself in vital losses that become suicidal whether abruptly or gradually as a living death.

Due to his interdependent complexity man lives in perpetual crisis. He must belong to a whole that is larger than himself, for otherwise he is doomed to perish. At the center of his subjective experience he knows himself as uniquely different and he naturally wants to be himself. He is one person who wants to be one. And yet his complex diversities thwart his unity, and the meeting of opposites must always be his peculiar problem. As a creature of multiple relationships he is pulled in many directions, and wherever he turns he will undergo the tensions of diversity. Suffering this "torn-to-pieces-hood" (as William James called it), the person will seek to integrate his diverse relationships into living unity. But then as he struggles to unify his dynamic goal strivings, he finds them in conflict with each other and resisting his efforts to bring them into working harmony. He is caught in a network of entangling contradictions that distort his perceptions and put him at war within his own personality.

I am related to Me as a biological organism surging with vital impulses and needs demanding satisfaction. This dimension, which Freud named the id, he characterized as a seething cauldron of libidinous drives, sexual excitement, appetitive cravings, and aggressive urges to reckless assertion and gratification. These drives he found in conflict with another dimension of ideal norms and standards which he named the superego. Between these unyielding oppositions the ego seeks to find some basis for unification and by devious ways represses one and restrains the other, projects here and sublimates there, in the best compromises he can find to settle the conflict. These dimensions we have aligned upon the vertical axis of the cross to indicate the upward thrust of individual development from the primitive impulses of vitality toward the ideal goal of mature aspiration personalized as Thou. (See Fig. III, p. 233.)

I am also related to It as a creature who depends upon a physical environment as the ground of my incoming resources and outgoing activity. Here again insatiable desires to possess and incorporate values from the environment may result in behavior typical of exploitation, to use for my own pleasure and purpose whatever I can seize from the world around me. Belonging in the possessive mood seeks to extend the area of mine by appropriating ever more to my domain. Other persons may also be taken possessively into the area of mine, or excluded therefrom, resulting in violent conflicts over human rights. My relation to things will then conflict with my relation to persons. These dimensions relating I to It and We are aligned upon the horizontal axis of the cross to indicate the outward reach of personal growth along inclusive directions. (See Fig. III, p. 233.)

Personal life is therefore crucial. Every meeting is a crisis, more so than we often realize, even though our anxiety may reveal a foreboding glimpse of impending contest. It might be easier to cope with these crises if we could give undivided attention to one meeting at a time. But our meetings coincide at the same time on different sectors and we are confronted with simultaneous demands for multiple responses. Like a man surrounded by friends or enemies, he may face one only by turning his back on the others, exposing his inability to deal equally with their many demands. And even while frantically trying to meet these external relations, he is struggling within himself to cope with the conflicting desires and uncertainties of his own contradictions. His predicament is both critical and chronic.

In such a predicament, choices have to be made. They are laid upon us by the very necessity of this crisis in which the choice of a person may be decisive. Is the contest worth the struggle or shall I give up in despair? Shall I seek to save myself or to give myself vicariously for others? Shall I resist the evil and fight against the enemies, or decide to love and forgive them? Shall I meet this alone in heroic independence or consecrate my life to God with whom and for whom I will bear the full cost of doing his will?

For two thousand years men have turned toward a man on a cross who faced these dilemmas and made these decisive choices. When threatened with ignominy and death he did not despair but went steadfastly forward. Confronted with a crucial choice he chose to save others rather than himself. Seized by mortal enemies he did not fight back but loved and forgave them. Wrestling with this costly alternative he decided not to seek his own will but to consecrate himself in life and death to the will of the unfailing and everloving Thou.

He called himself Son of Man, and well he might as the prototype of all men, for whom he bore their griefs and afflictions in vicarious compassion. He belonged to them as their representative in the tragic yet glorious predicament of man. The cross was his own; it was made for him according to his dimensions, and he accepted it as his mission to complete the work of God in man. Stretched upon the cross he suffered the full measure of human conflict, yet he would not give up his mission of relating opposites in creative unification. He knew the anguish of body and spirit, deserted by friends and nailed by enemies to the cross, yet he did not shrink therefrom. He saw the soldiers casting lots for his garments and realized the bitter indignity of things preferred to persons in a world of exploitation and possession. He felt the violent impact of prejudice and hate when scornful men hurl their fury against other men. He stood on the verge of lonely separation from God in the terror of those awful moments when he was apparently defeated and forsaken, yet he crossed over the chasm of despair to the unfailing love of God to whom he committed his spirit.

The cross of Jesus stands for the crisis in our personal existence. Every person in some way is stretched upon a cross by the inherent structure of his being. For he is a creature of dynamic relationships so deeply intersecting as to keep him forever going and coming in the restless search for fulfillment. He is torn apart by his strivings in many directions, yet involved in them all to the extent he cannot let go or give up the quest for wholeness. So he seeks to extend the range of his life across one boundary after another until he empties himself in outgoing activities. Then feeling hollow at the center he may cast off one relation after another in desperate efforts to unify the shreds of his fractional selfhood. But this egocentric striving shrinks the boundaries of life and leaves him isolated as well as empty and forlorn in the tragic defeat of alienation which is known as sin.

The saving work of Jesus was to relate men to God by eternally creative love. Suffering in his own person the worst that men could do to him, he did not retaliate but forgave them in undying love. This love he insisted was not his own but the creative love of God overflowing through him to them. Even at the depth of his sorrow when his cause appeared to be utterly lost, he found, amazingly, that God had not forsaken him, but suffered there with him upon the cruel cross. His spirit was revived in the hour of death, as he ascended this upward dimension in the consuming love of God. The eternal dynamic of this love overflows to other persons with a creative renewal of life in ever-widening relationships. In speaking of this creative event as atonement, we see therein the at-one-ment of God and man which draws man to man in a new oneness of forgiving love.

Wherever this occurs we discover belonging in a larger sense. The creative work of this love has this aim: that they may all be one.

The glory which thou hast given me I have given them, that they may be one even as we are one, I in them and thou in me, that they may become perfectly one, so that the world may know that thou hast sent me and hast loved them even as thou hast loved me. (John 17:22-23.)

There is no coercion in this love. No person can force another person to give him love, for love is an act of essential freedom. The deepest meaning of love is the act of free choice by which a person chooses a person. And when a person gives love by voluntary choice, who can stop him from loving? But the unity of force cannot endure, for it is a chain no stronger than its weakest link. To force another is to break the link of love, leaving nothing but convenience, which of all conditions is most temporary; it lasts only so long as it is convenient. Eros, or self-seeking love, is as temporary as the self-giving love is enduring, because the latter is voluntary and renewed again in every faithful choice. Agape is the New Testament love of God which overflows into the voluntary giving revealed in Jesus. By choosing this love a person may rise above the vicious circle of self-seeking which turns his striving back upon himself, and may enter upon a new course of self-giving which is eternally creative and faithfully outgoing for the sake of other persons.

Persons become creative through belonging. For no one is self-sufficient; and the way of growth is through enlarging relationships. The desire to be one is defeated by standing apart; it is accomplished by meeting other persons through self-giving love in which to become a part of a larger whole, i.e., a community of persons.

The intriguing mystery of life is that our belonging is greater than we know. The little person, whether he be six or sixty, is the one of local relationships. The little girl who said to me, "Why, I know almost everything myself, and I'm only in the first grade," was astonished that a grown man could still be going to school to learn more. The man of sixty who can find nothing to keep him growing, when he retires from the business which occupied his energies, will decline and die from acute loss of belonging. But the intrepid explorer will take no boundary as final; he will not be contained by confining walls or stopped in his tracks by fear of the unknown.

The genius of discovery in science as well as religion is to see the particulars of this locale in relation to a universal system of greater wholeness. In such discovery no event is complete in itself but has meaning as related to larger perspectives. Much of life is engaged in proximate striving for the next meal or the next task to be done, but this will be empty and repetitive routine unless one can lift the eyes to a more distant goal and see how each step leads on to some more ultimate meaning. Is it not the ultimate we seek most persistently through every intermediate step? So it is that human life is forever restless, pressing over one boundary after another to fulfill this unquenchable thirst for wholeness.

The natural sciences intend to stop short of the ultimate mysteries. For purposes of clarification, scientists delimit a field of investigation. Their task is to reduce complex data to a few simple principles, as when Einstein brought the space-time-energy of physics into a unifying mathematical formula. Under these ascetic restrictions has come astonishing progress, by submitting a limited unit of operation to hypothesis, verification, and application. In our optimistic moods we are comforted to manage a segment of the unknown and reduce the mystery to human knowledge. Yet the reality we seek to know is ever more than our scientific theories and simple formulas. If we forget this we practice self-deception, as scientific dogmatists and arrogant sophisticates, in the easy fallacy of mistaking the part for the whole. "Our horizons have shrunk," as one scientist declared. "We are so encapsulated in ourselves and our own concerns as to be cut off from the universe." [8]

To be aware of limits is a humbling experience essential to learning. But to settle down complacently before these limitations with no curiosity for what is beyond them is to surrender the vocation of truth-seeking. The scientist as scientist will remain within the delimitations of his particular science, but as a truth-seeking human being he will need to ask more ultimate questions.

The psychologist as psychologist cannot speak of God in supernatural terms if he has already restricted his scientific operations to the field of human behavior in the dimensions of natural science. Yet as a person he has a transcendent capacity to look beyond self-imposed limits and to seek the ultimate meaning of life. He may clearly see that he as a person is related to some reality beyond the human scene investigated by the behavioral sciences. He recognizes with the astron-

[8] Alphonse Maeder, "A New Concept of the Psychotherapist's Role," *Journal of Psychotherapy as a Religious Process,* II (January, 1955), 45.

omer how far his universe extends beyond the planet earth and the race of men who dwell precariously upon it. He knows that physicists have renounced materialism as a myth of the past century, that reality is ultimately more than anything we can reduce to human observation and measure. Yet everything seems to be related to everything else in our universe, and he will not deny the systematic orderliness of this vast reality where causes and effects go on progressively in a network of dynamic relationships.

If he has meditated deeply upon the complexities of this reality within and beyond the human venture, he is not likely to be dogmatic in hasty generalizations. He will not feel inclined to hoist the atheistic flag, for he realizes that infinite knowledge is required to say there is no God. And he is quite ready to admit that his knowledge is not infinite but finite. For this reason he is more inclined to be agnostic, cautiously affirming that he has not yet concluded his search, and is therefore seeking to pursue it with open mind. He may recall with Voltaire that there are no atheists, but only iconoclasts who smash the idols man sets before him by his own invention. Ultimate Being cannot be denied; it is rather our view of it that is to be corrected as true or false. If the psychologist denies, he refers to human folly; and if he affirms, it is man's own hypothesis to hold in humble yet persisting exploration.

It may, after all, be a contradiction to seek what is beyond science by scientific means. It may in fact be a better procedure for a scientist to employ his scientific method to pursue limited goals within the sphere of the natural order as scientists agree to perceive it, and then to claim as a person the right and responsibility to pursue religious goals by methods that move beyond the field of scientific operations. This need not fall into a dualism of double truth or parallel lines which never meet, if a person will seek to relate natural and supernatural in his own experience as emerging discovery. Whatever we know as familiar and local enough to use as a means or instrument to our purpose, we call natural. It has finite meaning and value as subordinate to a purpose that goes beyond it. But whenever we discover a Being that transcends our designs and evidently operates from a larger purpose, not subordinate to our desire but acting from a higher center of intention beyond our own, this we call supernatural. Such a Being has infinite meaning and value that goes beyond our finite use or comprehension.

If I go to work as a scientist my job is to reduce the unknown to manageable and predictable simplicity in order to control its complexity for human purposes. This is the legitimate procedure of a natural science. But as a person I must go beyond science to deal with the ultimate considerations of what Being requires or expects of me. In relation to things a person is supernatural, for his purposes transcend the nature of physical objects. In relation to ultimate Being a person is finite, for he cannot control or use what transcends his own nature. But even as he is finite, man has infinite potentialities, for he is able to transcend himself in gathering intentions of the past and projecting them to future goals. Knowing himself as finite, yet he takes up particulars, one by one, and relates them into perspectives of whole meaning. He is not able to renounce his ultimates nor to deal with them scientifically. In his ethical obligations to achieve the good as well as in his religious aspirations to wrestle with and devote himself to a larger destiny, he will have to reach out beyond his natural science. He will need a religious methodology to discover the full meaning of religion irreducible to sense data or scientific categories.

To fulfill his responsibility as a person, therefore, no man can escape becoming a philosopher and theologian. He belongs to an expanding circle of relationships that move out beyond the orbits of local events in the here and now. Even while he experiences the present moment he perceives a larger series of related meanings and values. As he dresses in the morning for the work of the day, or prepares for a journey of extended duration, he will be relating himself to the beyond. Even in his laboratory, peering through the microscope and searching for the meaning of a section of tissue, the scientist is setting the local item in a larger context. He may not fully realize how much his larger frame of reference is contributing to his presuppositions and hypotheses. Before he entered the laboratory he had a philosophy from which he approached his work, and when he turns the key at the end of the day he starts off for other goals in view of his overall principles. The person is forever related to these ultimate beliefs which govern his behavior and perceptions in every situation.

3. Being

I must ultimately confront Being. Whatever scientific limitations I may place upon my field of operations are like a room into which I enter for some purpose, in which to eat or sleep, to talk with my family, or to study in quiet meditation. And then when that task is over, I go on to the outdoor world where boundaries are crossed and life is viewed in other perspectives. So every local situation is temporary until we move on to larger dimensions and more ultimate relationships. Being is confronted in the small room as well as the open field, for each moment is set in time and eternity, while each event is a meeting of many dimensions. Wherever I stand it is possible to turn slowly

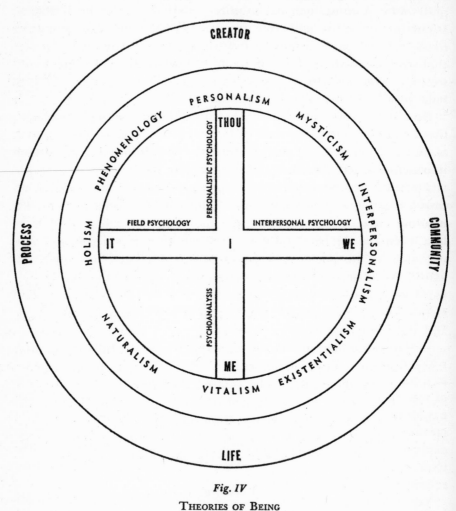

Fig. IV

THEORIES OF BEING

around and view the whole panorama in successive directions. From this center of experience as each person perceives his relationships, he confronts Being and seeks to interpret this meaning in some perspective.

In Fig. IV on p. 274, we find a series of outlooks toward Being along the directions of psychologies we have been exploring. Each psychology of personality moves out toward a philosophy which acts as a frame of reference in seeking to understand the ultimate meaning of life. Some psychologists are more vocal than others about their philosophy. Pure psychologists may even deny they have a philosophy, as tantamount to betraying the certainty of a delimited natural science to the diffused uncertainty of boundless speculation. And yet if a psychologist is to gain self-understanding and make the unconscious conscious, he will not want to hide his philosophy but will bring it to the light of critical examination.

How do psychoanalysts view the ultimate Being which they confront? We may infer from what they say that *Life* is the dynamic cause of human behavior. The energy upsurging in personality Freud names libido, to indicate the lusty and irrepressible biotic urges striving for satisfaction. That these life impulses are basically erotic he could never doubt, and we agree that whatever more they become they are not less vital than psychosexuality. This will to live, to create and preserve life, is the insistent demand that life fulfill its potentialities. The life urge may be blunted by disappointment, repressed by anxiety, or even denied when tortured by remorse and guilt. But though hidden it is never stamped out or extinguished, however it may be diverted, so long as life continues. As the will to live declines, the life itself cannot survive but perishes with it.

In this view of Life as the ultimate we have a philosophy of vitalism, which enthrones the life principle as the real and undefeatable power at work in personality. To Freud, in the context of his scientific frame of reference, this was associated with naturalism[9]—the hypothesis that nature is all there is to find, with no expectation of gaining by other means what natural science cannot give. In this naturalistic position he distrusted religion as a fantasy of wishing for what is illusory rather than real, obsessed rather than sensible. He did not distinguish neurotic religion from mature religion.

Yet as exponent of the unconscious he is associated with existentialism, in accenting the irrationality of man and the pathos of existence

[9] For a review of these philosophies, see *A History of Philosophical Systems*, ed. Vergilius Ferm (New York: Philosophical Library, 1950).

as he struggles with irreconcilable conflicts which he can modify but never resolve. By his devotion to the individual person through psychotherapy and research, he emphasized the uniqueness of concrete individuality rather than the common denominator of abstract universals. He repudiated the attempt to construct a complete world view by the self-sufficient intellect but dealt analytically with whatever existence he encountered in man himself. In this approach, he seems to be congenial with the vitalism of Nietzsche, Bergson, and Dilthey; and, though differing, not uncongenial with the existentialism of Kierkegaard.

Coming to Lewin and the field psychologists, we hear little of ultimate Being, for they are busily engaged in exploring the local scene, particularly the relation of a person to his nearest environment. Life space is the totality of possible events in the interaction of a person and his immediate psychological environment, beyond which is the "foreign hull." Yet no person or force is isolated; every event is related to other events in larger context. The total situation is determinative and must always be consulted to grasp the meaning of individual behavior. What we find in the field theory is a holistic philosophy, seeking everywhere the whole pattern of coexisting forces by which to perceive the relationships of each event. Only a system as a whole can be true or false, adequate or inadequate, to empirical facts. If we do not yet have the knowledge to determine this whole system, then we must construct a tentative field and work step by step toward larger understanding of the Gestalt in which any part depends upon every other part.

In developing this holistic approach, Kurt Lewin was cognizant of the theory of relativity as developed by Einstein and Maxwell. He was also conversant with the mathematical theory of topology and found its principles useful in exploring part-whole relations. He began to apply these principles to psychological research and eventually to call his theory topological psychology,[10] indicating that each event belongs to a larger whole of interacting forces to be studied in relation to each other. With this concept of dynamic fields, he approached every situation of individual and group behavior.

This view is akin to the holism of such philosophers as Whitehead and Wieman who subordinate the person to a whole process of inter-

[10] *Principles of Topological Psychology.*

acting forces. The Being is evidently a *process* or field of ever-moving tension systems which determine the individual. At one side this holistic philosophy is supported by a naturalism which views the system of nature as the ultimate frame of reference. At the other side is phenomenology, which develops a system of constructs or pure psychology as transcendental to worldly perceiving (Husserl). The topological space of Lewin is not the physical environment but the symbolic or mathematical concept of contemporary relations. The theorist does not deal with objective reality directly but with conceptual images to represent the facts of the psychological world open to influences from outside.

Personalistic psychology implies a philosophy of personalism. To avoid confusing these frames of reference, Allport as psychologist separates his position from the philosophy of personalism. Other personalists, like Stern or Brightman, hold their psychology in the perspective of a personalistic philosophy. When followed across the boundaries of psychology this trail is evidently moving toward a view of ultimate Being as *Creator*. If the Creator exercises functional autonomy, we may infer the characteristics of personality such as intelligent foresight, creative purpose, and ability to organize raw materials into whole designs. Yet to personify Being may mean to fall into the anthropomorphic fallacy of creating God in our own image. The personalist recognizes that every form of knowledge, scientific as well as theological, must project the frame of our perception upon the objective reality we seek to understand. In humility we must remember that whatever we perceive is relative to the observer as Kant insisted, and what is out there apart from the observer (*Ding-an-Sich*) we can only infer from the categories of our finite experience.

To transcend these limitations and avow that we do not confine Being to our halting categories or make God like us as one of a class, we may refer to the Creator as Ultra-Person. He is greater than any person we know in the poverty of our finitude, yet he cannot be less than the highest and richest potentialities we find in personality. As the Ultra-Person he is transcendent above his creation, yet also immanent in his ability to communicate and participate with finite persons in their strivings to achieve values.

Personalism affirms the worth and dignity of persons above things and impersonal events. It is supported on one side by phenomenology, which dignifies the person as knower with capacity to construct theory and perceive meanings that transcend sensuous perceptions. On the other side it is congenial with mysticism, which finds spirit more real than matter and seeks by immediate experience to meet Being in religious communion of spirit with spirit. In this sense, mystics like Schweitzer and Buber may be dualistic (person communing with Ultra-Person) ; yet other mystics, as in Hinduism, may be nondualistic and pantheistic in believing that I am Thou. A pantheist might associate himself with holistic philosophy in holding the Process more ultimate than the person. A dualistic mystic seeking communion of I and Thou would be congenial with interpersonalism.

Sullivan has not been vocal about these ultimate questions, as he was working within a naturalistic frame of reference. Yet he was evidently moving in the direction of *Community* as the ultimate consideration of his interpersonalism. Beginning as he did with the relation of person to person in a two-group, he moved out in the final period of his life to concern for the world community as he worked with UNESCO and the World Federation for Mental Health. Other interpersonalists like Moreno and Kunkel, as well as the present writer, have tried to articulate a philosophy of interpersonalism.

Moreno[11] portrays God as the Father of all, who freely gives his creative energy to all creatures in every event and experience of spontaneous relationships. Spontaneity everywhere arises from the creative activity of God moving through interpersonal relations. Interpersonal theology is cocreationism, for where God is there spontaneity comes to most creative expression, and this is the basis for all experimental procedures where persons explore their relationships with other persons. As we rise in spontaneity we become cocreators with the Creator in our sphere of interaction.

Kunkel[12] denies that psychology is a natural science, but rather it is a philosophical science which from his viewpoint he is willing to call "theocentric." In his religious psychology the ego is the sham-center of life; the real self is not I but we. Our true self is a religious experience, yet more than our conscious personality; it is also the creativity of the Creator working in and through the person. He who truly finds himself finds God. From I, growth moves to We, and then to He.

[11] Jacob L. Moreno, *Das Testament des Vaters,* published in 1920, reissued as *The Words of the Father* in 1941, revised as *The Psychodrama of God* (New York: Beacon House, 1947).

[12] *In Search of Maturity.*

"There is no experience of God without the experience of the human We-relationship." [13] Our obligations toward ourselves and others are not contradictory, for as we mature we seek with others the highest fulfillment of our aspirations in the positive relationships of community.

This is not pantheism, for persons are real though interdependent. As persons confront each other with reverent appreciation, they enhance the value of their relationships in a community of mutual respect and love. God is the ultimate Creator of the cosmic community of persons. For it is by the religious experience of meeting the infinite Thou in reverent devotion that we discover the potential value in every finite thou. In this experience interpersonalism is supported on one side by ethical mysticism. On the other side it may find something congenial in existentialism, which insists that the real is greater than the rational (contra Hegel), and the person is as profound as the mystery of existence in all its dimensions. It is no wonder that existentialists emphasize different aspects of existence, from the tragic dilemmas of Sartre and "no exit," to the heroic affirmation of theistic Being in Tillich. Common to all is their discovery of the deeper significance of subjectivity congenial with the person-to-person dimension of interpersonalism, even while returning to complete the circle by affirming the irrational depth dimension of psychoanalysis.

Obviously, we do not exhaust or adequately expound the logical implications of these theories by circumnavigating them in this cursory way. It might appear that each of the four dimensions has a different logic by which to proceed. Psychoanalysis employs a reductive logic by which the complexities of human behavior are reduced to the basic Life principle, or libido. Field theory employs an inductive logic by which each event is referred to a larger context, or Process, i.e., a force field of dynamic wholeness. Personalism employs a productive logic by which the diverse energies and motivations of life attain functional autonomy in a maturity of creative integration which indicates a Creator as ultimate. Interpersonalism employs a conductive logic by which to validate the relations of persons with persons in Community.

It is also obvious that we do not exhaust religious experiences by one of these dimensions alone. To demonstrate the diversity of religious experience, we might locate the founders of different religions on this

[13] *Ibid.,* p. viii.

circle design, or mandala of four dimensions. Buddha employed the reductive logic of psychoanalysis in reducing the complexities of suffering life to the basic demand of insatiable desire, which he sought to control at its source by renunciation. His way of peace was motivated by compassion for the sufferings of others and his creative decision to change the law of karma by sacrificial devotion. In the first austerity of self-denial this enlightenment might appear negative; but as he came to his disciples and they taught other disciples, Buddhism has expanded from Hinayana (lesser vehicle) to Mahayana (greater vehicle) and become a religion of merciful kindness and community service.

Lao-tze employed the inductive logic of field theory in seeking the Tao, or principle of reason in nature. Believing implicitly that nature is good, he taught the *wu-wei* doctrine of noninterference with natural processes. Discerning that nature is greater in scope than what appears to the senses, he sought to follow the Tao from the local to the universal, and to relate the single event to the onmoving destiny of the whole. We know little of Lao-tze as a historic person, except the legend that as he was starting on a westward journey, he was persuaded to write down the sage wisdom contained in the *Tao Tê Ching*. But the religious contribution of Taoism has been to mingle with Buddhism and Confucianism and thereby to enrich the culture of China with a creative tolerance, to accept and appreciate the power of dynamic repose in the relations of heaven and earth, and of man with his fellow men.

Confucious followed the interpersonal dimension and devoted his energies to improving human relations. His creative contribution was to gather up the ancient wisdom of China and systematize it in the Five Classics, to which were added the Four Books edited by his disciples to include his own sayings. It was his genius to show that persons are to respect each other by honorable and faithful relationships. Taking the family as the basic pattern of human life, he sought to regulate the relation of the child to his father, of younger brother to older brother, of wife to husband, of friend to friend, and citizen to ruler. These are mutual responsibilities, and to regulate them he developed the law of reciprocity—that each person should do to others only what he would want others to do to him—and thereby we may live in a responsible society where all will be brothers.

Moses was confronted by a message from a burning bush that called him to deliver his people from Egyptian bondage and to lead them

toward a promised land. His religious dimension was theistic personalism and he founded Judaism upon a covenant between the Creator
and his people. His God was a transcendent Ultra-Person who offered
them a theocracy in which if they would obey his laws, he would bless
and multiply them. The keynote of this religion is ethical monotheism,
with unfaltering devotion to the functional autonomy of the Eternal
Creator. "Hear, O Israel: the Lord our God is one Lord: and thou
shalt love the Lord thy God with all thine heart, and with all thy
soul, and with all thy might." (Deut. 6:4-5 K.J.V.) "Thou shalt love
thy neighbour as thyself." (Lev. 19:18 K.J.V.) The creative upsurge of
this people has been one of the great religious contributions of mankind, giving birth to two other world religions. (Matt. 22:37-40).

Of these, Islam was founded by Mohammed, who acknowledged the
Old Testament and gave his followers another testament, the Koran.
In his teaching we have a lofty view of the same transcendent Creator
who cares for his people on earth and expects of them obedience to his
will. Every person is subject to the one god Allah and will find blessed-
ness by faithful prayer and loyal service to him. Inspired by a mounting
enthusiasm, the faithful have found in this ethical monotheism a motivation and meaning to answer the riddles and enlarge the potentialities
of human existence. They are ardent personalists in their devotion to
the autonomous Creator whose self-originating purpose and power are
the ultimate resource of the growing life that is seeking maturity by
conscious integration. Zoroaster founded his religion also in this dimension where the transcendent God contends against the forces of evil.

The founder of Christianity is not easy to locate upon one of these
dimensions, for he actually pulls them all together into a remarkable
integration. We shall, therefore, place him at the center of the circle.
This may well be due to my ethnocentric prejudice, and I will be the
first to grant the possibility. For no one can escape his cultural heritage,
and there is no reason to expect that I will not be influenced by mine.
The reader will need to keep in mind that I speak as a Christian, and
will constantly make allowance for my orientation.

Jesus is symbolized by the cross because he stretched himself upon it
and identified his being with all of the human dimensions. At the foot
of the cross is Life; and Jesus declared, "I came that they may have
life, and have it abundantly" (John 10:10). He did not despise the
body with its biological hungers, nor did he consider the feet as less

than the head, for he stooped to wash his disciples' feet and healed the ills of the body as of equal concern with the mind.

As we face Jesus on the cross, one of his arms stretches along the I-It dimension relating the person to his impersonal environment. He declined to worship the kingdom of world power or to let himself be made king of an earthly kingdom, yet he knew the pangs of physical hunger and acknowledged the right of all to be fed. Affirming that man shall not live by bread alone, yet he taught his disciples to pray, "Give us this day our daily bread," and not to neglect sharing that bread with others. At the last supper when he broke the bread and gave his disciples to eat, he also fed the enemy who was to betray him. He gave himself freely and completely to meet the needs of those who hungered for bread and more than bread.

The other arm of Jesus stretches out to the thief hanging upon another cross. In fact both arms reach out to suffering men on either side, with whom he suffers as intensely as they, and whose sins and sorrows he takes upon himself, with forgiving love and the undying hope that "today you will be with me in Paradise" (Luke 23:43). The I-We dimension is witnessed by his life as well as the verbal invitation he uttered. "Come to me all who labor and are heavy-laden, and I will give you rest" (Matt 11:28); and "Greater love has no man than this, that a man lay down his life for his friends" (John 15:13).

At the head of the cross Jesus was looking toward God the Father, as the son he was, perplexed in anguish to cry out, "My God, why!" In this cry he spoke for every man, woman, or child who suffers the distress of anxious finitude and bitter loss. He was alone on that cross, and the loneliness was almost beyond human endurance. Yet he was not alone, for he found God there with him suffering the agony of that crucial hour. And because his perception of God was undimmed and his faith unshattered, he could say with his last breath, "Father, into thy hands I commit my spirit!" (Luke 23:46).

It appears to me that Jesus is at the center of the circle, in this way drawing together the meaning of its several dimensions into one unified perception of human existence in relation to ultimate Being. Life and the Creator of life, dynamic Process and the Community which persons achieve through interpersonal relationships—all these dimensions are joined in the cross of Jesus. If this is true other religions will not be reduced to rivals but enhanced as great historical streams of eternal life, through which the loving Creator reaches out to his many children.

Ultimate Being in fact surrounds us, and wherever we turn or in whatever direction we go, there is a meeting in which some revelation answers the honest and faithful searcher. Man's quest for wholeness takes him on many journeys pressing across one boundary after another. The restless activism so characteristic of western man demonstrates the earnest devotion with which he engages in the quest. But there is a compulsive drive here, an almost frantic effort to escape, as if to flee from the emptiness within himself. In America we have produced more goods than we can consume, and surrounded ourselves with marvelous machines unknown before in human history. And yet the rewards of our labors are too external to satisfy the inner need of the human soul.

This we may note as the tragic fallacy of our secular civilization. It comes to give us stones for bread, and to clutch the husks as the chief prize while neglecting the deeper spiritual nutriment we hunger for within. When we turn to its religious institutions for guidance we find them also preoccupied with externals. We enter magnificent temples, richly appointed with historic symbols, where rituals are performed in ceremonious precision by vested choirs and by clergy who lead in the vocal repetition of traditional creeds and formularies. Here is the form of religion to recite in unison as a mighty congregation speaking with one voice that all may hear and tremble at the power of this institution.

But what is the trembling vitality of religious experience? In the temple vision of Isaiah it was not the majesty of the Creator high and lifted up above the smoke of incense, but the personal visitation that brought the fire from the altar to the lips of the worshiper, to enter within and change his inner motivation. The religious quest for wholeness is not met by adding external things to the historic collection, and wherever religions multiply externals they offer substitutes for the genuine experience of new life. What we seek in religious discovery is a meeting within, a visitation of ultimate Being at the center of personality.

No founder of a great religion was occupied with externals; in fact, it was the externalism of religion he was protesting against and setting aside for a deeper and more vital, truly centered experience. He was not dealing with life at the periphery but insisting we come to the heart of it, for out of the heart are the issues of life (Prov. 4:23). In this sense Jesus is not alone at the center of the circle design, for other religious seers are turning there too, in search of deeper self-understanding.

In his search for ultimate Being, man has crossed one frontier after another, yet his finite knowledge is a tiny circle of light in a vast and boundless mystery. The religious person does not wait for perfect knowledge to comprehend all mysteries. From his humility he is willing to receive God into his heart. To meet God at the center of life he responds in love to the Infinite Love.

BIBLIOGRAPHY

Alexander, Franz, and Ross, Helen, eds. *Dynamic Psychiatry*. University of Chicago Press, 1952.

Allport, Gordon W. *Becoming: Basic Considerations for a Psychology of Personality*. New Haven, Conn.: Yale University Press, 1955.

——. *The Individual and His Religion: A Psychological Interpretation*. New York: The Macmillan Co., 1950.

——. *The Nature of Personality*. Cambridge, Mass.: Addison-Wesley Publishing Co., Inc., 1950.

——. *The Nature of Prejudice*. Cambridge, Mass.: Addison-Wesley Publishing Co., Inc., 1954.

——. *Personality: A Psychological Interpretation*. New York: Henry Holt & Co., Inc., 1937.

Angyal, András. *Foundations for a Science of Personality*. New York: Commonwealth Fund, 1941.

Ansbacher, Heinz L. and Rowena R., eds. *The Individual Psychology of Alfred Adler*. New York: Basic Books, Inc., 1956.

Bertocci, Peter A. "Personality," *Encyclopedia of Psychology*. Ed. P. L. Harriman. New York: Philosophical Library, Inc., 1946.

Blake, R. R., and Ramsey, G. V., eds. *Perception: An Approach to Personality*. New York: Ronald Press Co., 1951.

Boisen, Anton T. *The Exploration of the Inner World*. New York: Harper & Bros., 1936.

——. *Religion in Crisis and Custom*. New York: Harper & Bros., 1955.

Bonthius, Robert H. *Christian Paths to Self-Acceptance*. New York: King's Crown Press, 1948.

Braatoy, Trygve. *Fundamentals of Psychoanalytic Technique*. New York: John Wiley & Sons, Inc., 1954.

Brand, H. *The Study of Personality*. New York: John Wiley & Sons, Inc., 1954.

Brennan, Robert E. *Thomistic Psychology: A Philosophic Analysis of the Nature of Man*. New York: The Macmillan Co., 1941.

Bretall, Robert W., ed. *A Kierkegaard Anthology*. Princeton, N.J.: Princeton University Press, 1946.

Brightman, Edgar S. *Personality and Religion*. New York: The Abingdon Press, 1934.

——. *Persons and Values*. Boston University Press, 1952.

——. *A Philosophy of Religion*. Englewood Cliffs, N.J.: Prentice-Hall, Inc., 1940.

Brunner, Emil. *Man in Revolt*. Tr. O. Wyon. Philadelphia: Westminster Press, 1947.

Buber, Martin. *I and Thou.* Tr. R. G. Smith. New York: Charles Scribner's Sons, 1937.

———. *Between Man and Man.* Tr. R. G. Smith. New York: The Macmillan Co., 1948.

Cantril, Hadley. *The "Why" of Man's Experience.* New York: The Macmillan Co., 1951.

Cartwright, Dorwin, and Zander, A. F., eds. *Group Dynamics: Research and Theory.* Evanston, Ill. Row, Peterson & Co., 1953.

De Forest, Izette. *The Leaven of Love.* New York: Harper & Bros., 1954.

DeWolf, L. H. *The Religious Revolt Against Reason.* New York: Harper & Bros., 1949.

Dollard, John, *et al. Frustration and Aggression.* New Haven, Conn.: Yale University Press, 1939.

———. and Miller, N. E. *Personality and Psychotherapy.* New York: McGraw-Hill Book Co., Inc., 1950.

English, O. S., and Pearson, G. H. J. *Emotional Problems of Living.* New York: W. W. Norton & Co., Inc., 1945; 1955.

Evans, Jean. *Three Men: An Experiment in the Biography of Emotion.* New York: Alfred A. Knopf, Inc., 1954.

Fenichel, Otto. *The Psychoanalytic Theory of Neurosis.* New York: W. W. Norton & Co., Inc., 1945.

Frankl, Viktor. *The Doctor and the Soul.* New York: Alfred A. Knopf, Inc., 1955.

Freud, Anna. *The Ego and the Mechanisms of Defence.* London: Hogarth Press, 1937.

Freud, Sigmund. *Autobiography.* Tr. J. Strachey. New York: W. W. Norton & Co., Inc., 1935.

———. *Beyond the Pleasure Principle.* Tr. James Strachey. London: Hogarth Press, 1955.

———. *Collected Papers.* 5 vols. Tr. J. Riviere, *et al.* London: Hogarth Press, 1924.

———. *The Ego and the Id.* Tr. J. Riviere. London: Hogarth Press, 1927.

———. *The Future of an Illusion.* Tr. W. D. Robson-Scott. London: Hogarth Press, 1928.

———. *New Introductory Lectures on Psycho-Analysis.* Tr. W. J. H. Sprott. London: Hogarth Press, 1933.

———. *An Outline of Psychoanalysis.* Tr. J. Strachey. London: Hogarth Press, 1949.

Fromm, Erich. *Man for Himself.* New York: Rinehart & Co., Inc., 1947.

———. *Psychoanalysis and Religion.* New Haven, Conn.; Yale University Press, 1950.

———. *The Art of Loving.* New York: Harper & Bros., 1956.

Hiltner, Seward. *The Counselor in Counseling.* New York and Nashville: Abingdon Press, 1952.

Horney, Karen. *Neurosis and Human Growth.* New York: W. W. Norton & Co., Inc., 1950.

———. *The Neurotic Personality of Our Time.* New York: W. W. Norton & Co., Inc., 1937.

———. *Our Inner Conflicts*. New York: W. W. Norton, & Co., Inc., 1945.

Howe, Reuel L. *Man's Need and God's Action*. Greenwich, Conn.: Seabury Press, Inc., 1953.

Hunt, J. McV., ed. *Personality and the Behavior Disorders*. 2 vols. New York: Ronald Press Co., 1944.

James, William. *Varieties of Religious Experience*. New York: Longmans Green & Co., 1902.

Johnson, Paul E. *Christian Love*. New York and Nashville: Abingdon Press, 1951.

———. *Psychology of Pastoral Care*. New York and Nashville: Abingdon Press, 1953.

———. *Psychology of Religion*. New York: and Nashville: Abingdon Press, 1945.

Jones, Ernest. *The Life and Work of Sigmund Freud*. 3 vols. New York: Basic Books, Inc., 1953-57.

Joy, Chas. R., ed. *Albert Schweitzer: An Anthology*. Boston: Beacon Press, Inc., 1947.

Jung, Carl G. *The Development of Personality*. New York: Pantheon Books, Inc., 1954.

———. *The Integration of the Personality*. Tr. S. M. Dell. New York: Farrar & Rinehart, Inc., 1939.

———. *Psychological Reflections: An Anthology*. Ed. Jolande Jacobi. New York: Pantheon Books, Inc., 1951.

———. *Psychological Types*. New York: Harcourt Brace & Co., Inc., 1923.

———. *Psychology and Religion*. New Haven, Conn.: Yale University Press, 1938.

Kaufmann, W. A. *Nietzsche*. Princeton, N.J.: Princeton University Press, 1950.

Kierkegaard, Søren. *The Concept of Dread*. Tr. W. Lowrie. Princeton, N.J.: Princeton University Press, 1944.

———. *The Sickness Unto Death*. Tr. Walter Lowrie. Princeton, N.J.: Princeton University Press, 1941.

Kluckhohn, Clyde K., and Murray, Henry A., eds. *Personality in Nature, Society, and Culture*. New York: Alfred A. Knopf, Inc., 1948; 1953.

Knight, R. P., and Friedman, C. R., eds. *Psychoanalytic Psychiatry and Psychology*. New York: International Universities Press, Inc., 1954.

Krech, David, and Klein, George S., eds. *Theoretical Models and Personality Theory*. Durham, N. C.: Duke University Press, 1952.

Kunkel, Fritz. *Character, Growth, Education*. Trs. Keppel-Compton and B. Druitt. Philadelphia: J. B. Lippincott, Co., 1938.

———. *In Search of Maturity*. New York: Charles Scribner's Sons, 1943.

Lecky, Prescott. *Self-Consistency: A Theory of Personality*. New York: Island Press Coop., Inc., 1945.

Lewin, Kurt. *A Dynamic Theory of Personality*. New York: McGraw-Hill Book Co., Inc., 1935.

———. *Field Theory in Social Science*. Ed. Dorwin Cartwright. New York: Harper & Bros. 1951.

———. *Principles of Topological Psychology*. New York: McGraw-Hill Book Co., Inc., 1936.

Linton, Ralph. *The Cultural Background of Personality*. New York: Appleton-Century-Crofts, Inc., 1945.

Maeder, Alphonse. *Ways to Psychic Health*. New York: Charles Scribner's Sons, 1953.

Maslow, A. H. *Motivation and Personality*. New York: Harper & Bros., 1954.

————, and Mittelmann, B. *Principles of Abnormal Psychology*. New York: Harper & Bros., 1951.

May, Rollo. *Man's Search for Himself*. New York: W. W. Norton & Co., Inc., 1953.

Menninger, Karl A. and Jeanetta L. *Love Against Hate*. New York: Harcourt Brace & Co., Inc., 1942.

Moreno, Jacob L. *Who Shall Survive?* New York: Beacon House, Inc., 1953.

Mowrer, O. H. *Learning Theory and Personality Dynamics*. New York: Ronald Press & Co., 1950.

————, et al. *Psychotherapy: Theory and Research*. New York: Ronald Press Co., 1953.

Mullahy, Patrick, ed. *The Contributions of Harry Stack Sullivan*. New York: Thos. Nelson & Sons, 1952.

————. *A Study of Interpersonal Relations*. New York: Thos. Nelson & Sons, 1949.

Murphy, Gardner. *Personality: A Biosocial Approach to Origins and Structure*. New York: Harper & Bros., 1947.

Murray, Henry A. *Explorations in Personality*. New York: Oxford University Press, 1938.

Newcomb, Theodore M. *Social Psychology*. New York: Dryden Press, 1950.

Niebuhr, Reinhold. *The Nature and Destiny of Man: A Christian Interpretation*. 2 vols. New York: Charles Scribner's Sons, 1941.

————. *The Self and the Dramas of History*. New York: Charles Scribner's Sons, 1955.

Nygren, Anders. *Agape and Eros*. 2 vols. New York: The Macmillan Co. 1932-39.

Oates, Wayne E. *Religious Factors in Mental Illness*. New York: Association Press, 1955.

Outler, Albert C. *Psychotherapy and the Christian Message*. New York: Harper & Bros., 1954.

Rank, Otto. *Psychology and the Soul*. Tr. W. D. Turner. Philadelphia: University of Pennsylvania Press, 1950.

————. *Truth and Reality*. Tr. Jessie Taft. New York: Alfred A. Knopf, Inc., 1936.

————. *Will Therapy*. Tr. Jessie Taft. New York: Alfred A. Knopf, Inc., 1936.

Riesman, David. *The Lonely Crowd*. New Haven, Conn.: Yale University Press, 1950.

Roberts, David E. *The Grandeur and Misery of Man*. New York: Oxford University Press, 1955.

————. *Psychotherapy and a Christian View of Man*. New York: Charles Scribner's Sons, 1950.

Rogers, Carl R. *Client-Centered Therapy*. Boston: Houghton Mifflin Co., 1951.

————, and Dymond, R. F. *Psychotherapy and Personality Change*. University of Chicago Press, 1954.

Ruesch, Jurgen, and Bateson, Gregory. *Communication: The Social Matrix of Psychiatry*. New York: W. W. Norton, & Co., Inc., 1951.

Saul, Leon J. *Emotional Maturity: The Development and Dynamics of Personality.* Philadelphia: J. B. Lippincott Co., 1947.

Scheidlinger, Saul. *Psychoanalysis and Group Behavior.* New York: W. W. Norton & Co., Inc., 1952.

Sherrill, Lewis J. *Guilt and Redemption.* Richmond, Va.: John Knox Press, 1945; 1956.

Smith, F. V. *The Explanation of Human Behaviour.* New York: The Macmillan Co., 1952.

Snygg, Donald, and Combs, A. W. *Individual Behavior: A New Frame of Reference for Psychology.* New York: Harper & Bros., 1949.

Stern, William. *General Psychology from the Personalistic Standpoint.* Tr. H. D. Spoerl. New York: The Macmillan Co. 1938.

Sullivan, Harry Stack. *Conceptions of Modern Psychiatry.* New York: W. W. Norton & Co., Inc., 1940; 1953.

———. *The Interpersonal Theory of Psychiatry.* New York: W. W. Norton, & Co., Inc., 1953.

———. *The Psychiatric Interview.* New York: W. W. Norton & Co., Inc., 1954.

Suttie, Ian D. *The Origins of Love and Hate.* New York: Julian Press, Inc., 1935; 1952.

Thurman, Howard. *The Creative Encounter.* New York: Harper & Bros., 1954.

Tillich, Paul. *Biblical Religion and the Search for Ultimate Reality.* University of Chicago Press, 1955.

———. *Systematic Theology.* Vol I. University of Chicago Press, 1951.

———. *The Courage to Be.* New Haven, Conn.: Yale University Press, 1952.

Weatherhead, Leslie. *Psychology, Religion, and Healing.* New York and Nashville: Abingdon Press, 1952.

Weiss, Paul. *Man's Freedom.* New Haven, Conn.: Yale University Press, 1950.

White, Robert W. *Lives in Progress: A Study of the Natural Growth of Personality.* New York: Dryden Press, 1952.

White, Victor. *God and the Unconscious.* London: Harvill Press, 1952.

Wise, Carroll A. *Pastoral Counseling: Its Theory and Practice.* New York: Harper & Bros., 1951.

———. *Psychiatry and the Bible.* New York: Harper & Bros., 1956.

Wolff, Werner. *Values and Personality: An Existential Psychology of Crisis.* New York: Grune & Stratton, Inc., 1950.

INDEX

~~~~~~

Sunday, Billy, 200
Sunday school, 31
Superconscious, 257
Superego, 54-58, 114, 164, 167, 251-53, 267
Supernatural, 272-73
Suttie, Ian D., 225, 226, 289
Symbols, 135, 136

Taft, J, 221, 288
Tao Tê Ching, 280
Taoism, 180
Teacher (s) , 95, 178
Teaching, 137
Temperament, 29
Tenderness, 69
Tension (s) , 68, 114, 115
Theologian (s) , 120, 126, 133
Theology, 19, 135
Therapeutic team, 211
Therapy, 227
  client-centered, 227
  group, 213
  shock, 214
Threat (s) , 186, 187
Tillich, Paul, 19, 127, 230, 279, 289
Toilet training, 51, 54, 57, 225
Topological psychology, 48, 276
Trait, 146
Transference, 225
Trinity, 255
Truth, 133, 134
Turner, W. D., 288
Typology, 210

Unconscious, 27, 54, 160, 163, 234, 238, 239, 246
UNESCO, 278
Union Theological Seminary, 197

Value (s) , 101, 119, 125, 127, 129, 136-38, 146, 153, 176, 177, 231, 244, 263

Values (s) —*cont'd*
  cultural, 69
  religious, 154
  spiritual, 138, 164
Vitalism, 274, 275
Vitality, 239
Vocation, 63, 93, 137

War, 178-80
Weaning, 57
Weatherhead, Leslie, 289
Weiss, Paul, 263, 289
Wells, F. L., 204
White, Robert W., 289
White, Victor, 289
Whitehead, A. N., 276
Wieman, H. N., 276
Will, 54
Wise, Carroll A., 219, 289
Wish, 50, 58
Wolff, Werner, 289
Womb, 57
Woodson, Joseph F., 185, 208
Worcester, Elwood, 203
Worcester State Hospital, 204, 205, 221
World (s)
  inner, 18
  outer, 18
World Council of Churches, 193
World Federation for Mental Health, 278
Wundt, W., 5
Wyon, O., 285

X factor, 209

Y.M.C.A., 198
Yoga, 178
Youth, 68
Youth group (s) , 33

Zander, Alvin, 26, 248, 286
Zoroaster, 281